C-4604   CAREER EXAMINATION SERIES

This is your
PASSBOOK for...

Clerk-Typist III

Test Preparation Study Guide
Questions & Answers

NATIONAL LEARNING CORPORATION®

COPYRIGHT NOTICE

This book is SOLELY intended for, is sold ONLY to, and its use is RESTRICTED to individual, bona fide applicants or candidates who qualify by virtue of having seriously filed applications for appropriate license, certificate, professional and/or promotional advancement, higher school matriculation, scholarship, or other legitimate requirements of education and/or governmental authorities.

This book is NOT intended for use, class instruction, tutoring, training, duplication, copying, reprinting, excerption, or adaptation, etc., by:

1) Other publishers
2) Proprietors and/or Instructors of "Coaching" and/or Preparatory Courses
3) Personnel and/or Training Divisions of commercial, industrial, and governmental organizations
4) Schools, colleges, or universities and/or their departments and staffs, including teachers and other personnel
5) Testing Agencies or Bureaus
6) Study groups which seek by the purchase of a single volume to copy and/or duplicate and/or adapt this material for use by the group as a whole without having purchased individual volumes for each of the members of the group
7) Et al.

Such persons would be in violation of appropriate Federal and State statutes.

PROVISION OF LICENSING AGREEMENTS – Recognized educational, commercial, industrial, and governmental institutions and organizations, and others legitimately engaged in educational pursuits, including training, testing, and measurement activities, may address request for a licensing agreement to the copyright owners, who will determine whether, and under what conditions, including fees and charges, the materials in this book may be used them. In other words, a licensing facility exists for the legitimate use of the material in this book on other than an individual basis. However, it is asseverated and affirmed here that the material in this book CANNOT be used without the receipt of the express permission of such a licensing agreement from the Publishers. Inquiries re licensing should be addressed to the company, attention rights and permissions department.

All rights reserved, including the right of reproduction in whole or in part, in any form or by any means, electronic or mechanical, including photocopying, recording, or by any information storage and retrieval system, without permission in writing from the Publisher.

Copyright © 2024 by
National Learning Corporation

212 Michael Drive, Syosset, NY 11791
(516) 921-8888 • www.passbooks.com
E-mail: info@passbooks.com

PASSBOOK® SERIES

THE *PASSBOOK® SERIES* has been created to prepare applicants and candidates for the ultimate academic battlefield – the examination room.

At some time in our lives, each and every one of us may be required to take an examination – for validation, matriculation, admission, qualification, registration, certification, or licensure.

Based on the assumption that every applicant or candidate has met the basic formal educational standards, has taken the required number of courses, and read the necessary texts, the *PASSBOOK® SERIES* furnishes the one special preparation which may assure passing with confidence, instead of failing with insecurity. Examination questions – together with answers – are furnished as the basic vehicle for study so that the mysteries of the examination and its compounding difficulties may be eliminated or diminished by a sure method.

This book is meant to help you pass your examination provided that you qualify and are serious in your objective.

The entire field is reviewed through the huge store of content information which is succinctly presented through a provocative and challenging approach – the question-and-answer method.

A climate of success is established by furnishing the correct answers at the end of each test.

You soon learn to recognize types of questions, forms of questions, and patterns of questioning. You may even begin to anticipate expected outcomes.

You perceive that many questions are repeated or adapted so that you can gain acute insights, which may enable you to score many sure points.

You learn how to confront new questions, or types of questions, and to attack them confidently and work out the correct answers.

You note objectives and emphases, and recognize pitfalls and dangers, so that you may make positive educational adjustments.

Moreover, you are kept fully informed in relation to new concepts, methods, practices, and directions in the field.

You discover that you are actually taking the examination all the time: you are preparing for the examination by "taking" an examination, not by reading extraneous and/or supererogatory textbooks.

In short, this PASSBOOK®, used directedly, should be an important factor in helping you to pass your test.

CLERK-TYPIST III

DUTIES

Supervises and performs varied and complex clerical duties involving some typing; performs related duties as required.

SUBJECT OF EXAMINATION:

The written test designed to evaluate knowledge, skills and /or abilities in the following areas:

1. **Grammar/Usage/Punctuation** - The grammar and usage questions test for the ability to apply the basic rules of grammar and usage. The punctuation questions test for a knowledge of the correct placement of punctuation marks in sentences. You will be presented with sets of four sentences from each of which you must choose the sentence that contains a grammatical, usage, or punctuation error.
2. **Keyboarding practices** - These questions test for a knowledge of preferred practices in such areas as letter format, capitalization, hyphenation, plurals, possessives, word division, word and figure style for numbers, and common proofreading marks. In addition, there will be a passage to proofread followed by questions on how to correct the errors in the passage.
3. **Office practices** - These questions test for knowledge of generally agreed-upon practices governing the handling of situations which typists, stenographers, secretaries, and office assistants encounter in their work, as well as a knowledge of efficient and effective methods used to accomplish office tasks. The questions cover such topics as planning work flow; setting priorities; dealing effectively with staff, visitors, and callers; filing and retrieving information; safeguarding confidentiality; using office equipment; and making procedural decisions and recommendations which contribute to a well-managed office.
4. **Office record keeping** - These questions test your ability to perform common office record keeping tasks. The test consists of two or more "sets" of questions, each set concerning a different problem. Typical record keeping problems might involve the organization or collation of data from several sources; scheduling; maintaining a record system using running balances; or completion of a table summarizing data using totals, subtotals, averages and percents.
5. **Spelling** - These questions test for the ability to spell words that are used in written business communications.
6. **Supervision** - These questions test for knowledge of the principles and practices employed in planning, organizing, and controlling the activities of a work unit toward predetermined objectives. The concepts covered, usually in a situational question format, include such topics as assigning and reviewing work; evaluating performance; maintaining work standards; motivating and developing subordinates; implementing procedural change; increasing efficiency; and dealing with problems of absenteeism, morale, and discipline.

HOW TO TAKE A TEST

I. YOU MUST PASS AN EXAMINATION

A. WHAT EVERY CANDIDATE SHOULD KNOW

Examination applicants often ask us for help in preparing for the written test. What can I study in advance? What kinds of questions will be asked? How will the test be given? How will the papers be graded?

As an applicant for a civil service examination, you may be wondering about some of these things. Our purpose here is to suggest effective methods of advance study and to describe civil service examinations.

Your chances for success on this examination can be increased if you know how to prepare. Those "pre-examination jitters" can be reduced if you know what to expect. You can even experience an adventure in good citizenship if you know why civil service exams are given.

B. WHY ARE CIVIL SERVICE EXAMINATIONS GIVEN?

Civil service examinations are important to you in two ways. As a citizen, you want public jobs filled by employees who know how to do their work. As a job seeker, you want a fair chance to compete for that job on an equal footing with other candidates. The best-known means of accomplishing this two-fold goal is the competitive examination.

Exams are widely publicized throughout the nation. They may be administered for jobs in federal, state, city, municipal, town or village governments or agencies.

Any citizen may apply, with some limitations, such as the age or residence of applicants. Your experience and education may be reviewed to see whether you meet the requirements for the particular examination. When these requirements exist, they are reasonable and applied consistently to all applicants. Thus, a competitive examination may cause you some uneasiness now, but it is your privilege and safeguard.

C. HOW ARE CIVIL SERVICE EXAMS DEVELOPED?

Examinations are carefully written by trained technicians who are specialists in the field known as "psychological measurement," in consultation with recognized authorities in the field of work that the test will cover. These experts recommend the subject matter areas or skills to be tested; only those knowledges or skills important to your success on the job are included. The most reliable books and source materials available are used as references. Together, the experts and technicians judge the difficulty level of the questions.

Test technicians know how to phrase questions so that the problem is clearly stated. Their ethics do not permit "trick" or "catch" questions. Questions may have been tried out on sample groups, or subjected to statistical analysis, to determine their usefulness.

Written tests are often used in combination with performance tests, ratings of training and experience, and oral interviews. All of these measures combine to form the best-known means of finding the right person for the right job.

II. HOW TO PASS THE WRITTEN TEST

A. NATURE OF THE EXAMINATION

To prepare intelligently for civil service examinations, you should know how they differ from school examinations you have taken. In school you were assigned certain definite pages to read or subjects to cover. The examination questions were quite detailed and usually emphasized memory. Civil service exams, on the other hand, try to discover your present ability to perform the duties of a position, plus your potentiality to learn these duties. In other words, a civil service exam attempts to predict how successful you will be. Questions cover such a broad area that they cannot be as minute and detailed as school exam questions.

In the public service similar kinds of work, or positions, are grouped together in one "class." This process is known as *position-classification*. All the positions in a class are paid according to the salary range for that class. One class title covers all of these positions, and they are all tested by the same examination.

B. FOUR BASIC STEPS

1) Study the announcement

How, then, can you know what subjects to study? Our best answer is: "Learn as much as possible about the class of positions for which you've applied." The exam will test the knowledge, skills and abilities needed to do the work.

Your most valuable source of information about the position you want is the official exam announcement. This announcement lists the training and experience qualifications. Check these standards and apply only if you come reasonably close to meeting them.

The brief description of the position in the examination announcement offers some clues to the subjects which will be tested. Think about the job itself. Review the duties in your mind. Can you perform them, or are there some in which you are rusty? Fill in the blank spots in your preparation.

Many jurisdictions preview the written test in the exam announcement by including a section called "Knowledge and Abilities Required," "Scope of the Examination," or some similar heading. Here you will find out specifically what fields will be tested.

2) Review your own background

Once you learn in general what the position is all about, and what you need to know to do the work, ask yourself which subjects you already know fairly well and which need improvement. You may wonder whether to concentrate on improving your strong areas or on building some background in your fields of weakness. When the announcement has specified "some knowledge" or "considerable knowledge," or has used adjectives like "beginning principles of..." or "advanced ... methods," you can get a clue as to the number and difficulty of questions to be asked in any given field. More questions, and hence broader coverage, would be included for those subjects which are more important in the work. Now weigh your strengths and weaknesses against the job requirements and prepare accordingly.

3) Determine the level of the position

Another way to tell how intensively you should prepare is to understand the level of the job for which you are applying. Is it the entering level? In other words, is this the position in which beginners in a field of work are hired? Or is it an intermediate or advanced level? Sometimes this is indicated by such words as "Junior" or "Senior" in the class title. Other jurisdictions use Roman numerals to designate the level – Clerk I, Clerk II, for example. The word "Supervisor" sometimes appears in the title. If the level is not indicated by the title, check the description of duties. Will you be working under very close supervision, or will you have responsibility for independent decisions in this work?

4) Choose appropriate study materials

Now that you know the subjects to be examined and the relative amount of each subject to be covered, you can choose suitable study materials. For beginning level jobs, or even advanced ones, if you have a pronounced weakness in some aspect of your training, read a modern, standard textbook in that field. Be sure it is up to date and has general coverage. Such books are normally available at your library, and the librarian will be glad to help you locate one. For entry-level positions, questions of appropriate difficulty are chosen – neither highly advanced questions, nor those too simple. Such questions require careful thought but not advanced training.

If the position for which you are applying is technical or advanced, you will read more advanced, specialized material. If you are already familiar with the basic principles of your field, elementary textbooks would waste your time. Concentrate on advanced textbooks and technical periodicals. Think through the concepts and review difficult problems in your field.

These are all general sources. You can get more ideas on your own initiative, following these leads. For example, training manuals and publications of the government agency which employs workers in your field can be useful, particularly for technical and professional positions. A letter or visit to the government department involved may result in more specific study suggestions, and certainly will provide you with a more definite idea of the exact nature of the position you are seeking.

III. KINDS OF TESTS

Tests are used for purposes other than measuring knowledge and ability to perform specified duties. For some positions, it is equally important to test ability to make adjustments to new situations or to profit from training. In others, basic mental abilities not dependent on information are essential. Questions which test these things may not appear as pertinent to the duties of the position as those which test for knowledge and information. Yet they are often highly important parts of a fair examination. For very general questions, it is almost impossible to help you direct your study efforts. What we can do is to point out some of the more common of these general abilities needed in public service positions and describe some typical questions.

1) General information

Broad, general information has been found useful for predicting job success in some kinds of work. This is tested in a variety of ways, from vocabulary lists to questions about current events. Basic background in some field of work, such as sociology or economics, may be sampled in a group of questions. Often these are principles which have become familiar to most persons through exposure rather than through formal training. It is difficult to advise you how to study for these questions; being alert to the world around you is our best suggestion.

2) Verbal ability

An example of an ability needed in many positions is verbal or language ability. Verbal ability is, in brief, the ability to use and understand words. Vocabulary and grammar tests are typical measures of this ability. Reading comprehension or paragraph interpretation questions are common in many kinds of civil service tests. You are given a paragraph of written material and asked to find its central meaning.

3) Numerical ability

Number skills can be tested by the familiar arithmetic problem, by checking paired lists of numbers to see which are alike and which are different, or by interpreting charts and graphs. In the latter test, a graph may be printed in the test booklet which you are asked to use as the basis for answering questions.

4) Observation

A popular test for law-enforcement positions is the observation test. A picture is shown to you for several minutes, then taken away. Questions about the picture test your ability to observe both details and larger elements.

5) Following directions

In many positions in the public service, the employee must be able to carry out written instructions dependably and accurately. You may be given a chart with several columns, each column listing a variety of information. The questions require you to carry out directions involving the information given in the chart.

6) Skills and aptitudes

Performance tests effectively measure some manual skills and aptitudes. When the skill is one in which you are trained, such as typing or shorthand, you can practice. These tests are often very much like those given in business school or high school courses. For many of the other skills and aptitudes, however, no short-time preparation can be made. Skills and abilities natural to you or that you have developed throughout your lifetime are being tested.

Many of the general questions just described provide all the data needed to answer the questions and ask you to use your reasoning ability to find the answers. Your best preparation for these tests, as well as for tests of facts and ideas, is to be at your physical and mental best. You, no doubt, have your own methods of getting into an exam-taking mood and keeping "in shape." The next section lists some ideas on this subject.

IV. KINDS OF QUESTIONS

Only rarely is the "essay" question, which you answer in narrative form, used in civil service tests. Civil service tests are usually of the short-answer type. Full instructions for answering these questions will be given to you at the examination. But in case this is your first experience with short-answer questions and separate answer sheets, here is what you need to know:

1) Multiple-choice Questions

Most popular of the short-answer questions is the "multiple choice" or "best answer" question. It can be used, for example, to test for factual knowledge, ability to solve problems or judgment in meeting situations found at work.

A multiple-choice question is normally one of three types—
- It can begin with an incomplete statement followed by several possible endings. You are to find the one ending which *best* completes the statement, although some of the others may not be entirely wrong.
- It can also be a complete statement in the form of a question which is answered by choosing one of the statements listed.

- It can be in the form of a problem – again you select the best answer.

Here is an example of a multiple-choice question with a discussion which should give you some clues as to the method for choosing the right answer:

When an employee has a complaint about his assignment, the action which will *best* help him overcome his difficulty is to
  A. discuss his difficulty with his coworkers
  B. take the problem to the head of the organization
  C. take the problem to the person who gave him the assignment
  D. say nothing to anyone about his complaint

In answering this question, you should study each of the choices to find which is best. Consider choice "A" – Certainly an employee may discuss his complaint with fellow employees, but no change or improvement can result, and the complaint remains unresolved. Choice "B" is a poor choice since the head of the organization probably does not know what assignment you have been given, and taking your problem to him is known as "going over the head" of the supervisor. The supervisor, or person who made the assignment, is the person who can clarify it or correct any injustice. Choice "C" is, therefore, correct. To say nothing, as in choice "D," is unwise. Supervisors have and interest in knowing the problems employees are facing, and the employee is seeking a solution to his problem.

2) True/False Questions

The "true/false" or "right/wrong" form of question is sometimes used. Here a complete statement is given. Your job is to decide whether the statement is right or wrong.

SAMPLE: A roaming cell-phone call to a nearby city costs less than a non-roaming call to a distant city.

This statement is wrong, or false, since roaming calls are more expensive.

This is not a complete list of all possible question forms, although most of the others are variations of these common types. You will always get complete directions for answering questions. Be sure you understand *how* to mark your answers – ask questions until you do.

V. RECORDING YOUR ANSWERS

Computer terminals are used more and more today for many different kinds of exams.

For an examination with very few applicants, you may be told to record your answers in the test booklet itself. Separate answer sheets are much more common. If this separate answer sheet is to be scored by machine – and this is often the case – it is highly important that you mark your answers correctly in order to get credit.

An electronic scoring machine is often used in civil service offices because of the speed with which papers can be scored. Machine-scored answer sheets must be marked with a pencil, which will be given to you. This pencil has a high graphite content which responds to the electronic scoring machine. As a matter of fact, stray dots may register as answers, so do not let your pencil rest on the answer sheet while you are pondering the correct answer. Also, if your pencil lead breaks or is otherwise defective, ask for another.

Since the answer sheet will be dropped in a slot in the scoring machine, be careful not to bend the corners or get the paper crumpled.

The answer sheet normally has five vertical columns of numbers, with 30 numbers to a column. These numbers correspond to the question numbers in your test booklet. After each number, going across the page are four or five pairs of dotted lines. These short dotted lines have small letters or numbers above them. The first two pairs may also have a "T" or "F" above the letters. This indicates that the first two pairs only are to be used if the questions are of the true-false type. If the questions are multiple choice, disregard the "T" and "F" and pay attention only to the small letters or numbers.

Answer your questions in the manner of the sample that follows:

32. The largest city in the United States is
    A. Washington, D.C.
    B. New York City
    C. Chicago
    D. Detroit
    E. San Francisco

1) Choose the answer you think is best. (New York City is the largest, so "B" is correct.)
2) Find the row of dotted lines numbered the same as the question you are answering. (Find row number 32)
3) Find the pair of dotted lines corresponding to the answer. (Find the pair of lines under the mark "B.")
4) Make a solid black mark between the dotted lines.

VI. BEFORE THE TEST

Common sense will help you find procedures to follow to get ready for an examination. Too many of us, however, overlook these sensible measures. Indeed, nervousness and fatigue have been found to be the most serious reasons why applicants fail to do their best on civil service tests. Here is a list of reminders:

- Begin your preparation early – Don't wait until the last minute to go scurrying around for books and materials or to find out what the position is all about.
- Prepare continuously – An hour a night for a week is better than an all-night cram session. This has been definitely established. What is more, a night a week for a month will return better dividends than crowding your study into a shorter period of time.
- Locate the place of the exam – You have been sent a notice telling you when and where to report for the examination. If the location is in a different town or otherwise unfamiliar to you, it would be well to inquire the best route and learn something about the building.
- Relax the night before the test – Allow your mind to rest. Do not study at all that night. Plan some mild recreation or diversion; then go to bed early and get a good night's sleep.
- Get up early enough to make a leisurely trip to the place for the test – This way unforeseen events, traffic snarls, unfamiliar buildings, etc. will not upset you.
- Dress comfortably – A written test is not a fashion show. You will be known by number and not by name, so wear something comfortable.

- Leave excess paraphernalia at home – Shopping bags and odd bundles will get in your way. You need bring only the items mentioned in the official notice you received; usually everything you need is provided. Do not bring reference books to the exam. They will only confuse those last minutes and be taken away from you when in the test room.
- Arrive somewhat ahead of time – If because of transportation schedules you must get there very early, bring a newspaper or magazine to take your mind off yourself while waiting.
- Locate the examination room – When you have found the proper room, you will be directed to the seat or part of the room where you will sit. Sometimes you are given a sheet of instructions to read while you are waiting. Do not fill out any forms until you are told to do so; just read them and be prepared.
- Relax and prepare to listen to the instructions
- If you have any physical problem that may keep you from doing your best, be sure to tell the test administrator. If you are sick or in poor health, you really cannot do your best on the exam. You can come back and take the test some other time.

VII. AT THE TEST

The day of the test is here and you have the test booklet in your hand. The temptation to get going is very strong. Caution! There is more to success than knowing the right answers. You must know how to identify your papers and understand variations in the type of short-answer question used in this particular examination. Follow these suggestions for maximum results from your efforts:

1) Cooperate with the monitor

The test administrator has a duty to create a situation in which you can be as much at ease as possible. He will give instructions, tell you when to begin, check to see that you are marking your answer sheet correctly, and so on. He is not there to guard you, although he will see that your competitors do not take unfair advantage. He wants to help you do your best.

2) Listen to all instructions

Don't jump the gun! Wait until you understand all directions. In most civil service tests you get more time than you need to answer the questions. So don't be in a hurry. Read each word of instructions until you clearly understand the meaning. Study the examples, listen to all announcements and follow directions. Ask questions if you do not understand what to do.

3) Identify your papers

Civil service exams are usually identified by number only. You will be assigned a number; you must not put your name on your test papers. Be sure to copy your number correctly. Since more than one exam may be given, copy your exact examination title.

4) Plan your time

Unless you are told that a test is a "speed" or "rate of work" test, speed itself is usually not important. Time enough to answer all the questions will be provided, but this does not mean that you have all day. An overall time limit has been set. Divide the total time (in minutes) by the number of questions to determine the approximate time you have for each question.

5) **Do not linger over difficult questions**

If you come across a difficult question, mark it with a paper clip (useful to have along) and come back to it when you have been through the booklet. One caution if you do this – be sure to skip a number on your answer sheet as well. Check often to be sure that you have not lost your place and that you are marking in the row numbered the same as the question you are answering.

6) **Read the questions**

Be sure you know what the question asks! Many capable people are unsuccessful because they failed to *read* the questions correctly.

7) **Answer all questions**

Unless you have been instructed that a penalty will be deducted for incorrect answers, it is better to guess than to omit a question.

8) **Speed tests**

It is often better NOT to guess on speed tests. It has been found that on timed tests people are tempted to spend the last few seconds before time is called in marking answers at random – without even reading them – in the hope of picking up a few extra points. To discourage this practice, the instructions may warn you that your score will be "corrected" for guessing. That is, a penalty will be applied. The incorrect answers will be deducted from the correct ones, or some other penalty formula will be used.

9) **Review your answers**

If you finish before time is called, go back to the questions you guessed or omitted to give them further thought. Review other answers if you have time.

10) **Return your test materials**

If you are ready to leave before others have finished or time is called, take ALL your materials to the monitor and leave quietly. Never take any test material with you. The monitor can discover whose papers are not complete, and taking a test booklet may be grounds for disqualification.

VIII. EXAMINATION TECHNIQUES

1) Read the general instructions carefully. These are usually printed on the first page of the exam booklet. As a rule, these instructions refer to the timing of the examination; the fact that you should not start work until the signal and must stop work at a signal, etc. If there are any *special* instructions, such as a choice of questions to be answered, make sure that you note this instruction carefully.

2) When you are ready to start work on the examination, that is as soon as the signal has been given, read the instructions to each question booklet, underline any key words or phrases, such as *least, best, outline, describe* and the like. In this way you will tend to answer as requested rather than discover on reviewing your paper that you *listed without describing*, that you selected the *worst* choice rather than the *best* choice, etc.

3) If the examination is of the objective or multiple-choice type – that is, each question will also give a series of possible answers: A, B, C or D, and you are called upon to select the best answer and write the letter next to that answer on your answer paper – it is advisable to start answering each question in turn. There may be anywhere from 50 to 100 such questions in the three or four hours allotted and you can see how much time would be taken if you read through all the questions before beginning to answer any. Furthermore, if you come across a question or group of questions which you know would be difficult to answer, it would undoubtedly affect your handling of all the other questions.

4) If the examination is of the essay type and contains but a few questions, it is a moot point as to whether you should read all the questions before starting to answer any one. Of course, if you are given a choice – say five out of seven and the like – then it is essential to read all the questions so you can eliminate the two that are most difficult. If, however, you are asked to answer all the questions, there may be danger in trying to answer the easiest one first because you may find that you will spend too much time on it. The best technique is to answer the first question, then proceed to the second, etc.

5) Time your answers. Before the exam begins, write down the time it started, then add the time allowed for the examination and write down the time it must be completed, then divide the time available somewhat as follows:
   - If 3-1/2 hours are allowed, that would be 210 minutes. If you have 80 objective-type questions, that would be an average of 2-1/2 minutes per question. Allow yourself no more than 2 minutes per question, or a total of 160 minutes, which will permit about 50 minutes to review.
   - If for the time allotment of 210 minutes there are 7 essay questions to answer, that would average about 30 minutes a question. Give yourself only 25 minutes per question so that you have about 35 minutes to review.

6) The most important instruction is to *read each question* and make sure you know what is wanted. The second most important instruction is to *time yourself properly* so that you answer every question. The third most important instruction is to *answer every question*. Guess if you have to but include something for each question. Remember that you will receive no credit for a blank and will probably receive some credit if you write something in answer to an essay question. If you guess a letter – say "B" for a multiple-choice question – you may have guessed right. If you leave a blank as an answer to a multiple-choice question, the examiners may respect your feelings but it will not add a point to your score. Some exams may penalize you for wrong answers, so in such cases *only*, you may not want to guess unless you have some basis for your answer.

7) Suggestions
   a. Objective-type questions
      1. Examine the question booklet for proper sequence of pages and questions
      2. Read all instructions carefully
      3. Skip any question which seems too difficult; return to it after all other questions have been answered
      4. Apportion your time properly; do not spend too much time on any single question or group of questions

5. Note and underline key words – *all, most, fewest, least, best, worst, same, opposite,* etc.
6. Pay particular attention to negatives
7. Note unusual option, e.g., unduly long, short, complex, different or similar in content to the body of the question
8. Observe the use of "hedging" words – *probably, may, most likely,* etc.
9. Make sure that your answer is put next to the same number as the question
10. Do not second-guess unless you have good reason to believe the second answer is definitely more correct
11. Cross out original answer if you decide another answer is more accurate; do not erase until you are ready to hand your paper in
12. Answer all questions; guess unless instructed otherwise
13. Leave time for review

b. Essay questions
1. Read each question carefully
2. Determine exactly what is wanted. Underline key words or phrases.
3. Decide on outline or paragraph answer
4. Include many different points and elements unless asked to develop any one or two points or elements
5. Show impartiality by giving pros and cons unless directed to select one side only
6. Make and write down any assumptions you find necessary to answer the questions
7. Watch your English, grammar, punctuation and choice of words
8. Time your answers; don't crowd material

8) Answering the essay question

Most essay questions can be answered by framing the specific response around several key words or ideas. Here are a few such key words or ideas:

M's: manpower, materials, methods, money, management
P's: purpose, program, policy, plan, procedure, practice, problems, pitfalls, personnel, public relations
   a. Six basic steps in handling problems:
      1. Preliminary plan and background development
      2. Collect information, data and facts
      3. Analyze and interpret information, data and facts
      4. Analyze and develop solutions as well as make recommendations
      5. Prepare report and sell recommendations
      6. Install recommendations and follow up effectiveness

   b. Pitfalls to avoid
      1. *Taking things for granted* – A statement of the situation does not necessarily imply that each of the elements is necessarily true; for example, a complaint may be invalid and biased so that all that can be taken for granted is that a complaint has been registered

2. *Considering only one side of a situation* – Wherever possible, indicate several alternatives and then point out the reasons you selected the best one
3. *Failing to indicate follow up* – Whenever your answer indicates action on your part, make certain that you will take proper follow-up action to see how successful your recommendations, procedures or actions turn out to be
4. *Taking too long in answering any single question* – Remember to time your answers properly

IX. AFTER THE TEST

Scoring procedures differ in detail among civil service jurisdictions although the general principles are the same. Whether the papers are hand-scored or graded by machine we have described, they are nearly always graded by number. That is, the person who marks the paper knows only the number – never the name – of the applicant. Not until all the papers have been graded will they be matched with names. If other tests, such as training and experience or oral interview ratings have been given, scores will be combined. Different parts of the examination usually have different weights. For example, the written test might count 60 percent of the final grade, and a rating of training and experience 40 percent. In many jurisdictions, veterans will have a certain number of points added to their grades.

After the final grade has been determined, the names are placed in grade order and an eligible list is established. There are various methods for resolving ties between those who get the same final grade – probably the most common is to place first the name of the person whose application was received first. Job offers are made from the eligible list in the order the names appear on it. You will be notified of your grade and your rank as soon as all these computations have been made. This will be done as rapidly as possible.

People who are found to meet the requirements in the announcement are called "eligibles." Their names are put on a list of eligible candidates. An eligible's chances of getting a job depend on how high he stands on this list and how fast agencies are filling jobs from the list.

When a job is to be filled from a list of eligibles, the agency asks for the names of people on the list of eligibles for that job. When the civil service commission receives this request, it sends to the agency the names of the three people highest on this list. Or, if the job to be filled has specialized requirements, the office sends the agency the names of the top three persons who meet these requirements from the general list.

The appointing officer makes a choice from among the three people whose names were sent to him. If the selected person accepts the appointment, the names of the others are put back on the list to be considered for future openings.

That is the rule in hiring from all kinds of eligible lists, whether they are for typist, carpenter, chemist, or something else. For every vacancy, the appointing officer has his choice of any one of the top three eligibles on the list. This explains why the person whose name is on top of the list sometimes does not get an appointment when some of the persons lower on the list do. If the appointing officer chooses the second or third eligible, the No. 1 eligible does not get a job at once, but stays on the list until he is appointed or the list is terminated.

X. HOW TO PASS THE INTERVIEW TEST

The examination for which you applied requires an oral interview test. You have already taken the written test and you are now being called for the interview test – the final part of the formal examination.

You may think that it is not possible to prepare for an interview test and that there are no procedures to follow during an interview. Our purpose is to point out some things you can do in advance that will help you and some good rules to follow and pitfalls to avoid while you are being interviewed.

What is an interview supposed to test?

The written examination is designed to test the technical knowledge and competence of the candidate; the oral is designed to evaluate intangible qualities, not readily measured otherwise, and to establish a list showing the relative fitness of each candidate – as measured against his competitors – for the position sought. Scoring is not on the basis of "right" and "wrong," but on a sliding scale of values ranging from "not passable" to "outstanding." As a matter of fact, it is possible to achieve a relatively low score without a single "incorrect" answer because of evident weakness in the qualities being measured.

Occasionally, an examination may consist entirely of an oral test – either an individual or a group oral. In such cases, information is sought concerning the technical knowledges and abilities of the candidate, since there has been no written examination for this purpose. More commonly, however, an oral test is used to supplement a written examination.

Who conducts interviews?

The composition of oral boards varies among different jurisdictions. In nearly all, a representative of the personnel department serves as chairman. One of the members of the board may be a representative of the department in which the candidate would work. In some cases, "outside experts" are used, and, frequently, a businessman or some other representative of the general public is asked to serve. Labor and management or other special groups may be represented. The aim is to secure the services of experts in the appropriate field.

However the board is composed, it is a good idea (and not at all improper or unethical) to ascertain in advance of the interview who the members are and what groups they represent. When you are introduced to them, you will have some idea of their backgrounds and interests, and at least you will not stutter and stammer over their names.

What should be done before the interview?

While knowledge about the board members is useful and takes some of the surprise element out of the interview, there is other preparation which is more substantive. It *is* possible to prepare for an oral interview – in several ways:

1) Keep a copy of your application and review it carefully before the interview

This may be the only document before the oral board, and the starting point of the interview. Know what education and experience you have listed there, and the sequence and dates of all of it. Sometimes the board will ask you to review the highlights of your experience for them; you should not have to hem and haw doing it.

2) Study the class specification and the examination announcement

Usually, the oral board has one or both of these to guide them. The qualities, characteristics or knowledges required by the position sought are stated in these documents. They offer valuable clues as to the nature of the oral interview. For example, if the job involves supervisory responsibilities, the announcement will usually indicate that knowledge of modern supervisory methods and the qualifications of the candidate as a supervisor will be tested. If so, you can expect such questions, frequently in the form of a hypothetical situation which you are expected to solve. NEVER go into an oral without knowledge of the duties and responsibilities of the job you seek.

3) Think through each qualification required

Try to visualize the kind of questions you would ask if you were a board member. How well could you answer them? Try especially to appraise your own knowledge and background in each area, *measured against the job sought*, and identify any areas in which you are weak. Be critical and realistic – do not flatter yourself.

4) Do some general reading in areas in which you feel you may be weak

For example, if the job involves supervision and your past experience has NOT, some general reading in supervisory methods and practices, particularly in the field of human relations, might be useful. Do NOT study agency procedures or detailed manuals. The oral board will be testing your understanding and capacity, not your memory.

5) Get a good night's sleep and watch your general health and mental attitude

You will want a clear head at the interview. Take care of a cold or any other minor ailment, and of course, no hangovers.

What should be done on the day of the interview?

Now comes the day of the interview itself. Give yourself plenty of time to get there. Plan to arrive somewhat ahead of the scheduled time, particularly if your appointment is in the fore part of the day. If a previous candidate fails to appear, the board might be ready for you a bit early. By early afternoon an oral board is almost invariably behind schedule if there are many candidates, and you may have to wait. Take along a book or magazine to read, or your application to review, but leave any extraneous material in the waiting room when you go in for your interview. In any event, relax and compose yourself.

The matter of dress is important. The board is forming impressions about you – from your experience, your manners, your attitude, and your appearance. Give your personal appearance careful attention. Dress your best, but not your flashiest. Choose conservative, appropriate clothing, and be sure it is immaculate. This is a business interview, and your appearance should indicate that you regard it as such. Besides, being well groomed and properly dressed will help boost your confidence.

Sooner or later, someone will call your name and escort you into the interview room. *This is it.* From here on you are on your own. It is too late for any more preparation. But remember, you asked for this opportunity to prove your fitness, and you are here because your request was granted.

What happens when you go in?

The usual sequence of events will be as follows: The clerk (who is often the board stenographer) will introduce you to the chairman of the oral board, who will introduce you to the other members of the board. Acknowledge the introductions before you sit down. Do not be surprised if you find a microphone facing you or a stenotypist sitting by. Oral interviews are usually recorded in the event of an appeal or other review.

Usually the chairman of the board will open the interview by reviewing the highlights of your education and work experience from your application – primarily for the benefit of the other members of the board, as well as to get the material into the record. Do not interrupt or comment unless there is an error or significant misinterpretation; if that is the case, do not hesitate. But do not quibble about insignificant matters. Also, he will usually ask you some question about your education, experience or your present job – partly to get you to start talking and to establish the interviewing "rapport." He may start the actual questioning, or turn it over to one of the other members. Frequently, each member undertakes the questioning on a particular area, one in which he is perhaps most competent, so you can expect each member to participate in the examination. Because time is limited, you may also expect some rather abrupt switches in the direction the questioning takes, so do not be upset by it. Normally, a board member will not pursue a single line of questioning unless he discovers a particular strength or weakness.

After each member has participated, the chairman will usually ask whether any member has any further questions, then will ask you if you have anything you wish to add. Unless you are expecting this question, it may floor you. Worse, it may start you off on an extended, extemporaneous speech. The board is not usually seeking more information. The question is principally to offer you a last opportunity to present further qualifications or to indicate that you have nothing to add. So, if you feel that a significant qualification or characteristic has been overlooked, it is proper to point it out in a sentence or so. Do not compliment the board on the thoroughness of their examination – they have been sketchy, and you know it. If you wish, merely say, "No thank you, I have nothing further to add." This is a point where you can "talk yourself out" of a good impression or fail to present an important bit of information. Remember, *you close the interview yourself.*

The chairman will then say, "That is all, Mr. _____, thank you." Do not be startled; the interview is over, and quicker than you think. Thank him, gather your belongings and take your leave. Save your sigh of relief for the other side of the door.

How to put your best foot forward
Throughout this entire process, you may feel that the board individually and collectively is trying to pierce your defenses, seek out your hidden weaknesses and embarrass and confuse you. Actually, this is not true. They are obliged to make an appraisal of your qualifications for the job you are seeking, and they want to see you in your best light. Remember, they must interview all candidates and a non-cooperative candidate may become a failure in spite of their best efforts to bring out his qualifications. Here are 15 suggestions that will help you:

1) Be natural – Keep your attitude confident, not cocky
If you are not confident that you can do the job, do not expect the board to be. Do not apologize for your weaknesses, try to bring out your strong points. The board is interested in a positive, not negative, presentation. Cockiness will antagonize any board member and make him wonder if you are covering up a weakness by a false show of strength.

2) Get comfortable, but don't lounge or sprawl
Sit erectly but not stiffly. A careless posture may lead the board to conclude that you are careless in other things, or at least that you are not impressed by the importance of the occasion. Either conclusion is natural, even if incorrect. Do not fuss with your clothing, a pencil or an ashtray. Your hands may occasionally be useful to emphasize a point; do not let them become a point of distraction.

3) Do not wisecrack or make small talk
This is a serious situation, and your attitude should show that you consider it as such. Further, the time of the board is limited – they do not want to waste it, and neither should you.

4) Do not exaggerate your experience or abilities

In the first place, from information in the application or other interviews and sources, the board may know more about you than you think. Secondly, you probably will not get away with it. An experienced board is rather adept at spotting such a situation, so do not take the chance.

5) If you know a board member, do not make a point of it, yet do not hide it

Certainly you are not fooling him, and probably not the other members of the board. Do not try to take advantage of your acquaintanceship – it will probably do you little good.

6) Do not dominate the interview

Let the board do that. They will give you the clues – do not assume that you have to do all the talking. Realize that the board has a number of questions to ask you, and do not try to take up all the interview time by showing off your extensive knowledge of the answer to the first one.

7) Be attentive

You only have 20 minutes or so, and you should keep your attention at its sharpest throughout. When a member is addressing a problem or question to you, give him your undivided attention. Address your reply principally to him, but do not exclude the other board members.

8) Do not interrupt

A board member may be stating a problem for you to analyze. He will ask you a question when the time comes. Let him state the problem, and wait for the question.

9) Make sure you understand the question

Do not try to answer until you are sure what the question is. If it is not clear, restate it in your own words or ask the board member to clarify it for you. However, do not haggle about minor elements.

10) Reply promptly but not hastily

A common entry on oral board rating sheets is "candidate responded readily," or "candidate hesitated in replies." Respond as promptly and quickly as you can, but do not jump to a hasty, ill-considered answer.

11) Do not be peremptory in your answers

A brief answer is proper – but do not fire your answer back. That is a losing game from your point of view. The board member can probably ask questions much faster than you can answer them.

12) Do not try to create the answer you think the board member wants

He is interested in what kind of mind you have and how it works – not in playing games. Furthermore, he can usually spot this practice and will actually grade you down on it.

13) Do not switch sides in your reply merely to agree with a board member

Frequently, a member will take a contrary position merely to draw you out and to see if you are willing and able to defend your point of view. Do not start a debate, yet do not surrender a good position. If a position is worth taking, it is worth defending.

14) Do not be afraid to admit an error in judgment if you are shown to be wrong

The board knows that you are forced to reply without any opportunity for careful consideration. Your answer may be demonstrably wrong. If so, admit it and get on with the interview.

15) Do not dwell at length on your present job

The opening question may relate to your present assignment. Answer the question but do not go into an extended discussion. You are being examined for a *new* job, not your present one. As a matter of fact, try to phrase ALL your answers in terms of the job for which you are being examined.

Basis of Rating

Probably you will forget most of these "do's" and "don'ts" when you walk into the oral interview room. Even remembering them all will not ensure you a passing grade. Perhaps you did not have the qualifications in the first place. But remembering them will help you to put your best foot forward, without treading on the toes of the board members.

Rumor and popular opinion to the contrary notwithstanding, an oral board wants you to make the best appearance possible. They know you are under pressure – but they also want to see how you respond to it as a guide to what your reaction would be under the pressures of the job you seek. They will be influenced by the degree of poise you display, the personal traits you show and the manner in which you respond.

ABOUT THIS BOOK

This book contains tests divided into Examination Sections. Go through each test, answering every question in the margin. We have also attached a sample answer sheet at the back of the book that can be removed and used. At the end of each test look at the answer key and check your answers. On the ones you got wrong, look at the right answer choice and learn. Do not fill in the answers first. Do not memorize the questions and answers, but understand the answer and principles involved. On your test, the questions will likely be different from the samples. Questions are changed and new ones added. If you understand these past questions you should have success with any changes that arise. Tests may consist of several types of questions. We have additional books on each subject should more study be advisable or necessary for you. Finally, the more you study, the better prepared you will be. This book is intended to be the last thing you study before you walk into the examination room. Prior study of relevant texts is also recommended. NLC publishes some of these in our Fundamental Series. Knowledge and good sense are important factors in passing your exam. Good luck also helps. So now study this Passbook, absorb the material contained within and take that knowledge into the examination. Then do your best to pass that exam.

EXAMINATION SECTION

EXAMINATION SECTION
TEST 1

DIRECTIONS: Each question or incomplete statement is followed by several suggested answers or completions. Select the one that BEST answers the question or completes the statement. *PRINT THE LETTER OF THE CORRECT ANSWER IN THE SPACE AT THE RIGHT.*

1. As the supervisor of a staff of clerical employees performing various types of work, you are responsible for the accuracy and efficiency with which their work is performed.
   Of the following actions you may take to insure the accuracy of their work, the MOST practical one is for you to

   A. review each operation completed by a staff member before permitting the employee to proceed to the next operation
   B. keep a record of every error made by an employee and use this record to determine whether a careless employee should be transferred or discharged
   C. assign work in such a way that every operation is performed independently by two employees
   D. determine what errors are likely to occur and set up safeguards to prevent the occurrence of these errors

   1.____

2. Assume that you are the supervisor of a small clerical unit. One of your subordinates has violated a staff regulation by failing to inform you that he will be absent on a certain day.
   Of the following, the MOST appropriate action for you to take first is to

   A. discuss this matter with your immediate superior
   B. find out the reason for his failure to obey this staff regulation
   C. determine what disciplinary action other supervisors have taken in similar cases
   D. take no action if his absence did not interfere with the work of the unit; reprimand him if it did

   2.____

3. A newly appointed clerk is assigned to a unit of an agency at a time when the supervisor of the unit is very busy and has little time to devote to instructing the new employee in the work he is to perform.
   Of the following, the MOST appropriate method of training this employee is for the supervisor to

   A. instruct the new employee to observe several experienced clerks at work and question them regarding any aspect of the work he does not understand
   B. delegate the job of training this employee to an employee in the unit who is qualified to instruct him
   C. assign the new employee a simple task and inform him that more complex and varied duties will be given him when the supervisor is less busy
   D. have the employee spend his time reading the agency's annual reports and the laws, rules, and regulations governing its work

   3.____

4. As a supervisor, you may find it necessary to consult with your superior before taking action on some matters.
   Of the following, the action for which it is MOST important that you obtain the prior approval of your superior is one that involves

   4.____

1

A. assuming additional functions for your unit
B. rotating assignments among your staff members
C. initiating regular meetings of your staff
D. assigning certain members of your staff to work overtime on an emergency job

5. Suppose that a clerk who is employed in a unit under your supervision performs his work quickly but carelessly. He is about to be transferred to another unit in your department. The chief of this other unit asks you for your opinion of this employee's work habits.
Of the following, the MOST appropriate reply for you to make is to

A. point out this employee's good qualities only since he may correct his bad qualities after his transfer is effected
B. say nothing good or bad about this employee, thus permitting him to start his new assignment with a clean slate
C. inform the unit chief that this clerk performed his work speedily but was careless
D. emphasize this employee's good points and minimize his bad points

6. When subordinates request his advice in solving problems encountered in their work, a certain bureau chief occasionally answers the request by first asking the subordinate what he thinks should be done.
This action by the bureau chief is, on the whole,

A. *desirable* because it stimulates subordinates to give more thought to the solution of problems encountered
B. *undesirable* because it discourages subordinates from asking questions
C. *desirable* because it discourages subordinates from asking questions
D. *undesirable* because it undermines the confidence of subordinates in the ability of their supervisor

7. Of the following factors that may be considered by a unit head in dealing with the tardy subordinate, the one which should be given LEAST consideration is the

A. frequency with which the employee is tardy
B. effect of the employee's tardiness upon the work of other employees
C. willingness of the employee to work overtime when necessary
D. cause of the employee's tardiness

8. Of the following, the action that is likely to contribute MOST to the prestige of a supervisor is for him to

A. expect all his subordinates to perform with equal efficiency any tasks assigned to them
B. observe the same rules of conduct that he expects his subordinates to observe
C. seek their advice on his personal problems and offer them his advice on their personal problems
D. be always frank and outspoken to his subordinates in pointing out their faults

9. Although an employee under your supervision frequently protests when receiving a monotonous assignment, he nevertheless performs the assigned task efficiently. His protests, however, disturb the other employees and interfere with their work.
Of the following actions you may take in handling this employee, the MOST desirable one is for you to

A. point out to him the effect of his conduct on the staff's work and request his cooperation in accepting such assignments
B. arrange to issue such assignments to him when the other members of his staff are not present
C. inform him that you will request his transfer to another unit unless he puts a halt to his unjustifiable protests
D. ask other members of the staff to tell him that he is disturbing them by his protests

10. Assume that you are the supervisor of a small clerical unit which tabulates data prepared by another unit. One of your employees calls your attention to what appears to be an erroneous figure.
Of the following, the MOST acceptable advice for you to give this employee is to tell him to

    A. omit the figure containing the apparent error and continue with the tabulation
    B. make whatever change in the erroneous figure that appears warranted and notify the supervisor of the unit which prepared the data that errors are being made by his staff
    C. accept the questionable figure as correct and continue with the tabulation since there is no certainty that an error has been made
    D. ask the supervisor of the unit that prepared the data to have the questionable figure checked for accuracy and corrected if it is erroneous

10._____

11. A clerk in an agency informs Mr. Brown, an applicant for a license issued by the agency, that the application filed by him was denied because he lacks a year and six months of required experience. Shortly after the applicant leaves the agency's office, the clerk realizes that Mr. Brown lacks only six months of required experience rather than a year and six months.
Of the following, the MOST desirable procedure to be followed in connection with this matter is that

    A. a printed copy of the requirements should be sent to Mr. Brown
    B. a letter explaining and correcting the error should be sent to Mr. Brown
    C. no action should be taken because Mr. Brown is not qualified at the present time for the license
    D. a report of this matter should be prepared and attached to Mr. Brown's application for reference if Mr. Brown should file another application

11._____

12. Mr. Stone, who has been recently placed in charge of a clerical unit staffed with ten employees, plans to institute several radical changes in the procedures of his unit.
Of the following actions he may take before adopting any of the revisions, the MOST desirable one is for Mr. Stone to

    A. distribute to each staff member a memorandum describing the revised procedures and requesting the staff's cooperation in giving the revised procedures a fair trial
    B. issue to each staff member a memorandum describing the proposed changes and inviting him to submit his written criticism of these proposed changes
    C. issue to each staff member a memorandum describing the proposed changes and notifying him of the time and date of a staff conference to be held on the merits of the proposed changes
    D. discuss the proposed changes with each staff member independently and obtain his opinion of the proposed changes

12._____

13. An assignment completed by Frank King is returned to him by his unit supervisor for certain changes. Frank King objects to making these changes.
Of the following, the MOST appropriate action for the unit supervisor to take first is to

    A. permit Frank King to present his arguments against making these changes
    B. inform Frank King that he is free to take the matter up with a higher authority
    C. reprimand Frank King for objecting and assign another employee to make these changes
    D. state briefly that his decision is final and indicate by his manner that further discussion would be useless

14. A properly conducted job analysis will reveal the qualities essential for efficient job performance.
Of the following, the MOST accurate implication of this statement is that job analysis

    A. enables the supervisor to standardize procedures
    B. aids the supervisor in fitting the man to the job
    C. is helpful to the supervisor in scheduling work
    D. assists the supervisor in estimating costs of jobs

15. All of us who are employed by a government agency are, figuratively speaking, living in glass houses.
Of the following, this quotation MOST nearly means that employees of government agencies are

    A. basically secure in their positions
    B. more closely supervised than are those in private industry
    C. not free to exercise initiative
    D. subject to constant surveillance

16. So important to good supervision is effective leadership that some supervisors who are well equipped in this respect have compensated for deficiencies in other supervisory qualities.
On the basis of this statement, the MOST accurate of the following statements is that

    A. supervisory ability is the most valuable attribute a leader can have
    B. effective leaders are generally deficient in other supervisory qualities
    C. other supervisory qualities may be substituted for leadership ability
    D. good leaders may make good supervisors even though lacking in other supervisory qualities

17. The improvement in skill and the development of proper attitudes are essential factors in the building of correct work habits.
Of the following, the MOST valid implication of this statement for a supervisor is that

    A. the more skilled an employee is, the better will be his attitude toward his work
    B. developing proper attitudes in subordinates toward their work is more time-consuming for the supervisor than improving their skill
    C. the improvement of a worker's skill is only part of a supervisor's job
    D. correct work habits are established in order to either improve the skill of workers or develop in them a proper attitude toward their work

Questions 18-21.

DIRECTIONS: Questions 18 through 21 are based upon the situation described below. Consider the facts given in this situation when answering these questions.

SITUATION: *You are the supervisor of a small unit in a large department. In order to assist your staff in handling a peak work load, ten temporary clerks have been hired for a period of two months.*

18. Of the following actions you may take before assigning specific tasks to these temporary employees, the MOST appropriate action is for you to

    A. designate one of their number as your supervisory assistant
    B. find out what clerical experience and training each one has had
    C. ask each member of this group to indicate the type of work he prefers to do
    D. escort this group throughout the department, introducing each temporary employee to all the unit heads in the department

18.____

19. The ten temporary employees have been grouped into two teams of five employees each, and the two teams have been given different assignments. After working with his group for several days, an employee in one group asks to be transferred to the other group.
Of the following reasons for transferring this employee to the other group, the LEAST acceptable one is that

    A. there is a clash in temperament between him and some of the other members of his group
    B. he can perform the work assigned to the other group more efficiently than he can perform the work assigned to his group
    C. the work assigned to the other group is less monotonous than that assigned to his group
    D. the work assigned to his present group compels him to take frequent rest periods because of a physical disability

19.____

20. One of the temporary employees informs you that he has a suggestion for improving the method of performing the work assigned to his group.
Of the following actions, the MOST desirable one for you to take is to

    A. ignore his suggestion since he knows little about the purpose of the assignment
    B. ask him to try out the suggestion before submitting it to you
    C. have him discuss it with his co-workers before submitting it to you
    D. listen to his suggestion and take appropriate action

20.____

21. A temporary clerk who had been decreasing the amount of work he performed and who had also been attempting to induce other temporary clerks to reduce their production was twice cautioned by you to cease these practices. On each occasion, he promised to discontinue these improper practices and to perform his work conscientiously and cooperatively. Soon thereafter, he is detected for the third time attempting to persuade the other temporary clerks to shirk their duties.
Of the following, the MOST appropriate action for you to take is to

21.____

A. reprimand him for his improper conduct and have him transferred immediately to another unit
B. remind him that he may not be employed again as a temporary clerk if he continues his unethical practices
C. call a meeting of the temporary staff and warn them that anyone whose production falls below average will be discharged
D. report his improper practices to your immediate superior and recommend that this employee's services be terminated

22. As a supervisor in an agency, you receive a letter from the head of a civic organization requesting information which you are not permitted to divulge.
In preparing your letter of reply, it is MOST desirable that you

    A. begin with a pleasant phrase or statement and conclude with a brief statement denying the request
    B. limit your reply to a brief statement denying the request
    C. place the denial of the request between a pleasant opening phrase or statement and a cordial closing statement
    D. begin with a denial of the request and conclude with a pleasant closing statement

23. Of the following, it is LEAST essential for a supervisor, in assigning work to a subordinate, to issue written instructions when the

    A. supervisor will be on hand to check the work
    B. instructions are to be passed on to other employees
    C. assignment involves many details
    D. subordinate is to be held strictly accountable for the work performed

24. The suggestion is made that all the secretaries assigned to the bureau chiefs of a certain agency can be transferred to a newly established central transcribing unit which is to be staffed with stenographers and typists. Of the following, the MOST probable effect of reassigning these secretaries would be that

    A. the quality of the stenographic and typing work performed by the secretaries would deteriorate
    B. the bureau chiefs would be burdened with much of the routine work that is now performed by their secretaries
    C. typing and stenographic work would be performed less expeditiously and with frequent delays
    D. the development of understudies for bureau chiefs would be greatly hampered

25. In a large agency where both men and women are employed as clerks, certain duties may be assigned more appropriately to women than to men.
Of the following, the assignment that is generally MOST appropriate for a woman clerk is

    A. sorting and filing 3x5 index cards
    B. issuing supplies from the agency's stockroom to employees presenting requisitions
    C. serving at an information desk during the hours from 7:00 P.M. to 11:00 P.M. for a period of two months
    D. collecting outgoing mail from the various offices of the agency and delivering incoming mail to these offices

26. A unit supervisor discovers several errors in the work performed by a subordinate. 26.____
In dealing with this subordinate, it is LEAST desirable for the supervisor to

   A. give his criticism immediately rather than at a later date
   B. make it clear to the subordinate that he is criticizing the subordinate and not the subordinate's work
   C. praise, when possible, some commendable aspect of the subordinate's work before making the adverse criticism
   D. make sure that his criticism is not overheard by other employees

27. The status of the morale of a staff is usually a good indication of the quality of the leader- 27.____
ship displayed by the supervisor of the staff.
Of the following, the BEST indication of the existence of high morale among a staff is that

   A. the employees are prompt in reporting for work
   B. the staff is always willing to subordinate personal desires to attain group objectives
   C. it is seldom necessary for the staff to work overtime
   D. the subordinates and their superior meet socially after working hours

28. The use of standard practices and procedures in large organizations is often essential in 28.____
order to insure a smooth, efficient, and controlled flow of work. A strict adherence to standard practices and procedures to the extent that unnecessary delay is created is known, in general, as *red tape*.
On the basis of this statement, the MOST accurate of the following statements is that

   A. although the use of standard practices and procedures promotes efficiency, it also creates unnecessary delays and *red tape*
   B. in order to insure a smooth, efficient, and controlled plan of work, *red tape* should be eliminated by a strict adherence to standard practices and procedures
   C. *red tape* is a necessary evil which invariably creeps into any large organization which uses standard practices and procedures
   D. *red tape* exists when delay takes place as a result of a too rigid conformity with standard practices and procedures

29. The tasks of government are imposed not only by law but also by public opinion, which at 29.____
any time may be made into law. Government agencies must, therefore, strive to anticipate and fulfill the needs of the public.
Of the following, the MOST valid implication of this statement is that the

   A. satisfaction of the needs of the public is one of the obligations of a government agency
   B. law prescribes what tasks government agencies should perform and public opinion determines how these tasks should be performed
   C. tasks imposed by law on a government agency have priority over those imposed by public opinion
   D. functions of a government agency should be carried out in accordance with the letter, rather than the spirit, of the law

30. The manner in which an employee performs on the job rather than his potential ability is 30.____
the true test of his value to his employer.
The one of the following which is NOT an implication of the above statement is a(n)

A. employee of great potential ability may be of little or no value to his employer
B. supervisor should observe the manner in which his subordinates perform their work
C. employee's potential ability is of no significance in determining his fitness for a specific job
D. employee should attempt to perform his work to the best of his ability

31. No routine will automatically bring itself into proper relation with changing conditions. Of the following situations, the one which MOST NEARLY exemplifies the truth of this statement is a

    A. change in the rules governing the submission or reports by employees working in the field is found to be impractical and the previous procedure is reinstituted
    B. long established method of filing papers in a bureau is found to be inadequate because of changes in the functions of the bureau
    C. long established method of distributing orders to the staff is found to work effectively when the size of the staff is considerably increased
    D. change in the rules governing hours of attendance at work proves distasteful to many employees

32. Interest is essentially an attitude of continuing attentiveness, found where activity is satisfactorily self-expressive. Whenever work is so circumscribed that the chance for self-expression or development is denied, monotony is present.
On the basis of this statement, it is MOST accurate to state that

    A. tasks which are repetitive in nature do not permit self-expression and, therefore, create monotony
    B. interest in one's work is increased by financial and non-financial incentives
    C. jobs which are monotonous can be made self-expressive by substituting satisfactory working conditions
    D. workers whose tasks afford them no opportunity for self-expression find such tasks to be monotonous

33. The first step in an organizational study is the reading of the basic documents. There is some documentary basis for any governmental organization, outlining the purposes for which it was established, conferring certain powers, and imposing certain limitations on the conferred powers. This statement indicates that in making an organization study, one should FIRST

    A. review all the authoritative material in the field of government administration and organization
    B. arrange the functions of the organization on a functional chart in accordance with the official documents
    C. study the laws and authorities under which the organization operates
    D. outline the purposes for which the organization study was originally established

34. His attitude is as provincial as an isolationist country's unwillingness to engage in any international trade whatever, on the ground that it will be required to buy something from outsiders which could possibly be produced by local talent, although not as well and not as cheaply. This statement is MOST descriptive of the attitude of the division chief in a government agency who

A. wishes to restrict promotions to supervisory positions in his division exclusively to employees in his division
B. refuses to delegate responsible tasks to subordinates qualified to perform these tasks
C. believes that informal on-the-job training of new staff members is superior to formal training methods
D. frequently makes personal issues out of matters that should be handled on an impersonal basis

35. A trainee was paid a weekly wage of $480.00 for a 40-hour work week. As a result of a new labor contract, he is paid $494.00 a week for a 38-hour work week with time-and-one-half pay for time worked in excess of 38 hours in any work week.
If he continues to work 40 hours weekly under the new contract, the amount by which his average hourly rate for a 40-hour work week under the new contract exceeds the hourly rate previously paid him lies between _____ and _____, inclusive.

   A. $1.02; $1.06   B. $1.08; $1.16   C. $1.18; $1.26   D. $1.28; $1.36

36. The problem of inadequate storage space arising from the large number of inactive records stored in city agencies can be solved MOST satisfactorily with the aid of _____ equipment.

   A. photostat   B. microfilm
   C. IBM sorting   D. digital printing

37. To say that an employee is *erudite* means MOST NEARLY that he is

   A. scholarly
   B. insecure
   C. efficient
   D. punctual

38. The forms design section of a city agency recommended that the sizes of forms used by the agency be limited to the sizes that can be cut with the least amount of waste from either 17" x 22" or 17" x 28" sheets.
Of the following, the size that does NOT comply with this recommendation is

   A. 4 1/2" x 5 1/2"   B. 3 3/4" x 4 1/4"
   C. 3 1/2" x 4 1/4"   D. 4 1/4" x 2 3/4"

39. The number of investigations conducted by an agency in 2007 was 3,600. In 2008, the number of investigations conducted was one-third more than in 2007. The number of investigations conducted in 2009 was three-fourths of the number conducted in 2008. It is anticipated that the number of investigations conducted in 2010 will be equal to the average of the three preceding years.
On the basis of this information, the MOST accurate of the following statements is that the number of investigations conducted in

   A. 2007 is larger than the number anticipated for 2010
   B. 2008 is smaller than the number anticipated for 2010
   C. 2009 is equal to the number conducted in 2007
   D. 2009 is larger than the number anticipated for 2010

40. *The office manager thought it advisable to MOLLIFY his subordinate.*
    The word *mollify* as used in this sentence means MOST NEARLY

    A. reprimand B. caution C. calm D. question

41. *The bureau chief adopted a DILATORY policy.* The word *dilatory* as used in this sentence means MOST NEARLY

    A. tending to cause delay
    B. acceptable to all affected
    C. severe but fair
    D. prepared with great care

42. *He complained about the PAUCITY of requests.* The word *paucity* as used in this sentence means MOST NEARLY

    A. great variety
    B. unreasonableness
    C. unexpected increase
    D. scarcity

43. To say that an event is *imminent* means MOST NEARLY that it is

    A. near at hand
    B. unpredictable
    C. favorable or happy
    D. very significant

44. *The general manager delivered a LAUDATORY speech.*
    The word *laudatory* as used in this sentence means MOST NEARLY

    A. clear and emphatic
    B. lengthy
    C. introductory
    D. expressing praise

45. *We all knew of his AVERSION for performing statistical work.*
    The word *aversion* as used in this sentence means MOST NEARLY

    A. training
    B. dislike
    C. incentive
    D. lack of preparation

46. *The engineer was CIRCUMSPECT in making his recommendations.* The word *circumspect* as used in this sentence means MOST NEARLY

    A. hostile B. outspoken C. biased D. cautious

47. To say that certain clerical operations were *obviated* means MOST NEARLY that these operations were

    A. extremely distasteful
    B. easily understood
    C. made unnecessary
    D. very complicated

48. *The interviewer was impressed with the client's DEMEANOR.* The word *demeanor* as used in this sentence means MOST NEARLY

    A. outward manner
    B. plan of action
    C. fluent speech
    D. extensive knowledge

49. To say that the information was *gratuitous* means MOST NEARLY that it was

    A. given freely
    B. deeply appreciated
    C. brief
    D. valuable

50. *The supervisor was unaware of this EXIGENCY.*
    The word *exigency* as used in this sentence means MOST NEARLY

    A. unexplained absence
    B. costly delay
    C. pressing need
    D. final action

51. *She considered the supervisor's action to be ARBITRARY.* The word *arbitrary* as used in this sentence means MOST NEARLY

    A. inconsistent
    B. justifiable
    C. appeasing
    D. dictatorial

52. *His report on the activities of the agency was VERBOSE.*
    The word *verbose* as used in this sentence means MOST NEARLY

    A. vivid   B. wordy   C. vague   D. oral

Questions 53-61.

DIRECTIONS: Questions 53 through 61 are to be answered SOLELY on the basis of the following information.

Assume that the following rules for computing service ratings are to be used experimentally in determining the service ratings of seven permanent employees. (Note that these rules are hypothetical and are NOT to be confused with the existing method of computing service ratings for employees.) The personnel record of each of these seven employees is given in Table II. You are to determine the answer to each of the questions on the basis of the rules given below for computing service ratings and the data contained in the personnel records of these seven employees.

All computations should be made as of the close of the rating period ending March 31, 2007.

RULES FOR COMPUTING SERVICE RATINGS

Service Rating
The service rating of each permanent competitive class employee shall be computed by adding the following three scores: (1) a basic score, (2) the employee's seniority score, and (3) the employee's efficiency score.

Seniority Score
An employee's seniority score shall be computed by crediting him with 1/2% per year for each year of service starting with the date of the employee's entrance as a permanent employee into the competitive class, up to a maximum of 15 years (7 1/2%). A residual fractional period of eight months or more shall be considered as a full year and credited with 1/2%. A residual fraction of from four to, but not including, eight months shall be considered as a half-year and credited with 1/4%. A residual fraction of less than four months shall receive no credit in the seniority score. For example, a person who entered the competitive class as a permanent employee on August 1, 1999 would, as of March 31, 2002, be credited with a seniority score of 1 1/2% for his two years and 8 months of service.

Efficiency Score
An employee's efficiency score shall be computed by adding the annual efficiency ratings received by him during his service in his PRESENT position. (Where there are negative efficiency ratings, such ratings shall be subtracted from the sum of the positive efficiency ratings.) An employee's annual efficiency rating shall be based on the grade he receives from his supervisor for his work performance during the annual efficiency rating period.

Basic Score

A basic score of 70% shall be given to each employee upon permanent appointment to a competitive class position.

An employee shall receive a grade of "A" for performing work of the highest quality and shall be credited with an efficiency rating of plus (+) 3%, An employee shall receive a grade of "F" for performing work of the lowest quality and shall receive an efficiency rating of minus (-) 2%. Table I, entitled "Basis for Determining Annual Efficiency Ratings," lists the six grades of work performance with their equivalent annual efficiency ratings. Table I also lists the efficiency ratings to be assigned for service in a position for less than a year during the annual efficiency rating period. The annual efficiency rating period shall run from April 1 to March 31, inclusive.

TABLE I
BASIS FOE DETERMINING ANNUAL EFFICIENCY RATINGS

Quality of Work Performed	Grade Assigned A	Annual Efficiency Rating for Service in a Position for:		
		8 months to a full year	At least 4 months but less than 8 months	Less than 4 months
Highest Quality	A	+ 3%	+1½%	0%
Good Quality	B	+ 2%	+ 1%	0%
Standard Quality	C	+ 1%	+½%	0%
Substandard Quality	D	0%	0%	0%
Poor Quality	E	-1%	-½%	0%
Lowest Quality	F	-2%	-1%	0%

Appointment or Promotion during an Efficiency Rating Period

An employee who has been appointed or promoted during an efficiency rating period shall receive for that period an efficiency rating only for work performed by him during the portion of the period that he served in the position to which he was appointed or promoted. His efficiency rating for the period shall be determined in accordance with Table I.

Sample Computation of Service Rating

John Smith entered the competitive class as a permanent employee on December 1, 2002 and was promoted to his present position as a Clerk, Grade 3 on November 1, 2005. As a Clerk, Grade 3, he received a grade of "B" for work performed during the five-month period extending from November 1, 2005 to March 31, 2006 and a grade of "C" for work performed during the full annual period extending from April 1, 2006 to March 32, 2007.

On the basis of the Rules for Computing Service Ratings, John Smith should be credited with:

70 % basic score
2 1/4% seniority score - for 4 years and 4 months of service (from 12-1-02 to 3-31-07)
2 % efficiency score - for 5 months of "B" service and a full year of "C" service
74 1/4%

TABLE II
PERSONNEL RECORD OF SEVEN PERMANENT COMPETITIVE CLASS EMPLOYEES

Employee	Present Position	Date of Appointment or Promotion to Present Position	Date of Entry as Permanent Employee in Competitive Class
Allen	Clerk, Gr. 5	6-1-03	7-1-90
Brown	Clerk, Gr. 4	1-1-05	7-1-97
Cole	Clerk, Gr. 3	9-1-03	11-1-00
Fox	Clerk, Gr. 3	10-1-03	9-1-98
Green	Clerk, Gr. 2	12-1-01	12-1-01
Hunt	Clerk, Gr. 2	7-1-02	7-1-02
Kane	Steno, Gr. 3	11-16-04	3-1-01

	Grades Received Annually for Work Performed in Present Position					
Employee	4-1-01 to 3-31-02	4-1-02 to 3-31-03	4-1-03 to 3-31-04	4-1-04 to 3-31-05	4-1-05 to 3-31-06	4-1--06 to 3-31-07
Allen			C*	C	B	C
Brown				C*	C	B
Cole			A*	B	C	C
Fox			C*	C	D	C
Green	C*	D	C	D	C	C
Hunt		C*	C	E	C	C
Kane				B*	B	C

Explanatory Notes:
* Served in present position for less than a full year during this rating period. (Note date of appointment, or promotion, to present period.)

All seven employees have served continuously as permanent employees since their entry into the competitive class.

Questions 53 through 61 refer to the employees listed in Table II. You are to answer these questions SOLELY on the basis of the preceding Rules for Computing Service Ratings and on the information concerning these seven employees given in Table II. You are reminded that all computations are to be made as of the close of the rating period ending March 31, 2007. Candidates may find it helpful to arrange their computations on their scratch paper in an orderly manner since the computations for one question may also be utilized in answering another question.

53. The seniority score of Allen is
    A. 74%   B. 8 1/2%   C. 8%   D. 8 1/4%

54. The seniority score of Fox exceeds that of Cole by
    A. 1 1/2%   B. 2%   C. 1%   D. 3/4 1/4

55. The seniority score of Brown is
    A. equal to Hunt's
    B. twice Hunt's
    C. more than Hunt's by 1 1/2%
    D. less than Hunt's by 1/2%

56. Green's efficiency score is
    A. twice that of Kane
    B. equal to that of Kane
    C. less than Kane's by 1/2%
    D. less than Kane's by 1%

57. Of the following employees, the one who has the LOWEST efficiency score is
    A. Brown   B. Fox   C. Hunt   D. Kane

58. A comparison of Hunt's efficiency score with his seniority score reveals that his efficiency score is
    A. less than his seniority score by 1/2%
    B. less than his seniority score by 3/4%
    C. equal to his seniority score
    D. greater than his seniority score by 1/2%

59. Fox's service rating is
    A. 72 1/2% B. 74%   C. 76 1/2% D. 76 3/4%

60. Brown's service rating is
    A. less than 78%
    B. 78%
    C. 78 1/4%
    D. more than 78 1/4%

61. Cole's service rating exceeds Kane's by
    A. less than 2%
    B. 2%
    C. 2 1/4%
    D. more than 2 1/4%

Questions 62-71.

DIRECTIONS: Each of the sentences numbered 62 to 71 may be classified under one of the following four options:
(A) faulty; contains an error in grammar only
(B) faulty; contains an error in spelling only
(C) faulty; contains an error in grammar and an error in spelling
(D) correct; contains no error in grammar or in spelling

Examine each sentence carefully to determine under which of the above four options it is best classified. Then, in the correspondingly numbered space at the right, write the letter preceding the option which is the BEST of the four listed above.

62. A recognized principle of good management is that an assignment should be given to whomever is best qualified to carry it out.   62._____

63. He considered it a privilege to be allowed to review and summarize the technical reports issued annually by your agency.   63._____

64. Because the warehouse was in an inaccessable location, deliveries of electric fixtures from the warehouse were made only in large lots.   64._____

65. Having requisitioned the office supplies, Miss Brown returned to her desk and resumed the computation of petty cash disbursements.   65._____

66. One of the advantages of this chemical solution is that records treated with it are not inflammable.   66._____

67. The complaint of this employee, in addition to the complaints of the other employees, were submitted to the grievance committee.   67._____

68. A study of the duties and responsibilities of each of the various categories of employees was conducted by an unprejudiced classification analyst.   68._____

69. Ties of friendship with this subordinate compels him to withold the censure that the subordinate deserves.   69._____

70. Neither of the agencies are affected by the decision to institute a program for rehabilitating physically handicaped men and women.   70._____

71. The chairman stated that the argument between you and he was creating an intolerable situation.   71._____

Questions 72-75.

DIRECTIONS: Each of Questions 72 through 75 consists of a statement containing five words in capital letters. One of these capitalized words is not in keeping with the meaning which the statement is evidently intended to convey. The five words in capital letters in each statement are reprinted after the statement. In the correspondingly numbered space at the right, write the letter preceding the one of the five words which does MOST to spoil the true meaning of the statement.

72. The alert employee will find, EVEN in the best managed offices, violations of some of the rules of good office management. However, further study will reveal that the correction of such violations is by ALL means a SIMPLE matter, BUT requires research, time, patience, and often a high degree of MANAGERIAL ability.   72._____

   A. Even   B. All   C. Simple   D. But   E. Managerial

73. The information clerk in any organization must DELEGATE tact, courtesy, and good judgment in DEALING with callers, many of whom, on the other hand, DISREGARD business ETIQUETTE in their CONTACT with the information clerk.   73._____

   A. Delegate   B. Dealing   C. Disregard
   D. Etiquette   E. Contact

74. When the supervisor gives advancement or other rewards only to SUBORDINATES who have REQUESTED them, or shows a sincere INTEREST in the welfare of his staff, he is building FAVORABLE ATTITUDES.

    A. Subordinates B. Requested C. Interest
    D. Favorable E. Attitudes

75. An appointee to the City's civil service must be a bona fide resident of the City for at least three years immediately prior to his APPOINTMENT. An appointee who served in the Armed Forces retains as his legal address that place where he resided prior to his ENTRY into the MILITARY service, PROVIDED he has taken definite action to establish a new RESIDENCE.

    A. Appointment B. Entry C. Military
    D. Provided E. Residence

KEY (CORRECT ANSWERS)

1. D	16. D	31. B	46. D	61. A
2. B	17. C	32. D	47. C	62. A
3. B	18. B	33. C	48. A	63. D
4. A	19. C	34. A	49. A	64. B
5. C	20. D	35. D	50. C	65. D
6. A	21. D	36. B	51. D	66. B
7. C	22. C	37. A	52. B	67. A
8. B	23. A	38. B	53. A	68. D
9. A	24. B	39. C	54. C	69. C
10. D	25. A	40. C	55. B	70. C
11. B	26. B	41. A	56. C	71. A
12. C	27. B	42. D	57. B	72. B
13. A	28. D	43. A	58. D	73. A
14. B	29. A	44. D	59. D	74. B
15. D	30. C	45. B	60. B	75. D

EXAMINATION SECTION
TEST 1

DIRECTIONS: Each question or incomplete statement is followed by several suggested answers or completions. Select the one that BEST answers the question or completes the statement. *PRINT THE LETTER OF THE CORRECT ANSWER IN THE SPACE AT THE RIGHT.*

1. A supervisor may be required to help train a newly appointed clerk. Which of the following is LEAST important for a newly appointed clerk to know in order to perform his work efficiently?
   A. Acceptable ways of answering and recording telephone calls
   B. The number of files in the storage files unit
   C. The filing methods used by his unit
   D. Proper techniques for handling visitors

   1.____

2. In your agency you have the responsibility of processing clients who have appointments with agency representatives. On a particularly busy day, a client comes to your desk and insists that she must see the person handling her case although she has no appointment.
   Under the circumstances, your FIRST action should be to
   A. show her the full appointment schedule
   B. give her an appointment for another day
   C. ask her to explain the urgency
   D. tell her to return later in the day

   2.____

3. Which of the following practices is BEST for a supervisor to use when assigning work to his staff?
   A. Give workers with seniority the most difficult jobs
   B. Assign all unimportant work to the slower workers
   C. Permit each employee to pick the job he prefers
   D. Make assignments based on the workers' abilities

   3.____

4. In which of the following instances is a supervisor MOST justified in giving commands to people under his supervision? When
   A. they delay in following instructions which have been given to them clearly
   B. they become relaxed and slow about work, and he wants to speed up their production
   C. he must direct them in an emergency situation
   D. he is instructing them on jobs that are unfamiliar to them

   4.____

5. Which of the following supervisory actions or attitudes is MOST likely to result in getting subordinates to try to do as much work as possible for a supervisor? He
   A. shows that his most important interest is in schedules and production goals
   B. consistently pressures his staff to get the work out

   5.____

C. never fails to let them know he is in charge
D. considers their abilities and needs while requiring that production goals be met

6. Assume that a supervisor has been explaining certain regulations to a new clerk under his supervision.
The MOST efficient way for the supervisor to make sure that the clerk has understood the explanation is to
    A. give him written materials on the regulations
    B. ask him if he has any further questions about the regulations
    C. ask him specific questions based on what has just been explained to him
    D. watch the way he handles a situation involving these regulations

6.____

7. One of your unit clerks has been assigned to work for a Mr. Jones in another office for several days. At the end of the first day, Mr. Jones, saying the clerk was not satisfactory, asks that she not be assigned to him again. This clerk is one of your most dependable workers, and no previous complaints about her work have come to you from any other outside assignments.
To get to the root of this situation, your FIRST action should be to
    A. ask Mr. Jones to explain in what way her work was unsatisfactory
    B. ask the clerk what she did that Mr. Jones considered unsatisfactory
    C. check with supervisors for whom she previously worked to see if your own rating of her is in error
    D. tell Mr. Jones to pick the clerk he would prefer to have work for him the next time

7.____

8. A senior typist, still on probation, is instructed to type, as quickly as possible, one section of a draft of a long, complex report. Her part must be typed and readable before another part of the report can be written. Asked when she can have the report ready, she gives her supervisor an estimate of a day longer than she knows it will actually take. She then finishes the job a day sooner than the date given her supervisor.
The judgment shown by the senior typist in giving an overestimate of time in a situation like this is, in general,
    A. *good*, because it prevents the supervisor from thinking she works slowly
    B. *good*, because it keeps unrealistic supervisors from expecting too much
    C. *bad*, because she should have used the time left to further check and proofread her work
    D. *bad*, because schedules and plans for other parts of the project may have been based on her false estimate

8.____

9. Suppose a new clerk, still on probation, is placed under your supervision and refuses to do a job you ask him to do.
What is the FIRST thing you should do?
    A. Explain that you are the supervisor and he must follow your instructions
    B. Tell him he may be suspended if he refuses
    C. Ask someone else to do the job and rate him accordingly
    D. Ask for his reason for objecting to the request

9.____

10. As a supervisor of a small group of people, you have blamed worker A for something that you later find out was really done by worker B.
   The BEST thing for you to do now would be to
   A. say nothing to worker A but criticize worker B for his mistake while worker A is near so that A will realize that you know who made the mistake
   B. speak to each worker separately, apologize to worker A for your mistake, and discuss worker B's mistake with him
   C. bring both workers together, apologize to worker A for your mistake, and discuss worker B's mistake with him
   D. say nothing now but be careful about mixing up worker A with worker B in the future

11. You have just learned one of your staff is grumbling that she thinks you are not pleased with her work. As far as you're concerned, this isn't true at all. In fact, you've paid no particular attention to this worker lately because you've been very busy. You have just finished preparing an important report and *breaking in* a new clerk.
   Under the circumstances, the BEST thing to do is
   A. ignore her; after all, it's just a figment of her imagination
   B. discuss the matter with her now to try to find out and eliminate the cause of this problem
   C. tell her not to worry about it; you haven't had time to think about her work
   D. make a note to meet with her at a later date in order to straighten out the situation

12. A most important job of a supervisor is to positively motivate employees to increase their work production.
   Which of the following LEAST indicates that a group of workers has been positively motivated?
   A. Their work output becomes constant and stable.
   B. Their cooperation at work becomes greater.
   C. They begin to show pride in the product of their work.
   D. They show increased interest in their work

13. Which of the following traits would be LEAST important in considering a person for a merit increase?
   A. Punctuality
   B. Using initiative successfully
   C. High rate of production
   D. Resourcefulness

14. Of the following, the action LEAST likely to gain a supervisor the cooperation of his staff is for him to
   A. give each person consideration as an individual
   B. be as objective as possible when evaluating work performance
   C. rotate the least popular assignments
   D. expect subordinates to be equally competent

15. It has been said that, for the supervisor, nothing can beat the *face-to-face* communication of talking to one subordinate at a time.
    This method is, however, LEAST appropriate to use when
    A. supervisor is explaining a change in general office procedure
    B. subject is of personal importance
    C. supervisor is conducting a yearly performance evaluation of all employees
    D. supervisor must talk to some of his employees concerning their poor attendance and punctuality

16. While you are on the telephone answering a question about your agency, a visitor comes to your desk and starts to ask you a question. There is no emergency or urgency in either situation, that of the phone call or that of answering the visitor's question.
    In this case, you should
    A. continue to answer the person on the telephone until you are finished and then tell the visitor you are sorry to have kept him waiting
    B. excuse yourself to the person on the telephone and tell the visitor that you will be with him as soon as you have finished on the phone
    C. explain to the person on the telephone that you have a visitor and must shorten the conversation
    D. continue to answer the person on the phone while looking up occasionally at the visitor to let him know that you know he is waiting

17. While speaking on the telephone to someone who called, you are disconnected.
    The FIRST thing you should do is
    A. hang up but try to keep your line free to receive the call back
    B. immediately get the dial tone and continually dial the person who called you until you reach him
    C. signal the switchboard operator and ask her to re-establish the connection
    D. dial O for Operator and explain that you were disconnected

18. The type of speech used by an office worker in telephone conversations greatly affects the communicator.
    Of the following, the BEST way to express your ideas when telephoning is with a vocabulary that consists mainly of _____ words.
    A. formal, intellectual sounding   B. often used colloquial
    C. technical, emphatic   D. simple, descriptive

19. Suppose a clerk under your supervision has taken a personal phone call and is at the same time needed to answer a question regarding an assignment being handled by another member of your office. He appears confused as to what he should do. How should you instruct him later as to how to handle a similar situation?
    You should tell him to
    A. tell the caller to hold on while he answers the question
    B. tell the caller to call back a little later

C. return the call during an assigned break
D. finish the conversation quickly and answer the question

20. You are asked to place a telephone call by your supervisor. When you place the call, you receive what appears to be a wrong number.
Of the following, you should FIRST
    A. check the number with your supervisor to see if the number he gave you is correct
    B. ask the person on the other end what his number is and who he is
    C. check with the person on the other end to see if the number you dialed is the number you received
    D. apologize to the person on the other end for disturbing him and hang up

20._____

Questions 21-30.

DIRECTIONS: WORD MEANING
Each of Questions 21 through 30 contains a word in capitals followed by four suggested meanings of the word. For each question, choose the BEST meaning and write the letter of the best meaning in the space at the right.

21. ACCURATE
    A. correct   B. useful   C. afraid   D. careless

21._____

22. ALTER
    A. copy   B. change   C. repeat   D. agree

22._____

23. DOCUMENT
    A. outline   B. agreement   C. blueprint   D. record

23._____

24. INDICATE
    A. listen   B. show   C. guess   D. try

24._____

25. INVENTORY
    A. custom   B. discovery   C. warning   D. list

25._____

26. ISSUE
    A. annoy   B. use up   C. give out   D. gain

26._____

27. NOTIFY
    A. inform   B. promise   C. approve   D. strength

27._____

28. ROUTINE
    A. path   B. mistake   C. habit   D. journey

28._____

29. TERMINATE
    A. rest   B. start   C. deny   D. end

29._____

30. TRANSMIT
    A. put in   B. send   C. stop   D. go across

30._____

Questions 31-35.

DIRECTIONS: READING COMPREHENSION
Questions 31 through 35 test how well you understand what you read. It will be necessary for you to read carefully because your answers to these questions should be based SOLELY on the information given in the following paragraphs.

The recipient gains an impression of a typewritten letter before he begins to read the message. Factors which provide for a good first impression include margins and spacing that are visually pleasing, formal parts of the letter which are correctly placed according to the style of the letter, copy which is free of obvious erasures and over-strikes, and transcript that is even and clear. The problem for the typist is that of how to produce that first, positive impression of her work.

There are several general rules which a typist can follow when she wishes to prepare a properly spaced letter on a sheet of letterhead. Ordinarily, the width of a letter should not be less than four inches nor more than six inches. The side margins should also have a desirable relation to the bottom margin and the space between the letterhead and the body of the letter. Usually the most appealing arrangement is when the side margins are even and the bottom margin is slightly wider than the side margins. In some offices, however, standard line length is used for all business letters, and the secretary then varies the spacing between the date line and the inside address according to the length of the letter.

31. The BEST title for the above paragraphs would be
    A. Writing Office Letters
    B. Making Good First Impressions
    C. Judging Well-Typed Letters
    D. Good Placing and Spacing for Office Letters

32. According to the above paragraphs, which of the following might be considered the way in which people very quickly judge the quality of work which has been typed?
    By
    A. measuring the margins to see if they are correct
    B. looking at the spacing and cleanliness of the typescript
    C. scanning the body of the letter for meaning
    D. reading the date line and address for errors

33. What, according to the above paragraphs, would be definitely UNDESIRABLE as the average line length of a typed letter?
    A. 4"   B. 5"   C. 6"   D. 7"

34. According to the above paragraphs, when the line length is kept standard, the secretary
    A. does not have to vary the spacing at all since this also is standard
    B. adjusts the spacing between the date line and inside address for different lengths of letters
    C. uses the longest line as a guideline for spacing between the date line and inside address
    D. varies the number of spaces between the lines

35. According to the above paragraphs, side margins are MOST pleasing when they   35._____
    A. are even and somewhat smaller than the bottom margin
    B. are slightly wider than the bottom margin
    C. vary with the length of the letter
    D. are figured independently from the letterhead and the body of the letter

Questions 36-40.

DIRECTIONS: CODING

    Name of Applicant   H A N G S B R U K E
    Test Code   c o m p l e x i t y
    File Number   0 1 2 3 4 5 6 7 8 9

Assume that each of the above capital letters is the first letter of the name of an applicant, that the small letter directly beneath each capital letter is the test code for the applicant, and that the number directly beneath each code letter is the file number for the applicant.

In each of the following Questions 36 through 40, the test code letters and the file numbers in Columns 2 and 3 should correspond to the capital letters in Column 1. For each question, look at each column carefully and mark your answer as follows:
    If there is an error only in Column 2, mark your answer A.
    If there is an error only in Column 3, mark your answer B.
    If there is an error in both Columns 2 and 3, mark your answer C.
    If both Columns 2 and 3 are correct, mark your answer D.

The following sample question is given to help you understand the procedure.

SAMPLE QUESTION

Column 1	Column 2	Column 3
AKEHN	otyci	18902

In Column 2, the final test code letter *i* should be *m*. Column 3 is correctly coded in Column 1. Since there is an error only in Column 2, the answer is A.

	Column 1	Column 2	Column 3	
36.	NEKKU	mytti	29987	36._____
37.	KRAEB	txlye	86095	37._____
38.	ENAUK	ymoit	92178	38._____
39.	REANA	xeomo	69121	39._____
40.	EKHSE	ytcxy	97049	

8 (#1)

Questions 41-50.

DIRECTIONS: ARITHMETICAL REASONING
Solve the following problems.

41. If a secretary answered 28 phone calls and typed the addresses for 112 credit statements in one morning, what is the RATIO of phone calls answered to credit statements typed for that period of time?
    A. 1:4   B. 1:7   C. 2:3   D. 3:5

41.____

42. According to a suggested filing system, no more than 10 folders should be filed behind any one file guide, and from 15 to 25 file guides should be used in each file drawer for easy finding and filing.
    The MAXIMUM number of folders that a five-drawer file cabinet can hold to allow easy finding and filing is
    A. 550   B. 750   C. 1,100   D. 1,250

42.____

43. An employee had a starting salary of $32,902. He received a salary increase at the end of each year, and at the end of the seventh year, his salary was $36,738.
    What was his AVERAGE annual increase in salary over these seven years?
    A. $510   B. $538   C. $548   D. $572

43.____

44. The 55 typists and 28 senior clerks in a certain agency were paid a total of $1,943,200 in salaries for the year.
    If the average annual salary of a typist was $22,400, the average annual salary of a senior clerk was
    A. $25,400   B. $26,600   C. $26,800   D. $27,000

44.____

45. A typist has been given a three-page report to type. She has finished typing the first two pages. The first page has 283 words, and the second page has 366 words.
    If the total report consists of 954 words, how many words will she have to type on the third page of the report?
    A. 202   B. 287   C. 305   D. 313

45.____

46. In one day, Clerk A processed 30% more forms than Clerk B, and Clerk C processed 11/4 as many forms as Clerk A.
    If Clerk B processed 40 forms, how many MORE forms were processed by Clerk C?
    A. 12   B. 13   C. 21   D. 25

46.____

47. A clerk who earns a gross salary of $452 every week has the following deductions taken from her paycheck: 17½% for City, State, Federal taxes, and for Social Security, $1.20 for health insurance, and $6.10 for union dues.
    The amount of her take-home pay is
    A. $286.40   B. $312.40   C. $331.60   D. $365.60

47.____

48. In 2022 an agency spent $400 to buy pencils at a cost of $1 a dozen. If the agency used ¾ of these pencils in 2022 and used the same number of pencils in 2023, how many MORE pencils did it have to buy to have enough pencils for all of 2023?
   A. 1,200   B. 2,400   C. 3,600   D. 4,800

49. A clerk who worked in Agency X earned the following salaries: $30,070 the first year, $30,500 the second year, and $30,960 the third year. Another clerk who worked in Agency Y for three years earned $30,550 a year for two years and $30,724 the third year.
The DIFFERENCE between the average salaries received by both clerks over a three-year period is
   A. $98   B. $102   C. $174   D. $282

50. An employee who works over 40 hours in any week receives overtime payment for the extra hours at time and one-half (1½ times) his hourly rate of pay. An employee who earns $15.60 an hour works a total of 45 hours during a certain week.
His TOTAL pay for that week would be
   A. $624.00   B. $702.00   C. $741.00   D. $824.00

KEY (CORRECT ANSWERS)

1. B	11. B	21. A	31. D	41. A
2. C	12. A	22. B	32. B	42. D
3. D	13. A	23. D	33. D	43. C
4. C	14. D	24. B	34. B	44. A
5. D	15. A	25. D	35. A	45. C
6. C	16. B	26. C	36. B	46. D
7. A	17. A	27. A	37. C	47. D
8. D	18. D	28. C	38. D	48. B
9. D	19. C	29. D	39. A	49. A
10. B	20. C	30. B	40. C	50. C

TEST 2

DIRECTIONS: Each question or incomplete statement is followed by several suggested answers or completions. Select the one that BEST answers the question or completes the statement. *PRINT THE LETTER OF THE CORRECT ANSWER IN THE SPACE AT THE RIGHT.*

1. To tell a newly employed clerk to fill a top drawer of a four-drawer cabinet with heavy folders which will be often used and to keep lower drawers only partly filled is
    A. *good*, because a tall person would have to bend unnecessarily if he had to use a lower drawer
    B. *bad*, because the file cabinet may tip over when the top drawer is opened
    C. *good*, because it is the most easily reachable drawer for the average person
    D. *bad*, because a person bending down at another drawer may accidentally bang his head on the bottom of the drawer when he straightens up

1.____

2. If you have requisitioned a ream of paper in order to duplicate a single page office announcement, how many announcements can be printed from the one package of paper?
    A. 200   B. 500   C. 700   D. 1,000

2.____

3. In the operations of a government agency, a voucher is ORDINARILY used to
    A. refer someone to the agency for a position or assignment
    B. certify that an agency's records of financial transactions are accurate
    C. order payment from agency funds of a stated amount to an individual
    D. enter a statement of official opinion in the records of the agency

3.____

4. Of the following types of cards used in filing systems, the one which is generally MOST helpful in locating records which might be filed under more than one subject is the _____ card.
    A. cut
    B. tickler
    C. cross-reference
    D. visible index

4.____

5. The type of filing system in which one does NOT need to refer to a card index in order to find the folder is called
    A. alphabetic   B. geographic   C. subject   D. locational

5.____

6. Of the following, records management is LEAST concerned with
    A. the development of the best method for retrieving important information
    B. deciding what records should be kept
    C. deciding the number of appointments a client will need
    D. determining the types of folders to be used

6.____

7. If records are continually removed from a set of files without *charging* them to the borrower, the filing system will soon become ineffective.
   Of the following terms, the one which is NOT applied to a form used in a charge-out system is a
   A. requisition card
   B. out-folder
   C. record retrieval form
   D. substitution card

   7._____

8. A new clerk has been told to put 500 cards in alphabetical order. Another clerk suggests that she divide the cards into four groups such as A to F, G to L, M to R, and S to Z, and then alphabetize these four smaller groups.
   The suggested method is
   A. *poor*, because the clerk will have to handle the sheets more than once and will waste time
   B. *good*, because it saves time, is more accurate, and is less tiring
   C. *good*, because she will not have to concentrate on it so much when it is in smaller groups
   D. *bad*, because this method is much more tiring than straight alphabetizing

   8._____

9. The term that describes the equipment attached to an office computer is
   A. interface   B. network   C. hardware   D. software

   9._____

10. Suppose a clerk has been given pads of pre-printed forms to use when taking phone messages for others in her office. The clerk is then observed using scraps of paper and not the forms for writing her messages.
    It should be explained that the BEST reason for using the forms is that
    A. they act as a checklist to make sure that the important information is taken
    B. she is expected to do her work in the same way as others in the office
    C. they make sure that unassigned paper is not wasted on phone messages
    D. learning to use these forms will help train her to use more difficult forms

    10._____

11. Of the following, the one which is spelled INCORRECTLY is
    A. alphabetization
    B. reccommendation
    C. redaction
    D. synergy

    11._____

12. Of the following, the MAIN reason a stock clerk keeps a perpetual inventory of supplies in the storeroom is that such an inventory will
    A. eliminate the need for a physical inventory
    B. provide a continuous record of supplies on hand
    C. indicate whether a shipment of supplies is satisfactory
    D. dictate the terms of the purchase order

    12._____

13. As a supervisor, you may be required to handle different types of correspondence.
    Of the following types of letters, it would be MOST important to promptly seal which kind of letters?

    13._____

A. One marked *confidential*
B. Those containing enclosures
C. Any letter to be sent airmail
D. Those in which carbons will be sent along with the original

14. While opening incoming mail, you notice that one letter indicates that an enclosure was to be included but, even after careful inspection,, you are not able to find the information to which this refers.
Of the following, the thing that you should do FIRST is
   A. replace the letter in its envelope and return it to the sender
   B. file the letter until the sender's office mails the missing information
   C. type out a letter to the sender informing them of their error
   D. make a notation in the margin of the letter that the enclosure was omitted

14.____

15. You have been given a checklist and assigned the responsibility of inspecting certain equipment in the various offices of your agency.
Which of the following is the GREATEST advantage of the checklist?
   A. It indicates which equipment is in greatest demand.
   B. Each piece of equipment on the checklist will be checked only once.
   C. It helps to insure that the equipment listed will not be overlooked.
   D. The equipment listed suggests other equipment you should look for.

15.____

16. Your supervisor has asked you to locate a telephone number for an attorney named Jones, whose office is located at 311 Broadway and whose name is not already listed in your files.
The BEST method for finding the number would be for you to
   A. call the information operator and have her get it for you
   B. look in the alphabetical directory (white pages) under the name Jones at 311 Broadway
   C. refer to the heading Attorney in the yellow pages for the name Jones at 311 Broadway
   D. ask your supervisor who referred her to Mr. Jones, then call that person for the number

16.____

17. An example of material that should NOT be sent by first class mail is a
   A. carbon copy of a letter   B. postcard
   C. business reply card   D. large catalogue

17.____

18. Which of the following BEST describes *office work simplification*?
   A. An attempt to increase the rate of production by speeding up the movements of employees
   B. Eliminating wasteful steps in order to increase efficiency
   C. Making jobs as easy as possible for employees so they will not be overworked
   D. Eliminating all difficult tasks from an office and leaving only simple ones

18.____

19. The duties of a supervisor who is assigned the job of timekeeper may include all of the following EXCEPT
    A. computing and recording regular hours worked each day in accordance with the normal work schedule
    B. approving requests for vacation leave, sick leave, and annual leave
    C. computing and recording overtime hours worked beyond the normal schedule
    D. determining the total regular hours and total extra hours worked during the week

19.____

20. Suppose a clerk under your supervision accidentally opens a personal letter while handling office mail.
    Under such circumstances, you should tell the clerk to put the letter back in the envelope and
    A. take the letter to the person to whom it belongs and make sure he understands that the clerk did not read it
    B. try to seal the envelope so it won't appear to have been opened
    C. write on the envelope *Sorry, opened by mistake*, and put his initials on it
    D. write on the envelope *Sorry, opened by mistake*, but not put his initials on it

20.____

Questions 21-25.

DIRECTIONS: SPELLING
Each Question 21 through 25 consists of three words. In each question, one of the words may be spelled incorrectly or all three may be spelled correctly. For each question, if one of the words is spelled incorrectly, write the letter of the incorrect word in the space at the right. If all three words are spelled correctly, write the letter D in the space at the right.

SAMPLE I: (A) guide   (B) departmint   (C) stranger
SAMPLE II: (A) comply   (B) valuable   (C) window

In Sample Question I, *departmint* is incorrect. It should be spelled *department*. Therefore, B is the answer to Sample Question 1.
In Sample Question II, all three words are spelled correctly. Therefore D is the answer to Sample Question II.

21.	A. argument	B. reciept	C. complain	21.____
22.	A. sufficient	B. postpone	C. visible	22.____
23.	A. expirience	B. dissatisfy	C. alternate	23.____
24.	A. occurred	B. noticable	C. appendix	24.____
25.	A. anxious	B. guarantee	C. calender	25.____

Questions 26-30.

DIRECTIONS: ENGLISH USAGE
Each Question 26 through 30 contains a sentence. Read each sentence carefully to decide whether it is correct. Then, in the space at the right, mark your answer:
A. if the sentence is incorrect because of bad grammar or sentence structure
B. of the sentence is incorrect because of bad punctuation
C. if the sentence is incorrect because of bad capitalization
D. if the sentence is correct

Each incorrect sentence has only one type of error. Consider a sentence correct if it has no errors, although there may be other correct ways of saying the same thing.

SAMPLE QUESTION I: One of our clerks were promoted yesterday.
The subject of this sentence is *one*, so the verb should be *was promoted* instead of *were promoted*. Since the sentence is incorrect because of bad grammar, the answer to Sample Question I is A.

SAMPLE QUESTION II: Between you and me, I would prefer not going there.
Since this sentence is correct, the answer to Sample Question II is D.

26. The National alliance of Businessmen is trying to persuade private businesses to hire youth in the summertime. 26.____

27. The supervisor who is on vacation, is in charge of processing vouchers. 27.____

28. The activity of the committee at its conferences is always stimulating. 28.____

29. After checking the addresses again, the letters went to the mailroom. 29.____

30. The director, as well as the employees, are interested in sharing the dividends. 30.____

Questions 31-40.

DIRECTIONS: FILING
Each Question 31 through 40 contains four names. For each question, choose the name that should be FIRST if the four names are to be arranged in alphabetical order in accordance with the Rules for Alphabetical Filing given below. Read these rules carefully. Then, for each question, indicate in the correspondingly numbered space at the right the letter before the name that should be FIRST in alphabetical order.

RULES FOR ALPHABETICAL FILING

Names of People

1. The names of people are filed in strict alphabetical order, first according to the last name, then according to first name or initial, and finally according to middle name or initial. For example: George Allen comes before Edward Bell, and Leonard P. Reston comes before Lucille B. Reston.

2. When last names are the same, for example A. Green and Agnes Green, the one with the initial comes before the one with the name written out when the first initials are identical.

3. When first and last names are alike and the middle initial is given, for example John David Doe and John Devoe Doe, the names should be filed in the alphabetical order of the middle names.

4. When first and last names are the same, a name without a middle initial comes before one with a middle name or initial. For example, John Doe comes before both John A. Doe and John Alan Doe.

5. When first and last names are the same, a name with a middle initial comes before one with a middle name beginning with the same initial. For example: Jack R. Herts comes before Jack Richard Hertz.

6. Prefixes such as De, O', Mac, Mc, and Van are filed as written and are treated as part of the names to which they are connected. For example: Robert O'Dea is filed before David Olsen.

7. Abbreviated names are treated as if they were spelled out. For example: Chas. is filed as Charles and Thos. is filed as Thomas.

8. Titles and designations such as Dr., Mr., and Prof. are disregarded in filing.

Names of Organizations

1. The names of business organizations are filed according to the order in which each word in the name appears. When an organization name bears the name of a person, it is filed according to the rules for filing names of people as given above. For example, William Smith Service Co. comes before Television Distributors, Inc.

2. Where bureau, board, office or department appears as the first part of the title of a governmental agency, that agency should be filed under the word in the title expressing the chief function of the agency. For example: Bureau of the Budget would be filed as if written Budget, (Bureau of the). The Department of Personnel would be filed as if written Personnel (Department of).

3. When the following words are part of an organization, they are disregarded: the, of, and.

4. When there are numbers in a name, they are treated as if they were spelled out. For example: 10th Street Bootery is filed as Tenth Street Bootery.

SAMPLE QUESTION:
A. Jane Earl (2)
B. James A. Earle (4)
C. James Earl (1)
D. J. Earle (3)

The numbers in parentheses show the proper alphabetical order in which these names should be filed. Since the name that should be filed FIRST is James Earl, the answer to the sample question is C.

31. A. Majorca Leather Goods B. Robert Majorca and Sons
    C. Maintenance Management Corp. D. Majestic Carpet Mills
    31.____

32. A. Municipal Telephone Service B. Municipal Reference Library
    C. Municipal Credit Union D. Municipal Broadcasting System
    32.____

33. A. Robert B. Pierce B. R. Bruce Pierce
    C. Ronald Pierce D. Robert Bruce Pierce
    33.____

34. A. Four Seasons Sports Club B. 14 Street Shopping Center
    C. Forty Thieves Restaurant D. 42nd St. Theaters
    34.____

35. A. Franco Franceschini B. Amos Franchini
    C. Sandra Franceschia D. Lilie Franchinesca
    35.____

36. A. Chas. A. Levine B. Kurt Levene
    C. Charles Levine D. Kurt E. Levene
    36.____

37. A. Prof. Geo. Kinkaid B. Mr. Alan Kinkaid
    C. Dr. Albert A. Kinkade D. Kincade Liquors Inc.
    37.____

38. A. Department of Public Events B. Office of the Public Administrator
    C. Queensborough Public Library D. Department of Public Health
    38.____

39. A. Martin Luther King, Jr. Towers B. Metro North Plaza
    C. Manhattanville Houses D. Marble Hill Houses
    39.____

40. A. Dr. Arthur Davids B. The David Check Cashing Service
    C. A.C. Davidsen D. Milton Davidoff
    40.____

Questions 41-45.

DIRECTIONS: READING COMPREHENSION
Questions 41 through 45 test how well you understand what you read. It will be necessary for you to read carefully because your answers to these questions should be based SOLELY on the information given in the following paragraph.

Work standards presuppose an ability to measure work. Measurement in office management is needed for several reasons. First, it is necessary to evaluate the overall efficiency of the office itself. It is then essential to measure the efficiency of each particular section or unit and that of the individual worker. To plan and control the work of sections and units, one must have measurement. A program of measurement goes hand in hand with a program of standards. One can have measurement without standards, but one cannot have work standards without measurement. Providing data on amount of work done and time expended, measurement does not deal with the amount of energy expended by an individual although in many cases such energy may be in direct proportion to work output. Usually from two-thirds to three fourths of all work can be measured. However, less than two-thirds of all work is actually measured because measurement difficulties are encountered when office work is non-repetitive and irregular, or when it is primarily mental rather than manual. These obstacles are often used as excuses for non-measurement far more frequently than is justified.

41. According to the paragraph, an office manager cannot set work standards unless he can
    A. plan the amount of work to be done
    B. control the amount of work that is done
    C. estimate accurately the quantity of work done
    D. delegate the amount of work to be done to efficient workers

41.____

42. According to the paragraph, the type of office work that would be MOST difficult to measure would be
    A. checking warrants for accuracy of information
    B. recording payroll changes
    C. processing applications
    D. making up a new system of giving out supplies

42.____

43. According to the paragraph, the actual amount of work that is measured is _____ of all work.
    A. less than two-thirds
    B. two-thirds to three-fourths
    C. less than three-sixths
    D. more than three-fourths

43.____

44. Which of the following would be MOST difficult to determine by using measurement techniques?
    A. The amount of work that is accomplished during a certain period of time
    B. The amount of work that should be planned for a period of time
    C. How much time is needed to do a certain task
    D. The amount of incentive a person must have to do his job

44.____

45. The one of the following which is the MOST suitable title for the paragraph is:
    A. How Measurement of Office Efficiency Depends on Work Standards
    B. Using Measurement for Office Management and Efficiency
    C. Work Standards and the Efficiency of the Office Worker
    D. Managing the Office Using Measured Work Standards

45.____

Questions 46-50.

DIRECTIONS: INTERPRETING STATISTICAL DATA
Questions 46 through 50 are to be answered using the information given in the following table.

AGE COMPOSITION IN THE LABOR FORCE IN CITY A
(2010-2020)

	Age Group	2010	2015	2020
Men	14-24	8,430	10,900	14,340
	25-44	22,200	22,350	26,065
	45+	17,550	19,800	21,970
Women	14-24	4,450	6,915	7,680
	25-44	9,080	10,010	11,550
	45+	7,325	9,470	13,180

46. The GREATEST increase in the number of people in the labor force between 2010 and 2015 occurred among
   A. men between the ages of 14 and 24
   B. men age 45 and over
   C. women between the ages of 14 and 24
   D. women age 45 and over

47. If the total number of women of all ages in the labor force increases from 2020 to 2025 by the same number as it did from 2015 to 2020, the TOTAL number of women of all ages in the labor force in 2025 will be
   A. 27,425   B. 29,675   C. 37,525   D. 38,425

48. The total increase in number of women in the labor force from 2010 to 2015 differs from the total increase of men in the same years by being _____ than that of men.
   A. 770 less   B. 670 more   C. 770 more   D. 1,670 more

49. In the year 2010, the proportion of married women in each group was as follows: 1/5 of the women in the 14-24 age group, 1/4 of those in the 25-44 age group, and 2/5 of those 45 and over.
   How many married women were in the labor force in 2010?
   A. 4,625   B. 5,990   C. 6,090   D. 7,910

50. The 14-24 age group of men in the labor force from 2010 to 2020 increased by APPROXIMATELY
   A. 40%   B. 65%   C. 70%   D. 75%

KEY (CORRECT ANSWERS)

1. B	11. B	21. B	31. C	41. C
2. B	12. B	22. D	32. D	42. D
3. C	13. A	23. A	33. B	43. A
4. C	14. D	24. B	34. D	44. D
5. A	15. C	25. C	35. C	45. B
6. C	16. C	26. C	36. B	46. A
7. C	17. D	27. B	37. D	47. D
8. B	18. B	28. D	38. B	48. B
9. C	19. B	29. A	39. A	49. C
10. A	20. C	30. A	40. B	50. C

36

EXAMINATION SECTION
TEST 1

DIRECTIONS: Each question or incomplete statement is followed by several suggested answers or completions. Select the one that BEST answers the question or completes the statement. *PRINT THE LETTER OF THE CORRECT ANSWER IN THE SPACE AT THE RIGHT.*

1. When you select someone to serve as supervisor of your unit during your absence on vacation and at other times, it would generally be BEST to choose the employee who is

    A. able to move the work along smoothly without friction
    B. on staff longest
    C. liked best by the rest of the staff
    D. able to perform the work of each employee to be supervised

2. Successful supervision of handicapped persons employed in a department depends MOST on providing them with a work place and work climate

    A. which is safe and accident-free
    B. that requires close and direct supervision by others
    C. that requires the performance of routine, repetitive tasks under a minimum of pressure
    D. where they will be accepted by the other employees

3. Studies have indicated that when employees feel that their work is aimless and unchallenging, the allocation or payment of more money for this type of work is LIKELY to

    A. contribute little to increased production
    B. bring more status to this work
    C. increase employees' feelings of security
    D. give employees greater motivation

4. An employee's performance has fallen below established minimum standards of quantity and quality.
   The threat of monetary or other disciplinary action as a device for improving this employee's performance would PROBABLY be acceptable and most effective

    A. only if applied as soon as the performance fell below standard
    B. only after more constructive techniques have failed
    C. at any time provided the employee understands that the punishment will be carried out
    D. at no time

5. A supervisor must, on short notice, ask his staff to work overtime.
   Of the following, a technique that is MOST likely to win their willing cooperation would be to

    A. explain that occasional overtime is part of the job requirement
    B. explain that they will be doing him a personal favor which he will appreciate very much
    C. explain why the overtime is necessary
    D. promise them that they can take the extra time off in the near future

6. On checking a completed work assignment of an employee, the supervisor finds that the work was not done correctly because the employee had not understood his instructions. Of the following, the BEST way to prevent repetition of this situation next time is for the supervisor to

   A. ask the employee whether he fully understood the instructions and tell him to ask questions in the future whenever anything is unclear
   B. ask the employee to repeat the instructions given and test his understanding with several key questions
   C. give the instructions a second time, emphasizing the more complicated aspects of the job
   D. give work instructions in writing

7. If, as a supervisor, you find yourself pressured for time to handle all of your job responsibilities, the one of the following tasks which it would be MOST appropriate for you to delegate to a subordinate is

   A. attending a staff conference of unit supervisors to discuss the implementation of a new departmental policy
   B. making staff work assignments
   C. interviewing a new employee
   D. checking work of certain employees for accuracy

8. Suppose you are unavoidably late for work one morning. When you arrive at 10 o'clock, you find there are several matters demanding your attention.
   Which one of the following matters should you handle LAST?

   A. A visitor who had a 9:30 appointment with you has been waiting to see you since 9 o'clock
   B. An employee on an assignment which should have been completed that morning is absent, and the work will have to be reassigned
   C. Several letters which you dictated at the end of the previous day have been typed and are on your desk for signature and mailing
   D. Your superior called asking you to get certain information for him when you come in and to call him back

9. Suppose that you have assigned a typist to type a report containing considerable statistical and tabular material and have given her specific instructions as to how this material is to be laid out on each page. When she returns the completed report, you find that it was not prepared according to your instructions, but you may possibly be able to use it the way it was typed. When you question her, she states that she thought her layout was better, but you were unavailable for consultation when she began the work.
   Of the following, the BEST action for you to take is to

   A. criticize her for not doing the work according to your instructions
   B. have her retype the report
   C. praise her for her work but tell her she could have waited until she could consult you
   D. praise her for using initiative

10. Of the following, the MOST effective way for a supervisor to correct poor working habits of an employee which result in low and poor quality output is to give the employee

A. additional training
B. less demanding assignments until his work improves
C. continuous supervision
D. more severe criticism

11. Of the following, the BEST way for a supervisor to teach an employee how to do a new and somewhat complicated job is to

    A. assign him to observe another employee who is already skilled in this work and instruct him to consult this employee if he has any questions
    B. explain to him how to do it, then demonstrate how it is done, then observe and correct the employee as he does it, then follow up
    C. give him a written, detailed, step-by-step explanation of how to do the job and instruct him to ask questions if anything is unclear when he does the work
    D. teach him the easiest part of the job first, then the other parts one at a time, in order of their difficulty, as the employee masters the easier parts

12. After an employee has completed telling his supervisor about a grievance against a co-worker, the supervisor tells the employee that he will take action to remove the cause of the grievance.
    The action of the supervisor was

    A. *good* because ill feeling between subordinates interferes with proper performance
    B. *poor* because the supervisor should give both employees time to *cool off*
    C. *good* because grievances that appear petty to the supervisor are important to subordinates
    D. *poor* because the supervisor should tell the employee that he will investigate the matter before he comes to any conclusion

13. During work on an important project, one employee in a secretarial pool turns in several pages of typed copy, one page of which contains several errors.
    Of these four comments which her supervisor might possibly make, which one would be MOST constructive?

    A. "You did such a poor job on this; I'll have to have it done over."
    B. "You will have to do better more consistently than this if you want to be in charge of a secretarial pool yourself someday."
    C. "How come you made so many mistakes here? Your other pages were all right."
    D. "If my boss saw this, he'd be very displeased with you."

14. A supervisor has general supervision over a large, complex project with many employees. The work is subdivided among small units of employees, each with a senior clerk or senior stenographer in charge. At a staff meeting, after all work assignments have been made, the supervisor tells all the employees that they are to take orders only from their immediate supervisor and instructs them to let him know if any one else tries to give them orders.
    This instruction by the supervisor is

    A. *good* because it may prevent the issuance of orders by unauthorized persons which would interfere with the accomplishment of the assignment
    B. *poor* because employees should be instructed to take up such problems with their immediate supervisor

C. *good* because orders issued by immediate supervisors would be precise and directly related to the tasks of the assignments while those issued by others would not be
D. *poor* because it places upon all employees a responsibility which should not normally be theirs

15. A supervisor who is to direct a team of senior clerks and clerks and senior stenographers and stenographers in a complex project calls them together beforehand to inform them of the tasks each employee will perform on this job. Of the following, the CHIEF value of this action by the supervisor is that each member of this team will be able to

    A. work independently in the absence of the supervisor
    B. understand what he will do and how this will fit into the total picture
    C. share in the process of decision-making as an equal participant
    D. judge how well the plans for this assignment have been made

16. A supervisor who has both younger and older employees under his supervision may sometimes find that employee absenteeism seriously interferes with accomplishment of goals.
    Studies of such employee absenteeism have shown that the absences of employees

    A. under 35 years of age are usually unexpected and the absences of employees over 45 years of age are usually unnecessary
    B. of all age groups show the same characteristics as to length of absence
    C. under 35 years of age are for frequent, short periods while the absences of employees over 45 years of age are less frequent but of longer duration
    D. under 35 years of age are for periods of long duration and the absences of employees over 45 years of age are for periods of short duration

17. Suppose you have a long-standing procedure for getting a certain job done by your subordinates that is apparently a good one. Changes in some steps of the procedure are made from time to time to handle special problems that come up.
    For you to review this procedure periodically is desirable MAINLY because

    A. the system is working well
    B. checking routines periodically is a supervisor's chief responsibility
    C. subordinates may be confused as to how the procedure operates as a result of the changes made
    D. it is necessary to determine whether the procedure has become outdated or is in need of improvement

18. In conducting an interview, the BEST types of questions with which to begin the interview are those which the person interviewed is _____ to answer.

    A. willing and able
    B. willing but unable
    C. able to but unwilling
    D. unable and unwilling

19. In order to determine accurately a child's age, it is BEST for an interviewer to rely on

    A. the child's grade in school
    B. what the mother says
    C. birth records
    D. a library card

20. In his first interview with a new employee, it would be LEAST appropriate for a unit supervisor to

   A. find out the employee's preference for the several types of jobs to which he is able to assign him
   B. determine whether the employee will make good promotion material
   C. inform the employee of what his basic job responsibilities will be
   D. inquire about the employee's education and previous employment

21. If an interviewer takes care to phrase his questions carefully and precisely, the result will MOST probably be that

   A. he will be able to determine whether the person interviewed is being truthful
   B. the free flow of the interview will be lost
   C. he will get the information he wants
   D. he will ask stereotyped questions and narrow the scope of the interview

22. When, during an interview, is the person interviewed LEAST likely to be cautious about what he tells the interviewer?

   A. Shortly after the beginning when the questions normally suggest pleasant associations to the person interviewed
   B. As long as the interviewer keeps his questions to the point
   C. At the point where the person interviewed gains a clear insight into the area being discussed
   D. When the interview appears formally ended and goodbyes are being said

23. In an interview held for the purpose of getting information from the person interviewed, it is sometimes desirable for the interviewer to repeat the answer he has received to a question.
   For the interviewer to rephrase such an answer in his own words is good practice MAINLY because it

   A. gives the interviewer time to make up his next question
   B. gives the person interviewed a chance to correct any possible misunderstanding
   C. gives the person interviewed the feeling that the interviewer considers his answer important
   D. prevents the person interviewed from changing his answer

24. There are several methods of formulating questions during an interview. The particular method used should be adapted to the interview problems presented by the person being questioned.
   Of the following methods of formulating questions during an interview, the ACCEPTABLE one is for the interviewer to ask questions which

   A. incorporate several items in order to allow a cooperative interviewee freedom to organize his statements
   B. are ambiguous in order to foil a distrustful interviewee
   C. suggest the correct answer in order to assist an interviewee who appears confused
   D. would help an otherwise unresponsive interviewee to become more responsive

25. For an interviewer to permit the person being interviewed to read the data the interviewer writes as he records the person's responses on a routine departmental form is

   A. *desirable* because it serves to assure the person interviewed that his responses are being recorded accurately
   B. *undesirable* because it prevents the interviewer from clarifying uncertain points by asking additional questions
   C. *desirable* because it makes the time that the person interviewed must wait while the answer is written seem shorter
   D. *undesirable* because it destroys the confidentiality of the interview

26. Suppose that a stranger enters the office you are in charge of and asks for the address and telephone number of one of your employees.
   Of the following, it would be BEST for you to

   A. find out why he needs the information and release it if his reason is a good one
   B. explain that you are not permitted to release such information to unauthorized persons
   C. give him the information but tell him it must be kept confidential
   D. ask him to leave the office immediately

27. A member of the public approaches an employee who is at work at his desk. The employee cannot interrupt his work in order to take care of this person.
   Of the following, the BEST and MOST courteous way of handling this situation is for the employee to

   A. avoid looking up from his work until he is finished with what he is doing
   B. tell this person that he will not be able to take care of him for quite a while
   C. refer the individual to another employee who can take care of him right away
   D. chat with the individual while he continues with his work

28. You answer a phone call from a citizen who urgently needs certain information you do not have, but you think you know who may have it. He is angry because he has already been switched to two different offices.
   Of the following, it would be BEST for you to

   A. give him the phone number of the person you think may have the information he wants, but explain you are not sure
   B. tell him you regret you cannot help him because you are not sure who can give him the information
   C. advise him that the best way he can be sure of getting the information he wants is to write a letter to the agency
   D. get the phone number where he can be reached and tell him you will try to get the information he wants and will call him back later

29. Persons who have business with an agency often complain about the *red tape* which complicates or slows up what they are trying to accomplish.
   As a supervisor of a unit which deals with the public, the LEAST effective of the following actions which you could take to counteract this feeling on the part of a person who has business with your office is to

   A. assure him that your office will make every effort to take care of his matter as fast as possible
   B. tell him that because of the volume of work in your agency he must be patient with *red tape*

C. give him a reasonable date by which action on the matter he is concerned about will be completed and tell him to call you if he hasn't heard by then
D. give him an understanding of why the procedures he must comply with are necessary

30. If a receptionist is sorting letters at her desk and a caller appears to make an inquiry, the receptionist should

    A. ask the caller to have a seat and wait
    B. speak to the caller while continuing the sorting, looking up occasionally
    C. stop what she is doing and give undivided attention to the caller
    D. continue with the sorting until a logical break in the work is reached, then answer any inquiries

31. To avoid cutting off parts of letters when using an automatic letter opener, it is BEST to

    A. arrange all of the letters so that the addresses are right side up
    B. hold the envelopes up to the light to make sure their contents have not settled to the side that is to be opened
    C. strike the envelopes against a table or desk top several times so that the contents of all the envelopes settle to one side
    D. check the enclosures periodically to make sure that the machine has not been cutting into them

32. Requests to repair office equipment which appears to be unsafe should be given priority MAINLY because if repairs are delayed

    A. there may be injuries to staff
    B. there may be further deterioration of the equipment
    C. work flow may be interrupted
    D. the cost of repair may increase

33. Of the following types of documents, it is MOST important to retain and file

    A. working drafts of reports that have been submitted in final form
    B. copies of letters of good will which conveyed a message that could not be handled by phone
    C. interoffice orders for materials which have been received and verified
    D. interoffice memoranda regarding the routing of standard forms

34. Of the following, the BEST reason for discarding certain material from office files would be that the

    A. files are crowded
    B. material in the files is old
    C. material duplicates information obtainable from other sources in the files
    D. material is referred to most often by employees in an adjoining office

35. Of the following, the BEST reason for setting up a partitioned work area for the typists in your office is that

    A. an uninterrupted flow of work among the typists will be possible
    B. complaints about ventilation and lighting will be reduced
    C. the first-line supervisor will have more direct control over the typists
    D. the noise of the typewriters will be less disturbing to other workers

36. Of the following, the MAIN factor contributing to the expense of maintaining an office procedure manual would be the

    A. infrequent use of the manual
    B. need to revise it regularly
    C. cost of looseleaf binders
    D. high cost of printing

37. From the viewpoint of use of a typewriter to fill in a form, the MOST important design factor to consider is

    A. standard spacing
    B. box headings
    C. serial numbering
    D. vertical guide lines

38. Out-of-date and seldom used records should be removed PERIODICALLY from the files because

    A. overall responsibility for records will be transferred to the person in charge of the central storage files
    B. duplicate copies of every record are not needed
    C. valuable filing space will be regained and the time needed to find a current record will be cut down
    D. worthwhile suggestions on improving the filing system will result whenever this is done

39. In a certain office, file folders are constantly being removed from the files for use by administrators. At the same time, new material is coming in to be filed in some of these folders.
    Of the following, the BEST way to avoid delays in filing of the new material and to keep track of the removed folders is to

    A. keep a sheet listing all folders removed from the file, who has them, and a follow-up date to check on their return; attach to this list new material received for filing
    B. put an *out* slip in the place of any file folder removed, telling what folder is missing, date removed, and who has it; file new material received at front of files
    C. put a temporary *out* folder in place of the one removed, giving title or subject, date removed, and who has it; put into this temporary folder any new material received
    D. keep a list of all folders removed and who has them; forward any new material received for filing while a folder is out to the person who has it

40. Folders labeled *Miscellaneous* should be used in an alphabetic filing system MAINLY to

    A. provide quick access to recent material
    B. avoid setting up individual folders for all infrequent correspondents
    C. provide temporary storage for less important documents
    D. temporarily hold papers which will not fit into already crowded individual folders

41. Suppose that one of the office machines in your unit is badly in need of replacement. Of the following, the MOST important reason for postponing immediate purchase of a new machine would be that

    A. a later model of the machine is expected on the market in a few months
    B. the new machine is more expensive than the old machine
    C. the operator of the present machine will have to be instructed by the manufacturer in the operation of the new machine
    D. the employee operating the old machine is not complaining

42. If the four steps listed below for processing records were given in logical sequence, the one that would be the THIRD step is:

    A. Coding the records, using a chart or classification system
    B. Inspecting the records to make sure they have been released for filing
    C. Preparing cross-reference sheets or cards
    D. Skimming the records to determine filing captions

43. The suggestion that memos or directives which circulate among subordinates be initialed by each employee is a

    A. *poor* one because, with modern copying machines, it should be possible to supply every subordinate with a copy of each message for his personal use
    B. *good* one because it relieves the supervisor of blame for the action of subordinates who have read and initialed the messages
    C. *poor* one because initialing the memo or directive is no guarantee that the subordinate has read the material
    D. *good* one because it can be used as a record by the supervisor to show that his subordinates have received the message and were responsible for reading it

44. Of the following, the MOST important reason for microfilming office records is to

    A. save storage space needed to keep records
    B. make it easier to get records when needed
    C. speed up the classification of information
    D. shorten the time which records must be kept

45. Your office filing cabinets have become so overcrowded that it is difficult to use the files. Of the following, the MOST desirable step for you to take FIRST to relieve this situation would be to

    A. assign your assistant to spend some time each day reviewing the material in the files and to give you his recommendations as to what material may be discarded
    B. discard all material which has been in the files more than a given number of years
    C. submit a request for additional filing cabinets in your next budget request
    D. transfer enough material to the central storage room of your agency to give you the amount of additional filing space needed

46. Of the following, the USUAL order of the subdivisions in a standard published report is:

    A. Table of contents, body of report, index, appendix
    B. Index, table of contents, body of report, appendix
    C. Index, body of report, table of contents, appendix
    D. Table of contents, body of report, appendix, index

47. The BEST type of pictorial illustration to show the approximate percentage breakdown of the titles of employees in a department would be the

    A. flow chart   B. bar graph
    C. organization chart   D. line graph

48. You are reviewing a draft, written by one of your subordinates, of a report that is to be distributed to every bureau and division of your department.
Which one of the following would be the LEAST desirable characteristic of such a report?

   A. It gives information, explanations, conclusions, and recommendations for which purpose it was written.
   B. There is sufficient objective data presented to substantiate the conclusions reached and the recommendations made by the writer.
   C. The writing style and opinions of the writer are persuasive enough to win over to its conclusions those who read the report, although little data is given in support.
   D. It will be understood easily by the people to whom it will be distributed.

49. According to accepted practice, a business letter is addressed to an organization but marked for the attention of a specific individual whenever the sender wants

   A. only the person to whose attention the letter is sent to read the letter
   B. the letter to be opened and taken care of by someone else in the organization of the person for whose attention it is marked is away
   C. a reply only from the specific individual
   D. to improve the appearance and balance of the letter in cases where the company address is a long one

50. Which one of the following would be an ACCEPTABLE way to end a business letter?

   A. Hoping you will find this information useful, I remain
   B. Yours for continuing service
   C. I hope this letter gives you the information you need
   D. Trusting this gives you the information you desire, I am

KEY (CORRECT ANSWERS)

1. A	11. B	21. C	31. C	41. A
2. D	12. D	22. D	32. A	42. A
3. A	13. C	23. B	33. D	43. D
4. B	14. B	24. D	34. C	44. A
5. C	15. B	25. A	35. D	45. A
6. B	16. C	26. B	36. B	46. D
7. D	17. D	27. C	37. A	47. B
8. C	18. A	28. D	38. C	48. C
9. A	19. C	29. B	39. C	49. B
10. A	20. B	30. C	40. B	50. C

TEST 2

DIRECTIONS: Each question or incomplete statement is followed by several suggested answers or completions. Select the one that BEST answers the question or completes the statement. *PRINT THE LETTER OF THE CORRECT ANSWER IN THE SPACE AT THE RIGHT.*

1. You are replying to a letter from an individual who asks for a pamphlet put out by your agency. The pamphlet is out of print. A new pamphlet with a different title, but dealing with the same subject, is available.
   Of the following, it would be BEST that your reply indicate that

   A. you cannot send him the pamphlet he requested because it is out of print
   B. the pamphlet he requested is out of print, but he may be able to find it in the public library
   C. the pamphlet he requested is out of print, but you are sending him a copy of your agency's new pamphlet on the same subject
   D. since the pamphlet he requested is out of print, you would advise him to ask his friends or business acquaintances if they have a copy of it

   1._____

2. An angry citizen sends a letter to your agency claiming that your office sent him the wrong form and complaining about the general inefficiency of city workers. Upon checking, you find that an incorrect form was indeed sent to this person.
   In reply, you should

   A. admit the error, apologize briefly, and enclose the correct form
   B. send the citizen the correct form with a transmittal letter stating only that the form is enclosed
   C. send him the correct form without any comment
   D. advise the citizen that mistakes happen in every large organization and that you are enclosing the correct form

   2._____

3. It has been suggested that the language level of a letter of reply written by a government employee be geared no higher than the probable educational level of the person to whom the letter is written.
   This suggestion is a

   A. *good* one because it is easier for anyone to write letters simply, and this will make for a better reply
   B. *poor* one because it is not possible to judge, from one letter, the exact educational level of the writer
   C. *good* one because it will contribute to the recipient's comprehension of the contents of the letter
   D. *poor* one because the language should be at the simplest possible level so that anyone who reads the letter can understand it

   3._____

4. Suppose that a large bureau has 187 employees. On a particular day, approximately 14% of these employees are not available for work because of absences due to vacation, illness, or other reasons. Of the remaining employees, 1/7 are assigned to a special project while the balance are assigned to the normal work of the bureau.
   The number of employees assigned to the normal work of the bureau on that day is

   A. 112   B. 124   C. 138   D. 142

   4._____

5. Suppose that you are in charge of a typing pool of 8 typists. Two typists type at the rate of 38 words per minute; three type at the rate of 40 words per minute; three type at the rate of 42 words per minute. The average typewritten page consists of 50 lines, 12 words per line. Each employee works from 9 to 5 with one hour off for lunch.
   The total number of pages typed by this pool in one day is, on the average, CLOSEST to _____ pages.

   A. 205   B. 225   C. 250   D. 275

6. Suppose that part-time workers are paid $14.40 an hour, prorated to the nearest half hour, with pay guaranteed for a minimum of four hours if services are required for less than four hours. In one operation, part-time workers signed the time sheet as follows:

Worker	In	Out
A	8:00 A.M.	11:35 A.M.
B	8:30 A.M.	3:20 P.M.
C	7:55 A.M.	11:00 A.M.
D	8:30 A.M.	2:25 P.M.

   How much would total payment to these part-time workers amount to for this operation, assuming that those who stayed after 12 Noon were not paid for one hour which they took off for lunch?

   A. $268.80   B. $273.60   C. $284.40   D. $297.60

7. He wanted to *ascertain* the facts before arriving at a conclusion.
   The word *ascertain* means MOST NEARLY

   A. disprove   B. determine   C. convert   D. provide

8. Did the supervisor *assent* to her request for annual leave? The word *assent* means MOST NEARLY

   A. allude   B. protest   C. agree   D. refer

9. The new worker was fearful that the others would *rebuff* her.
   The word *rebuff* means MOST NEARLY

   A. ignore   B. forget   C. copy   D. snub

10. The supervisor of that office does not *condone* lateness. The word *condone* means MOST NEARLY

    A. mind   B. excuse   C. punish   D. remember

11. Each employee was instructed to be as *concise* as possible when preparing a report.
    The word *concise* means MOST NEARLY

    A. exact   B. sincere   C. flexible   D. brief

Questions 12-21.

DIRECTIONS: Below are 10 sentences numbered 12 to 21. Some of the sentences contain an error in spelling, word usage, or sentence structure, or punctuation. Some sentences are correct as they stand, although there may be other correct ways of expressing the same thought. All incorrect sentences contain only one error. Mark your answer to each question as follows:

A. if the sentence has an error in spelling
B. if the sentence has an error in punctuation or capitalization
C. if the sentence has an error in word usage or sentence structure
D. if the sentence is correct

12. Because the chairman failed to keep the participants from wandering off into irrelevant discussions, it was impossible to reach a consensus before the meeting was adjourned.   12.____

13. Certain employers have an unwritten rule that any applicant, who is over 55 years of age, is automatically excluded from consideration for any position whatsoever.   13.____

14. If the proposal to build schools in some new apartment buildings were to be accepted by the builders, one of the advantages that could be expected to result would be better communication between teachers and parents of schoolchildren.   14.____

15. In this instance, the manufacturer's violation of the law against deseptive packaging was discernible only to an experienced inspector.   15.____

16. The tenants' anger stemmed from the president's going to Washington to testify without consulting them first.   16.____

17. Did the president of this eminent banking company say; "We intend to hire and train a number of these disad-vantaged youths?"   17.____

18. In addition, today's confidential secretary must be knowledgable in many different areas: for example, she must know modern techniques for making travel arrangements for the executive.   18.____

19. To avoid further disruption of work in the offices, the protesters were forbidden from entering the building unless they had special passes.   19.____

20. A valuable secondary result of our training conferences is the opportunities afforded for management to observe the reactions of the participants.   20.____

21. Of the two proposals submitted by the committee, the first one is the best.   21.____

Questions 22-26.

DIRECTIONS: In Questions 22 through 26, choose the sentence which is BEST from the point of view of English usage suitable for a business letter or report.

22. A. It is the opinion of the Commissioners that programs which include the construction of cut-rate municipal garages in the central business district is inadvisable.   22.____
    B. Having reviewed the material submitted, the program for putting up cut-rate garages in the central business district seemed likely to cause traffic congestion.
    C. The Commissioners believe that putting up cut-rate municipal garages in the central business district is inadvisable.
    D. Making an effort to facilitate the cleaning of streets in the central business district, the building of cut-rate municipal garages presents the problem that it would encourage more motorists to come into the central city.

23.
 A. This letter, together with the reports, are to be sent to the principal.
 B. The reports, together with this letter, is to be sent to the principal.
 C. The reports and this letter is to be sent to the principal.
 D. This letter, together with the reports, is to be sent to the principal.

24.
 A. Each employee has to decide for themselves whether to take the examination.
 B. Each of the employees has to decide for himself whether to take the examination.
 C. Each of the employees has to decide for themselves whether to take the examination.
 D. Each of the employees have to decide for himself whether to take the examination.

25.
 A. The reason a new schedule is being prepared is that there has been a change in priorities.
 B. Because there has been a change in priorities is the reason why a new schedule is being made up.
 C. The reason why a new schedule is being made up is because there has been a change in priorities.
 D. Because of a change in priorities is the reason why a new schedule is being prepared.

26.
 A. The changes in procedure had an unfavorable affect upon the output of the unit.
 B. The increased output of the unit was largely due to the affect of the procedural changes.
 C. The changes in procedure had the effect of increasing the output of the unit.
 D. The increased output of the unit from the procedural changes were the effect.

Questions 27-33.

DIRECTIONS: Questions 27 through 33 are to be answered SOLELY on the basis of the information in the following extract, which is from a report prepared for Department X, which outlines the procedure to be followed in the case of transfers of employees.

Every transfer, regardless of the reason therefor, requires completion of the record of transfer, Form DT 411. To denote consent to the transfer, DT 411 should contain the signatures of the transferee and the personnel officer(s) concerned, except that, in the case of an involuntary transfer, the signatures of the transferee's present and prospective supervisors shall be entered in Boxes 8A and 8B, respectively, since the transferee does not consent. Only a permanent employee may request a transfer; in such cases, the employee's attendance record shall be duly considered with regard to absences, latenesses, and accrued overtime balances. In the case of an inter-district transfer, the employee's attendance record must be included in Section 8A of the transfer request, Form DT 410, by the personnel officer of the district from which the transfer is requested. The personnel officer of the district to which the employee requested transfer may refuse to accept accrued overtime balances in excess of ten days.

An employee on probation shall be eligible for transfer. If such employee is involuntarily transferred, he shall be credited for the period of time already served on probation. However, if such transfer is voluntary, the employee shall be required to serve the entire period of his probation in the new position. An employee who has occurred a disability which prevents him from performing his normal duties may be transferred during the period of such disability to other appropriate duties. A disability transfer requires the completion of either Form DT414 if the disability is job-connected, or Form DT 415 if it is not a job-connected disability. In either case, the personnel officer of the district from which the transfer is made signs in Box 6A of the first two copies and the personnel officer of the district to which the transfer is made signs in Box 6B of the last two copies; or, in the case of an intra-district disability transfer, the personnel officer must sign in Box 6A of the first two copies and Box 6B of the last two copies

27. When a personnel officer consents to an employee's request for transfer from his district, this procedure requires that the personnel officer sign Form(s)

    A. DT 411
    B. DT 410 and DT 411
    C. DT 411 and either Form DT 414 or DT 415
    D. DT 410 and DT 411, and either Form DT 414 or DT 415

28. With respect to the time record of an employee transferred against his wishes during his probationary period, this procedure requires that

    A. he serve the entire period of his probation in his present office
    B. he lose his accrued overtime balance
    C. his attendance record be considered with regard to absences and latenesses
    D. he be given credit for the period of time he has already served on probation

29. Assume you are a supervisor and an employee must be transferred into your office against his wishes.
    According to this procedure, the box you must sign on the record of transfer is

    A. 6A   B. 8A   C. 6B   D. 8B

30. Under this procedure, in the case of a disability transfer, when must Box 6A on Forms DT 414 and DT 415 be signed by the personnel officer of the district to which the transfer is being made?

    A. In all cases when either Form DT 414 or Form DT 415 is used
    B. In all cases when Form DT 414 is used and only under certain circumstances when Form DT 415 is used
    C. In all cases when Form DT 415 is used and only under certain circumstances when Form DT 414 is used
    D. Only under certain circumstances when either Form DT 414 or Form DT 415 is used

31. From the above passage, it may be inferred MOST correctly that the number of copies of Form DT 414 is

    A. no more than 2
    B. at least 3
    C. at least 5
    D. more than the number of copies of Form DT 415

32. A change in punctuation and capitalization only which would change one sentence into two and possibly contribute to somewhat greater ease of reading of this report extract would be MOST appropriate in the _____ sentence, _____ paragraph.

    A. 2nd; 1st
    B. 3rd; 1st
    C. next to the last; 2nd
    D. 2nd; 2nd

33. In the second paragraph, a word that is INCORRECTLY used is _____ in the _____ sentence.

    A. *shall;* 1st
    B. *voluntary;* 3rd
    C. *occurred;* 4th
    D. *intra-district;* last

Questions 34-38.

DIRECTIONS: Questions 34 through 38 are to be answered SOLELY on the basis of the information contained in the following passage.

Positive discipline minimizes the amount of personal supervision required and aids in the maintenance of standards. When a new employee has been properly introduced and carefully instructed, when he has come to know the supervisor and has confidence in the supervisor's ability to take care of him, when he willingly cooperates with the supervisor, that employee has been under positive discipline and can be put on his own to produce the quantity and quality of work desired. Negative discipline, the fear of transfer to a less desirable location, for example, to a limited extent may restrain certain individuals from overt violation of rules and regulations governing attendance and conduct which in governmental agencies are usually on at least an agency-wide basis. Negative discipline may prompt employees to perform according to certain rules to avoid a penalty such as, for example, docking for tardiness.

34. According to the above passage, it is reasonable to assume that in the area of discipline, the first-line supervisor in a governmental agency has GREATER scope for action in

    A. *positive* discipline because negative discipline is largely taken care of by agency rules and regulations
    B. *negative* discipline because rules and procedures are already fixed and the supervisor can rely on them
    C. *positive* discipline because the supervisor is in a position to recommend transfers
    D. *negative* discipline because positive discipline is reserved for people on a higher supervisory level

35. In order to maintain positive discipline of employees under his supervision, it is MOST important for a supervisor to

    A. assure each employee that he has nothing to worry about
    B. insist at the outset on complete cooperation from employees
    C. be sure that each employee is well trained in his job
    D. inform new employees of the penalties for not meeting standards

36. According to the above passage, a feature of negative discipline is that it

    A. may lower employee morale
    B. may restrain employees from disobeying the rules
    C. censures equal treatment of employees
    D. tends to create standards for quality of work

37. A REASONABLE conclusion based on the above passage is that positive discipline benefits a supervisor because

   A. he can turn over orientation and supervision of a new employee to one of his subordinates
   B. subordinates learn to cooperate with one another when working on an assignment
   C. it is easier to administer
   D. it cuts down, in the long run, on the amount of time the supervisor needs to spend on direct supervision

38. Based on the above passage, it is REASONABLE to assume that an important difference between positive discipline and negative discipline is that positive discipline

   A. is concerned with the quality of work and negative discipline with the quantity of work
   B. leads to a more desirable basis for motivation of the employee
   C. is more likely to be concerned with agency rules and regulations
   D. uses fear while negative discipline uses penalties to prod employees to adequate performance

Questions 39-50.

DIRECTIONS: Questions 39 through 50 are to be answered on the basis of the information given in the graph and chart below.

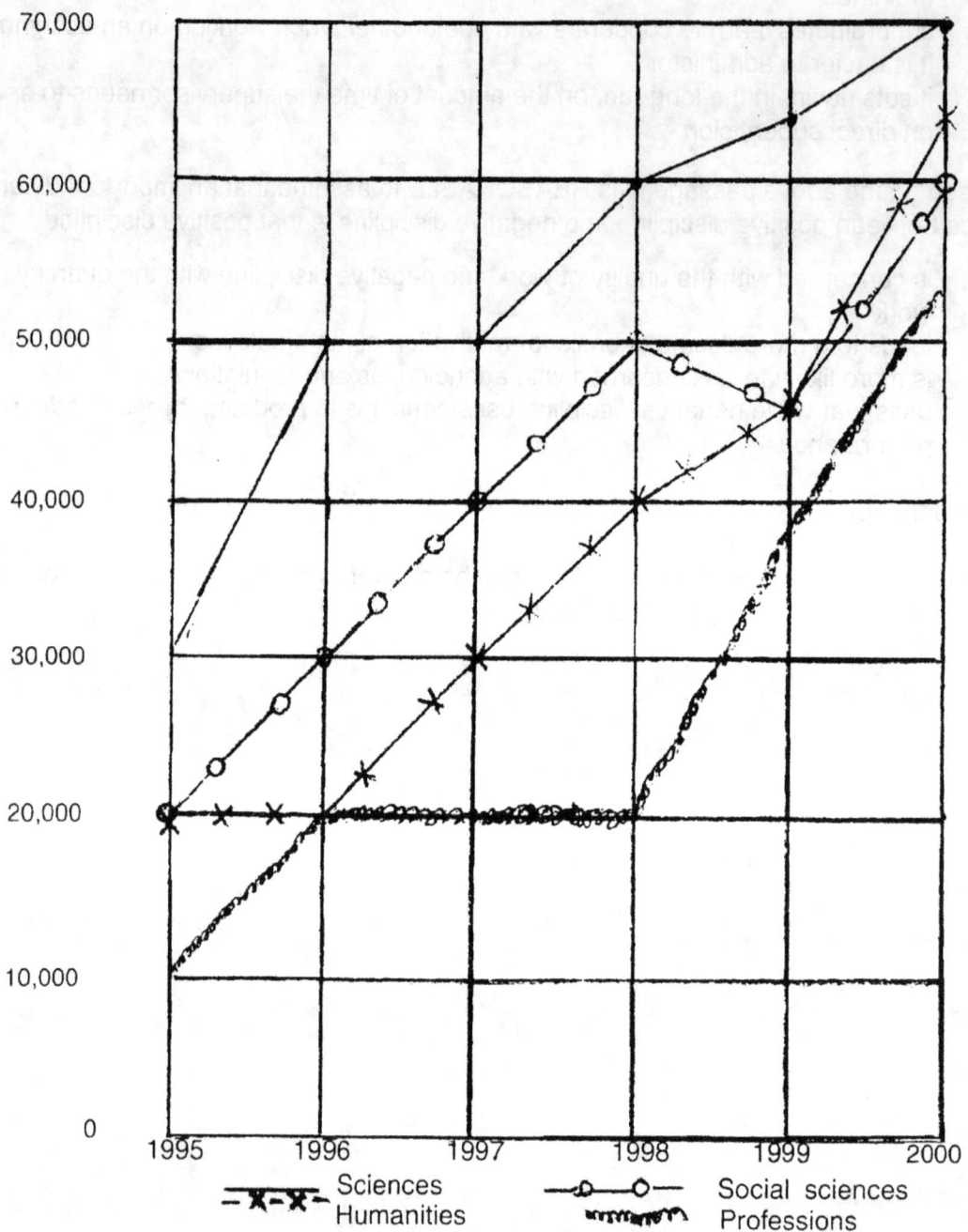

ENROLLMENT IN POSTGRADUATE STUDIES

Fields	Subdivisions	1999	2000
Sciences	Math	10,000	12,000
	Physical science	22,000	24,000
	Behavioral science	32,000	35,000
Humanities	Literature	26,000	34,000
	Philosophy	6,000	8,000
	Religion	4,000	6,000
	Arts	10,000	16,000
Social sciences	History	36,000	46,000
	Sociology	8,000	14,000
Professions	Law	2,000	2,000
	Medicine	6,000	8,000
	Business	30,000	44,000

39. The number of students enrolled in the social sciences and in the humanities was the same in _____ and _____.

    A. 1997; 1999
    B. 1995; 1999
    C. 1999; 2000
    D. 1996; 1999

40. A comparison of the enrollment of students in the various postgraduate studies shows that in every year from 1995 through 2000, there were more students enrolled in the _____ than in the _____.

    A. professions; sciences
    B. humanities; professions
    C. social sciences; professions
    D. humanities; sciences

41. The number of students enrolled in the humanities was GREATER than the number of students enrolled in the professions by the same amount in _____ of the years.

    A. two   B. three   C. four   D. five

42. The one field of postgraduate study to show a decrease in enrollment in one year compared to the year immediately preceding is

    A. humanities
    B. sciences
    C. professions
    D. social sciences

43. If the proportion of arts students to all humanities students was the same in 1997 as in 2000, then the number of arts students in 1997 was

    A. 7,500   B. 13,000   C. 15,000   D. 5,000

44. In which field of postgraduate study did enrollment INCREASE by 20 percent from 1997 to 1998?

    A. Humanities
    B. Professions
    C. Sciences
    D. Social sciences

45. The GREATEST increase in overall enrollment took place between

    A. 1995 and 1996
    B. 1997 and 1998
    C. 1998 and 1999
    D. 1999 and 2000

46. Between 1997 and 2000, the combined enrollment of the sciences and social sciences increased by

    A. 40,000   B. 48,000   C. 50,000   D. 54,000

47. If the enrollment in the social sciences had decreased from 1999 to 2000 at the same rate as from 1998 to 1999, then the social science enrollment in 2000 would have differed from the humanities enrollment in 2000 MOST NEARLY by

    A. 6,000   B. 8,000   C. 12,000   D. 22,000

48. In the humanities, the GREATEST percentage increase in enrollment from 1999 to 2000 was in

    A. literature   B. philosophy
    C. religion   D. arts

49. If the proportion of behavioral science students to the total number of students in the sciences was the same in 1996 as in 1999, then the increase in behavioral science enrollment from 1996 to 2000 was

    A. 5,000   B. 7,000   C. 10,000   D. 14,000

50. If enrollment in the professions increased at the same rate from 2000 to 2001 as from 1999 to 2000, the enrollment in the professions in 2001 would be MOST NEARLY

    A. 85,000   B. 75,000   C. 60,000   D. 55,000

KEY (CORRECT ANSWERS)

1. C	11. D	21. C	31. B	41. B
2. A	12. C	22. C	32. B	42. D
3. C	13. B	23. D	33. C	43. A
4. C	14. D	24. B	34. A	44. C
5. B	15. A	25. A	35. C	45. D
6. B	16. D	26. C	36. B	46. A
7. B	17. B	27. A	37. D	47. D
8. C	18. A	28. D	38. B	48. D
9. D	19. C	29. D	39. B	49. C
10. B	20. D	30. D	40. C	50. B

EXAMINATION SECTION
TEST 1

DIRECTIONS: Each question or incomplete statement is followed by several suggested answers or completions. Select the one that BEST answers the question or completes the statement. *PRINT THE LETTER OF THE CORRECT ANSWER IN THE SPACE AT THE RIGHT.*

1. You have recently been assigned to a new office and are expected to supervise six clerks.
   All of the following would be good introductory steps to take EXCEPT

   A. giving a clear presentation of yourself to the clerks, including a short summary of your recent work experience
   B. initiating informal discussions with each clerk concerning his work
   C. making a general survey of all the functions which each clerk has been performing
   D. making a list of the duties each clerk is required to perform and giving it to the clerk

   1.____

2. Your supervisor has advised you that a specific aspect of a job is being done incorrectly and you acknowledge the mistake.
   Of the following, the MOST efficient way of dealing with this situation is to

   A. call a meeting of the clerks who are performing this particular function and explain the correct method
   B. assume the blame and correct the errors as they are given to you
   C. speak with each clerk individually and carefully show each one the proper method
   D. distribute a set of written instructions covering all clerical procedures to the employees doing that particular job

   2.____

3. A new department regulation calls for a change in a particular method of processing new applications. Two clerks have complained to you that the new method is more time-consuming, and they prefer to do it the original way.
   Of the following, what is the MOST advisable thing to do?

   A. Discuss the situation with them and attempt to determine whether they are utilizing the method properly.
   B. Discuss the advantages of both methods with them and let them use the one that is more practical.
   C. Firmly instruct the clerks to proceed with the new method since it is not up to them to refute department policy.
   D. Tell them to survey the opinions of the other clerks on this matter and inform you of the results.

   3.____

4. A member of the clerical staff has recently begun reporting late for work rather regularly. On each occasion, the individual presented an excuse, but the latenesses continue.
   Of the following, the MOST advisable action for her supervisor to take is to

   A. have a staff meeting and stress the importance of being on time for work, without singling out the specific individual
   B. put a notice on the departmental office bulletin board, specifying and stressing that lateness can not be tolerated

   4.____

57

C. talk privately with the individual to determine whether there are any unusual circumstances that might be causing the lateness
D. send the individual a memorandum clearly indicating that continual lateness will result in disciplinary action

5. Assume that, as the supervisor of a unit, you have been asked to prepare a vacation schedule for your subordinate employees. The employees have had different lengths of service. Some of them have already submitted requests for certain weeks.
Of the following, which factor would be LEAST important in setting up this schedule?

    A. Your opinion of each employee's past work performance
    B. Each employee's preference for a vacation period
    C. The amount of work the unit is expected to accomplish during the vacation period
    D. The number of employees who have requested to go on vacation at the same time

6. Your superior finds that he must leave the office one day before he has had time to check and sign the day's correspondence. He asks you to proofread the letters, have corrections made where necessary, and then sign his name. You have never signed his name before.
Of the following, the BEST thing for you to do is to

    A. sign your superior's name in full, making it look as much like his handwriting as possible
    B. sign your superior's name and your own name in full as proof that you signed for him
    C. sign your superior's name in full and add your initials to show that the signature is not his own
    D. politely refuse to sign his name because it is forgery

7. The head of your office sometimes makes handwritten notations on original letters which he receives and requests that you mail the letters back to the sender. Of the following, the BEST action for you to take FIRST is to

    A. request that this practice be stopped because it does not provide for a record in the files
    B. request that this practice be stopped because it is not the customary way to respond to letters
    C. photocopy the letters so that there are copies for the file and then send the letters out
    D. ask the head of your office if he wants you to keep any record of the letters

8. The main function of most agency administrative offices is *information management*. Information that is received by an administrative office may be classified as active (information which requires the recipient to take some action) or passive (information which does not require action).
Which one of the following items received must clearly be treated as ACTIVE information?
A(n)

    A. confirmation of payment
    B. press release concerning an agency event
    C. advertisement for a new restaurant opening near the agency
    D. request for a student transcript

9. Which of the following statements about the use of the photocopy process is COR- 9._____
RECT?

   A. It is difficult to use.
   B. It can be used to reproduce color.
   C. It does not print well on colored paper.
   D. Once source documents have been used, they cannot be used again.

10. In order to get the BEST estimate of how long a repetitive office procedure should take, a 10._____
supervisor should find out how

   A. long it takes her best worker to do the procedure once on a typical day
   B. long it takes her best and worst workers to do the procedure once on a typical day
   C. much time her best worker spends on the procedure during a typical week and the total number of times the worker executes the procedure during the same week
   D. much time all her subordinates spend on the procedure during a typical week and the total number of times the procedure was executed during the same week by all employees

11. Of the following, the MOST suitable and appropriate way to make 250 copies of a partic- 11._____
ular form is to

   A. print all 250 copies on the office computer
   B. delegate the work to someone else
   C. reproduce it on a photocopying machine
   D. use an offset printing process

Questions 12-18.

DIRECTIONS: Questions 12 through 18 are to be answered on the basis of the extracts shown below from Federal withholding tables. These tables indicate the amounts which must be withheld from the employee's salary by his employer for Federal income tax and for social security. They are based on weekly earnings.

4 (#1)

INCOME TAX WITHHOLDING TABLE

The wages are -		And the number of withholding exemptions claimed is-					
At least	But less than	0	1	2	3	4	5
		The amount of income tax to be withheld shall be -					
$200	$205	$14.10	$11.80	$9.50	$7.20	$4.90	$2.80
205	210	14.90	12.60	10.30	8.00	5.70	3.50
210	215	15.70	13.40	11.10	8.80	6.50	4.20
215	220	16.50	14.20	11.90	9.60	7.30	5.00
220	225	17.30	15.00	12.70	10.40	8.10	5.80
225	230	18.10	15.80	13.50	11.20	8.90	6.60
230	235	18.90	16.60	14.30	12.00	9.70	7.40
235	240	19.70	17.40	15.10	12.80	10.50	8.20
240	245	20.50	18.20	15.90	13.60	11.30	9.00
245	250	21.30	19.00	16.70	14.40	12.10	9.80

SOCIAL SECURITY EMPLOYEE TAX TABLE

Wages		Tax to be withheld	Wages		Tax to be withheld
At least	But less than		At least	But less than	
$202.79	$202.99	$15.35	$229.72	$229.91	$16.75
202.99	203.18	15.36	229.91	230.10	16.76
203.18	203.37	15.37	230.10	230.29	16.77
203.37	203.56	15.38	230.29	230.49	16.78
203.56	203.75	15.39	230.49	230.68	16.79
203.75	203.95	15.40	230.68	230.87	16.80
203.95	204.14	15.41	230.87	231.06	16.81
204.14	204.33	15.42	231.06	231.25	16.82
204.33	204.52	15.43	231.25	231.45	16.83
204.52	204.72	15.44	231.45	231.64	16.84

Wages		Tax to be withheld	Wages		Tax to be withheld
At least	But less than		At least	But less than	
$222.02	$222.22	$16.35	$234.52	$234.72	$17.00
222.22	222.41	16.36	234.72	234.91	17.01
222.41	222.60	16.37	234.91	235.10	17.02
222.60	222.79	16.38	235.10	235.29	17.03
222.79	222.99	16.39	235.29	235.49	17.04
222.99	223.18	16.40	235.49	235.68	17.05
223.18	223.37	16.41	235.68	235.87	17.06
223.37	223.56	16.42	235.87	236.06	17.07
223.56	223.75	16.43	236.06	236.25	17.08
223.75	223.95	16.44	236.25	236.45	17.09

12. Dave Andes has wages of $242.75 for one week. He has claimed three withholding exemptions.
    What is the Federal income tax which should be withheld?

    A. $13.60   B. $15.90   C. $18.20   D. $20.50

    12._____

13. Mary Hodes has wages of $229.95 for one week.
    What is the Social Security tax which should be withheld?

    A. $16.75   B. $16.76   C. $16.77   D. $16.78

    13._____

14. Joe Jones had wages of $235.63 for one week. He has claimed two withholding exemptions.
    What is the Federal income tax which should be withheld?

    A. $12.80   B. $14.30   C. $15.10   D. $17.40

    14._____

15. Tom Stein had wages of $203.95 for one week. What is the Social Security tax which should be withheld?

    A. $15.40   B. $15.41   C. $16.05   D. $16.06

    15._____

16. Robert Helman had wages of $222.80 for one week. He has claimed one withholding exemption.
    If only Federal income tax and Social Security tax were deducted from his earnings for the same week, how much *take-home* pay should he have for the week?

    A. $191.41   B. $193.96   C. $194.12   D. $195.65

    16._____

17. Audrey Stein has wages of $203.00 for one week. She claimed no withholding exemptions.
    If only Federal income tax and Social Security tax were deducted from her earnings for the same week, how much *take-home* pay should she have for the week?

    A. $171.84   B. $172.34   C. $173.54   D. $175.84

    17._____

18. Anthony Covallo, who worked 28 hours in the past week, has a regular hourly rate of $7.25 per hour and earns a premium of time and a half for hours over 40. He has claimed four withholding exemptions.
    After Social Security tax and Federal income tax are deducted from his wages for the past week, how much pay does he have left?

    A. $180.98   B. $181.13   C. $182.29   D. $182.74

    18._____

19. In judging the adequacy of a standard office form, which of the following is LEAST important?
    _____ of the form.

    A. Date   B. Legibility   C. Size   D. Design

    19._____

20. Clear and accurate telephone messages should be taken for employees who are out of the office.
    Which of the following is of LEAST importance when taking a telephone message?

    A. Name of the person called
    B. Name of the caller

    20._____

C. Details of the message
D. Time of the call

21. Suppose that all office supplies are kept in a centrally located cabinet in the office. Of the following, which is usually the BEST policy to adhere to for distribution of supplies?

    A. Permit employees to stock up on all supplies to avoid frequent trips to the cabinet.
    B. Assign one employee to be in charge of distributing all supplies to other employees at frequent intervals.
    C. Inform employees that supplies should be taken in large quantities and only when needed.
    D. Keep cabinet closed and instruct employees that they must check with you before taking supplies.

Questions 22-25.

DIRECTIONS: Questions 22 through 25 are to be answered SOLELY on the basis of the following passage.

   Use of the systems and procedures approach to office management is revolutionizing the supervision of office work. This approach views an enterprise as an entity which seeks to fulfill definite objectives. Systems and procedures help to organize repetitive work into a routine, thus reducing the amount of decision-making required for its accomplishment. As a result, employees are guided in their efforts and perform only necessary work. Supervisors are relieved of any details of execution and are free to attend to more important work. Establishing work guides which require that identical tasks be performed the same way each, time permits standardization of forms, machine operations, work methods, and controls. This approach also reduces the probability of errors. Any error committed is usually discovered quickly because the incorrect work does not meet the requirement of the work guides. Errors are also reduced through work specialization which allows each employee to become thoroughly proficient in a particular type of work. Such proficiency also tends to improve the morale of the employees.

22. Of the following, which one BEST expresses the main theme of the above passage? The

    A. advantages and disadvantages of the systems and procedures approach to office management
    B. effectiveness of the systems and procedures approach to office management in developing skills
    C. systems and procedures approach to office management as it relates to office costs
    D. advantages of the systems and procedures approach to office management for supervisors and office workers

23. Work guides are LEAST likely to be used when

    A. standardized forms are used
    B. a particular office task is distinct and different from all others
    C. identical tasks are to be performed in identical ways
    D. similar work methods are expected from each employee

24. According to the above passage, when an employee makes a work error, it USUALLY   24.____

　　A. is quickly corrected by the supervisor
　　B. necessitates a change in the work guides
　　C. can be detected quickly if work guides are in use
　　D. increases the probability of further errors by that employee

25. The above passage states that the accuracy of an employee's work is INCREASED by   25.____

　　A. using the work specialization approach
　　B. employing a probability sample
　　C. requiring him to shift at one time into different types of tasks
　　D. having his supervisor check each detail of work execution

KEY (CORRECT ANSWERS)

1.	D	11.	C
2.	A	12.	A
3.	A	13.	B
4.	C	14.	C
5.	A	15.	B
6.	C	16.	A
7.	D	17.	C
8.	D	18.	D
9.	B	19.	A
10.	D	20.	D

21. B
22. D
23. B
24. C
25. A

TEST 2

DIRECTIONS: Each question or incomplete statement is followed by several suggested answers or completions. Select the one that BEST answers the question or completes the statement. *PRINT THE LETTER OF THE CORRECT ANSWER IN THE SPACE AT THE RIGHT.*

1. A certain supervisor often holds group meetings with subordinates to discuss the goals of the unit and manpower requirements for meeting objectives.
For the supervisor to hold such meetings is a

   A. *good* practice because it will aid both the supervisor and subordinates in planning and completing the unit's work
   B. *good* practice because it will prevent future problems from interfering with the unit's objectives
   C. *poor* practice because the supervisor has the sole responsibility for meeting objectives and should make manpower decisions without any advice
   D. *poor* practice because the subordinates will be allowed to set their own work quotas

1.____

2. Assume that you are a supervisor who has been asked to evaluate the work of a clerk who was transferred to your unit about six months ago.
Which one of the following, by itself, provides the BEST basis for making such an evaluation?

   A. Ask the clerk's former supervisor about the employee's previous work.
   B. Ask the clerk's co-workers for their opinions of the employee's work.
   C. Evaluate the quantity and quality of the employee's work over the six-month period.
   D. Observe the employee's performance from time to time during the next week and base your evaluation on these observations.

2.____

3. Which of the following would be the MOST desirable way for a supervisor to help improve the job performance of a particular subordinate?

   A. Criticize the employee's performance in front of other employees.
   B. Privately warn the employee that failure to meet work standards may lead to dismissal.
   C. Hold a meeting with this employee and other subordinates in which the need to improve the unit's performance is stressed.
   D. Meet privately with the employee and discuss both positive and negative aspects of the employee's work

3.____

4. Suppose that your office has a limited supply of a pamphlet which people may read in your office when they seek certain information, but another office in your building is supposed to have a large supply available for distribution to the public.
Which of the following would be the BEST thing for you to do when someone states that he has not been able to obtain one of these pamphlets?

   A. Tell him that he misunderstood the directions that other employees have given him and carefully direct him to the other office.
   B. Ask whether he has visited the other office and requested a copy from them.
   C. Let him take one of your office's copies of the pamphlet and then call the other office and ask why they have run out of copies for distribution.

4.____

D. Tell him that your office does its best to keep the public informed but that this might not be true of other offices.

5. On Monday, a clerk made many errors in completing a new daily record form. The supervisor explained the errors and had the clerk correct the form. On Tuesday, the clerk made fewer errors. Because he was very busy, the supervisor did not point out the errors to the clerk but corrected the errors himself. On Wednesday, the clerk made the same number of errors as on Tuesday. The supervisor reprimanded the clerk for making so many errors.
The supervisor's handling of this situation on Wednesday may be considered poor MAINLY because the

   A. clerk was not given enough time to complete each form properly
   B. supervisor should not have expected improvement without further training
   C. clerk was obviously incapable of completing the form
   D. supervisor should have continued to correct the errors himself

Questions 6-8.

DIRECTIONS: Questions 6 through 8 are to be answered SOLELY on the basis of the information contained in the following passage.

When using words like company, association, council, committee, and board in place of the full official name, the writer should not capitalize these short forms unless he intends them to invoke the full force of the institution's authority. In legal contracts, in minutes, or in formal correspondence where one is speaking formally and officially on behalf of the company, the term "Company" is usually capitalized, but in ordinary usage, where it is not essential to load the short form with this significance, capitalization would be excessive. (Example: The company will have many good openings for graduates this June.)

The treatment recommended for short forms of place names is essentially the same as that recommended for short forms of organizational names. In general, we capitalize the full form but not the short form. If Park Avenue is referred to in one sentence, then "the avenue" is sufficient in subsequent references. The same is true with words like building, hotel, station, and airport, which are capitalized when part of a proper name (Pan Am Building, Hotel Plaza, Union Station, O'Hare Airport) but are simply lower-cased when replacing these specific names.

6. The above passage states that USUALLY the short forms of names of organizations

   A. and places should not be capitalized
   B. and places should be capitalized
   C. should not be capitalized, but the short forms of names of places should be capitalized
   D. should be capitalized, but the short forms of names of places should not be capitalized

7. The above passage states that in legal contracts, in minutes, and in formal correspondence, the short forms of names of organizations should

   A. usually not be capitalized   B. usually be capitalized
   C. usually not be used   D. never be used

8. It can be INFERRED from the above passage that decisions regarding when to capitalize certain words

   A. should be left to the discretion of the writer
   B. should be based on generally accepted rules
   C. depend on the total number of words capitalized
   D. are of minor importance

9. The Central Terminal and the Gardens Terminal are located on Glover Street.
   In ordinary usage, if this sentence were to be followed by the sentence in the choices below, which form of the sentence would be CORRECT?

   A. Both Terminals are situated on the same street.
   B. Both terminals are situated on the same Street.
   C. Both terminals are situated on the same street.
   D. Both Terminals are situated on the same Street.

10. A stylus is a(n)

    A. implement for writing containing a cylinder of graphite
    B. implement for writing with ink or a similar fluid
    C. pointed implement used to write
    D. stick of colored wax used for writing

11. As a supervisor, you have the responsibility of teaching new employees the functions and procedures of your office after their orientation by the personnel office.
    Of the following, the BEST way to begin such instruction is to

    A. advise the new employee of the benefits and services available to him, over and above his salary
    B. discuss the negative aspects of the departmental procedures and indicate methods available to overcome them
    C. assist the new employee in understanding the general purpose of the office procedures and how they fit in with the overall operation
    D. give a detailed briefing of the operations of your office, its functions and procedures

12. Assume that you are the supervisor of a clerical unit. One of the duties of the employees in your unit is to conduct a brief interview with persons using the services of your agency for the first time. The purpose of the interview is to get general background information in order to best direct them to the appropriate division.
    A clerk comes to your office and says that a prospective client has just called her some rather unpleasant names, accused her of being nosey and meddlesome, and has stated emphatically that she refuses to talk with an *underling,* meaning the clerk. The young woman is almost in tears. Of the following, what is the FIRST action you should take?

    A. Immediately call the agency's protection officer, have him advise the client of the regulations, and tell her that she will be removed if she is not more polite.
    B. Calm the clerk, introduce yourself to the client, and quietly discuss the agency's services, regulations, and informational needs, and request that she complete the interview with the clerk.

C. Calm the clerk, have her return and firmly advise the client of the agency's rules concerning the need for this first interview.
D. Introduce yourself to the client and advise her that without an apology to the clerk and completion of the interview, she will not be given any service.

13. A recent high school graduate has just been assigned to the unit which you supervise. Which of the following would be the LEAST desirable technique to use with this employee?

    A. At any one time, give the new employee only as much detail about the job as the employee can absorb.
    B. Always tell the new employee the correct procedure, then demonstrate how it is accomplished.
    C. Assign the employee the same quantity and type of work that the other employees are doing to see if the employee can handle the job.
    D. Assume the employee is tense and be prepared to repeat procedures and descriptions.

14. Assume that you supervise a work unit of several employees. Which of the following is LEAST essential in assuring that the goals which you set for the unit are achieved?

    A. Establishing objectives and standards for the staff
    B. Providing justification for disciplinary action
    C. Measuring performance or progress of individuals against standards
    D. Taking corrective action where performance is less than expected

15. One of the clerks you supervise is often reluctant to accept assignments and usually complains about the amount of work expected, although the other clerks with the same assignments and workload seem quite happy.
    Of the following, the MOST accurate assumption that you can make about this clerk is that she

    A. will require additional observation and help
    B. will eventually have to be discharged or transferred
    C. is incompetent
    D. is overworked

Questions 16-21.

DIRECTIONS: Questions 16 through 21 are to be answered SOLELY on the basis of the airline timetable and the information appearing on the last page of this test.

Fact Situation:
An administrator wants you to purchase airline tickets for him so that he can attend a meeting being held in Chicago on Monday. He must leave from LaGuardia Airport in New York on Monday morning as late as possible but with arrival in Chicago no later than 9:00 A.M. He wishes to fly coach/economy class both ways. The meeting is due to end at 5:30 P.M., and he wishes to obtain the first plane after 6:45 P.M. going back to LaGuardia Airport. If all these requirements have been met, he would, if possible, also like to fly to and leave from Midway Airport in Chicago and go non-stop both ways.

16. You should obtain a ticket for the administrator from New York to Chicago on flight number

    A. 483 B. 201 C. 277 D. 539

17. You should obtain a ticket for the administrator from Chicago to New York on flight number

    A. 588 B. 692 C. 268 D. 334

18. The administrator decides to take limousines to and from both airports.
    If the limousine charge in Chicago is $52.50. and there is no reduced rate for a round-trip flight, what is the cost of the administrator's round-trip air fare PLUS limousine service?

    A. $827.50 B. $931.00 C. $963.00 D. $967.00

19. The administrator asked you whether he would be able to get breakfast on his flight to Chicago or whether he should go to the airport early and eat there before boarding the plane. He prefers to eat on the plane.
    Of the following, the BEST reply to make is:

    A. I will have to telephone the airport to find out
    B. You should eat at the airport
    C. A meal is served on the plane
    D. Only certain passengers get a meal on the plane

20. Of the following requests of the administrator concerning his travel arrangements, which one is IMPOSSIBLE to meet?

    A. Chicago arrival no later than 9 A.M.
    B. New York departure from LaGuardia Airport
    C. Non-stop flights both ways
    D. Chicago departure from Midway Airport

21. Suppose that it is necessary to take a first-class seat on the trip to Chicago although you have no problem reserving a coach/economy seat on the return trip.
    If there is no reduction in fare for round-trip flights, how much MORE will this trip cost than round-trip coach/ economy?

    A. $209 B. $236 C. $318 D. $636

22. Ms. X, a clerk under your supervision, has been working in the unit for a few weeks. Some of the other employees have complained to you that Ms. X has an annoying habit of constantly tapping her feet on the floor and it disturbs their work.
    The BEST thing for you to do is to

    A. ignore the complaints because the employees should be concerned only with their own habits
    B. speak with Ms. X privately and discuss the situation with her
    C. make a general announcement that employees should control their nervous habits
    D. observe Ms. X for a few weeks to see if the employees are correct, and then take action

23. Suppose you answer a telephone call from someone who states that he is a friend of one of your co-workers and needs the employee's new address in order to send an invitation. Your co-worker is on vacation but you know her address.
    Which of the following is the BEST action for you to take?

    A. Give the caller the address but ask the caller not to mention that you are the one who gave it out.
    B. Give the caller the address and leave a note for your co-worker stating what you did.
    C. Tell the caller you do not know the address but will give the employee's phone number if that will help.
    D. Offer to take his name and address and have your co-worker contact him.

24. Assume that you receive a telephone call in which the caller requests information which you know is posted in the office next to yours. You start to tell the caller you will transfer her call to the right office, but she interrupts you and says she has been transferred from office to office and is tired of getting a *run-around*. Of the following, the BEST thing for you to do is to

    A. give the caller the phone number of the office next to yours and quickly end the conversation
    B. give her the phone number of the office next to yours and tell her you will try to transfer her call
    C. ask her if she wants to hold on while you get the information for her
    D. tell the caller that she could have avoided the *run-around* by asking for the right office, and suggest that she come in person

25. Assume that your unit processes confidential forms which are submitted by persons seeking financial assistance. An individual comes to your office, gives you his name, and states that he would like to look over a form which he sent in about a week ago because he believes he omitted some important information.
    Of the following, the BEST thing for you to do FIRST is to

    A. locate the proper form
    B. call the individual's home telephone number to verify his identity
    C. ask the individual if he has proof of his identity
    D. call the security office

KEY (CORRECT ANSWERS)

1.	A	11.	C
2.	C	12.	B
3.	D	13.	C
4.	B	14.	B
5.	B	15.	A
6.	A	16.	A
7.	B	17.	D
8.	B	18.	B
9.	C	19.	C
10.	C	20.	D

21. C
22. B
23. D
24. C
25. C

EXAMINATION SECTION
TEST 1

DIRECTIONS: Each question or incomplete statement is followed by several suggested answers or completions. Select the one that BEST answers the question or completes the statement. *PRINT THE LETTER OF THE CORRECT ANSWER IN THE SPACE AT THE RIGHT.*

1. The ∧ or caret symbol is a proofreader's mark which means that a
   A. space should have been left between two words
   B. new paragraph should be indicated
   C. word, phrase, or punctuation mark should be inserted
   D. word that is abbreviated should be spelled out

   1._____

2. Of the following items, the one which should NOT be omitted from a typed inter-office memorandum is the
   A. salutation
   B. complementary closing
   C. formal signature
   D. names of those to receive copies

   2._____

3. A typed rough draft should be double-spaced and should have wide margins PRIMARILY in order to
   A. save time in making typing corrections
   B. provide room for making insertions and corrections
   C. insure that the report is well-organized
   D. permit faster typing of the draft

   3._____

4. In tabular reports, when a main heading, secondary heading, and single line of columnar headings are used, a triple space (2 blank lines) would be used after the _____ heading(s).
   A. main
   B. secondary
   C. columnar
   D. main and secondary

   4._____

5. You have been requested to type a letter to Mr. Brown, a district attorney of a small town.
   Of the following, the CORRECT salutation to use is Dear
   A. District Attorney Brown:
   B. Mr. District Attorney:
   C. Mr. Brown:
   D. Honorable Brown:

   5._____

6. A form letter that is sent to the public can be made to look more personal in appearance by doing all of the following EXCEPT
   A. using a meter stamp on the envelope of the letter
   B. having the letter signed with pen and ink
   C. using a good quality of paper for the letter
   D. matching the type used in the letter with that used for fill-ins

   6._____

7. A senior typist opens a word-processing application to instruct a typist to create a table that contains three column headings. Under each column heading are three items.
Of the following, which sequence should the senior typist tell the typist to use when creating this table?
   A. First type the headings, and then type the items under them, a column at a time
   B. type each heading with its column of items under it, one column at a time
   C. first type the column of items, then center the headings above them
   D. type the headings and items across the page line by line

7.____

8. When a letter is addressed to an agency and a particular person should see it, an *attention line* is used.
This attention line is USUALLY found
   A. on the envelope only
   B. above the address
   C. below the address
   D. after the agency named in the address

8.____

9. The typing technique of *justifying* is used to
   A. decide how wide margins of different sized letters should be
   B. make all the lines of copy end evenly on the right-hand margin
   C. center headings above columns on tabular typed material
   D. condense the amount of space that is needed to make a manuscript look presentable

9.____

10. The date line on a letter is typed correctly when the date is ALL on one line
    A. with the month written out
    B. with slashes between the numbers
    C. and the month is abbreviated
    D. with a period at the end

10.____

11. When considering how wide to make a column when typing a table, the BASIC rule to follow is that the column should be as wide as the longest
    A. item in the body of the column
    B. heading of all of the columns
    C. item in the body or heading of that column
    D. heading or the longest item in the body of any column on that page

11.____

12. When a lengthy quotation is included in a letter or a report, it must be indicated that it is quoted material. This may be done by
    A. enclosing the quotation in parentheses
    B. placing an exclamation point at the end of the quotation
    C. using the apostrophe marks
    D. indenting from the regular margins on the left and right

12.____

13. In order to reach the highest rate of speed and the greatest degree of accuracy while typing, it is LEAST important to
    A. maintain good posture
    B. keep the hands and arms at a comfortable level
    C. strike the keys evenly
    D. keep the typing action in the wrists

    13.____

14. It has been shown that the rate of typing and dictation drops when the secretary is not familiar with the language or topic of the copy.
    A practice that a supervisor might BEST advise to improve the knowledge and therefore increase the rate of typing dictation for such material would be for the secretary to
    A. plan a conference with her supervisor to discuss the subject matter
    B. read and review correspondence and related technical journals that come into the office
    C. recopy or retype previously transcribed material as practice
    D. withdraw sample materials from the files to take home for study

    14.____

15. The one of the following in which the tab key is NOT generally used is the
    A. placement of the complimentary close and signature line
    B. indentation of paragraphs
    C. placement of the date line
    D. centering of title headings

    15.____

16. In order for a business letter to be effective, it is LEAST important that it
    A. say what is meant simply and directly
    B. be written in formal language
    C. include all information the receiver needs to know
    D. be courteously written

    16.____

17. If you are momentarily called away from your desk while typing a report of a confidential nature, you should cover or turn the copy over and
    A. remove the page being typed from the computer and file the report
    B. ask someone to watch your desk for you
    C. close the document so that the page is not visible
    D. spread a folder over the computer screen to conceal it

    17.____

18. When typing a table that contains a column of figures and a column of words, the PROPER alignment of the column of figures and the column of words should be an even _____ the column of words.
    A. right-hand edge for the column of numbers and an even left-hand edge for
    B. right-hand edge for both the column of numbers and
    C. left-hand edge for the column of numbers and an even right-hand edge for
    D. left-hand edge for both the column of numbers and

    18.____

19. The word *re*, when used in a memorandum, refers to the information that is   19.____
    on the _____ line.
    A. identification   B. subject   C. attention   D. reference

20. Of the following uses of the period, the one which requires NO spacing after   20.____
    it when it is typed is when the period
    A. follows an abbreviation or an initial
    B. follows a figure or letter at the beginning of a line in a list of items
    C. comes between the initials that make up a single abbreviation
    D. comes at the end of a sentence

21. This mark is a proofreader's mark meaning the word   21.____
    A. is misspelled   B. should be underlined
    C. should be bold   D. should be capitalized

22. When typing a report that is double-spaced, the STANDARD recommended   22.____
    practice for indicating the start of new paragraphs is to
    A. double-space between paragraphs and indent the first word at least five
       spaces
    B. triple-space between paragraphs and indent the first word at least five
       spaces
    C. triple-space between paragraphs and type block style at the margin
    D. double-space between paragraphs and type block style at the margin

23. In order to center a heading on a sheet of paper once the center of the paper   23.____
    has been found, the EASIEST and MOST efficient method to use is
    A. note the scale at each end of the heading to be centered and divide by
       two
    B. backspace from the center of the paper one space for every two letters
       and spaces in the heading
    C. arrange the heading around the middle number on the computer
    D. use a ruler to mark off the amount of space from both sides of the center
       of the paper that should be taken up by the heading

24. You are about to type a single-spaced letter from a typewritten draft.   24.____
    In order to center this letter from top to bottom, your FIRST step should be to
    A. determine the number of spaces needed for the top and bottom margins
    B. determine the number of spaces needed for the left and right margins
    C. count the number of lines, including blank ones, which will be used for the
       letter
    D. subtract from the number of writing lines on the sheet of paper the
       number of lines that will not be used for the letter

25. When typing a table which lists several amounts of money and the total in a   25.____
    column, the dollar sign should be placed in front of the
    A. first dollar amount only
    B. total dollar amount only
    C. first and total dollar amounts only
    D. all of the amounts of money in the column

26. If a legal document is being prepared and requires necessary information to be typed into blank areas on preprinted legal forms, the margins for a line of typewritten material should be determined PRIMARILY by
    A. counting the total number of words to be typed
    B. the margins set for the pre-printed matter
    C. spacing backwards from the right margin rule
    D. the estimated width and height of the material to be entered

27. When checking for errors in material you've typed, it is BEST to
    A. proofread the material and use the spell-check function in combination
    B. give the material to someone else to review
    C. run the spell-check function and auto-correct all found errors
    D. proofread the material then e-mail it to another typist for final approval

28. Assume that Mr. Frank Foran is an acting official. In a letter written to him, the word *acting* would
    A. be used with the title in the address and in the salutation
    B. not be used with the title in the address
    C. be used with the title in the address but not in the salutation
    D. not be used with the title in the address or in the salutation

29. The software program that requires proficiency in typing in order to best utilize its MOST important features is
    A. Microsoft Excel   B. Adobe Reader
    C. Microsoft Word   D. Intuit QuickBooks

30. The MAIN reason for keeping a careful record of incoming mail is that
    A. greater speed and accuracy is obtained for answering outgoing mail
    B. this record is legal evidence
    C. it develops the efficiency of the office clerks
    D. the information may be useful some day

KEY (CORRECT ANSWERS)

1.	C	11.	C	21.	D
2.	D	12.	D	22.	A
3.	B	13.	D	23.	B
4.	B	14.	B	24.	C
5.	C	15.	D	25.	C
6.	A	16.	B	26.	B
7.	D	17.	C	27.	A
8.	C	18.	A	28.	C
9.	B	19.	B	29.	C
10.	A	20.	C	30.	A

TEST 2

DIRECTIONS: Each question or incomplete statement is followed by several suggested answers or completions. Select the one that BEST answers the question or completes the statement. *PRINT THE LETTER OF THE CORRECT ANSWER IN THE SPACE AT THE RIGHT.*

Questions 1-4.

DIRECTIONS: Questions 1 through 4 are to be answered SOLELY on the basis of the information contained in the following passage which is taken from a typing test.

Modern office methods, geared to ever higher speeds and aimed at ever greater efficiency, are largely the result of the typewriter. The typewriter is a substitute for handwriting; and, in the hands of a skilled typist, not only turns out letters and other documents at least three times faster than a penman can do the work, but turns out the greater volume more uniformly and legibly. With the use of carbon paper and onionskin paper, identical copies can be made at the same time.

The typewriter, besides its effect on the conduct of business and government, has had a very important effect on the position of women. The typewriter has done much to bring women into business and government, and today there are vastly more women than men typists. Many women have used the keys of the typewriter to climb the ladder to responsible managerial positions.

The typewriter, as its name implies, employs type to make an ink impression on paper. For many years, the manual typewriter was the standard machine used. Today, the electric typewriter is dominant, with electronic typewriters, word processors, and computers coming into wider use.

The mechanism of the office manual typewriter includes a set of keys arranged systematically in rows; a semicircular frame of type, connected to the keys by levers; the carriage or paper carrier; a rubber roller called a platen, against which the type strikes; and an inked ribbon which makes the impression of the type character when the key strikes it. This machine, once omnipresent, is an antique today.

1. The above passage mentions a number of good features of the combination of a skilled typist and a typewriter.
   Of the following, the feature which is NOT mentioned in the passage is
   A. speed   B. uniformity   C. reliability   D. legibility

   1.____

2. According to the above passage, a skilled typist can
   A. turn out at least five carbon copies of typed matter
   B. type at least three times faster than a penman can write
   C. type more than 80 words a minute
   D. readily move into a managerial position

   2.____

3. According to the above passage, which of the following is NOT part of the mechanism of a manual typewriter?
   A. Carbon paper
   B. Paper carrier
   C. Platen
   D. Inked ribbon

4. According to the above passage, the typewriter has helped
   A. men more than women in business
   B. women in career advancement into management
   C. men and women equally, but women have taken better advantage of it
   D. more women than men, because men generally dislike routine typing work

5. Standard rules for typing spacing have developed through usage. According to these rules, two spaces are left after a(n)
   A. colon
   B. comma
   C. hyphen
   D. opening parenthesis

6. Assume that you have to type the heading CENTERING TYPED HEADINGS on a piece of paper which extends from 0 to 100 on the typewriter scale. You want the heading to be perfectly centered on the paper.
   In order to find the proper point on the typewriter scale at which to begin typing, you should determine the paper's center point on the typewriter scale and then _____ the number of letters and spaces in the heading.
   A. add
   B. add one-half
   C. subtract
   D. subtract one-half

7. While typing from a rough draft, the practice of reading a line ahead of what you are now typing is considered to be a
   A. *good* practice; it may prepare your fingers for the words which you will be typing
   B. *good* practice; it may help you to review the subject matter contained in the material
   C. *poor* practice; it may increase your typing speed so that your accuracy is decreased
   D. *poor* practice; it may cause you to lose your concentration and make errors in the words you are presently typing

8. Assume that you are transcribing a letter and you are not sure how to divide a word at the end of a line you are typing.
   The BEST way to determine where to divide the word is by
   A. asking your supervisor
   B. asking the person who dictated the letter
   C. checking with other stenographers
   D. looking up the word in a dictionary

9. When taking proper care of a typewriter, it is NOT a desirable action to   9.____
   A. clean the feed rolls with a cloth
   B. dust the exterior surface of the machine
   C. oil the rubber parts of the machine
   D. use a type-cleaning brush to clean the keys

10. Of the following, the LEAST desirable action to take when typing a rough   10.____
    draft of a report is to
    A. cross out typing errors instead of erasing them
    B. double or triple space between lines
    C. provide large margins on all sides of the typing paper
    D. use letterhead or onionskin paper

11. The date line of every business letter should indicate the month, the day of   11.____
    the month, and the year.
    The MOST common practice when typing a date line is to type it as
    A. Jan. 12, 2018   B. January 12, 2018
    C. 1-12-18   D. 1/12/18

Questions 12-16.

DIRECTIONS: Questions 12 through 16 are to be answered SOLELY on the basis of the
              information provided in the following passage.

   A written report is a communication of information from one person to another. It is an
account of some matter especially investigated, however routine that matter may be. The
ultimate basis of any good written report is facts, which became known through observation and
verification. Good written reports may seem to be no more than general ideas and opinions.
However, in such cases, the facts leading to these opinions were gathered, verified, and
reported earlier, and the opinions are dependent upon these facts. Good style, proper form,
and emphasis cannot make a good written report out of unreliable information and bad
judgments but on the other hand, solid investigation and brilliant thinking are not likely to
become very useful until they are effectively communicated to others. If a person's work calls
for written reports, then his work is often no better than his written reports.

12. Based on the information in the above passage, it can be concluded that   12.____
    opinions expressed in a report should be
    A. based on facts which are gathered and reported
    B. emphasized repeatedly when they result from a special investigation
    C. kept to a minimum
    D. separated from the body of the report

13. In the above passage, the one of the following which is mentioned as a way   13.____
    of establishing facts is
    A. authority   B. communication
    C. reporting   D. verification

14. According to the above passage, the characteristic shared by ALL written reports is that they are
    A. accounts of routine matters
    B. transmissions of information
    C. reliable and logical
    D. written in proper form

14.____

15. Which of the following conclusions can LOGICALLY be drawn from the information given in the above passage?
    A. Brilliant thinking can make up for unreliable information in a report.
    B. One method of judging an individual's work is the quality of the written reports he is required to submit.
    C. Proper form and emphasis can make a good report out of unreliable information.
    D. Good written reports that seem to be no more than general ideas should be rewritten.

15.____

16. Which of the following suggested titles would be MOST appropriate for this passage?
    A. GATHERING AND ORGANIZING FACTS
    B. TECHNIQUES OF OBSERVATION
    C. NATURE AND PURPOSE OF REPORTS
    D. REPORTS AND OPINIONS: DIFFERENCES AND SIMILARITIES

16.____

Questions 17-25

DIRECTIONS: Each of Questions 17 through 25 consists of a sentence which may or may not be an example of good English usage. Examine each sentence, considering grammar, punctuation, spelling, capitalization, and awkwardness. Then choose the correct statement about it from the four choices below it. If the English usage in the sentence given is better than any of the changes suggested in Choices B, C, or D, pick choice A. Do NOT pick a choice that will change the meaning of the sentence.

17. We attended a staff conference on Wednesday the new safety and fire rules were discussed.
    A. This is an example of acceptable writing.
    B. The words *safety*, *fire*, and *rules* should begin with capital letters.
    C. There should be a comma after the word *Wednesday*.
    D. There should be a period after the word *Wednesday*, and the word *the* should begin with a capital letter.

17.____

18. Neither the dictionary or the telephone directory could be found in the office library.
    A. This is an example of acceptable writing.
    B. The word *or* should be changed to *nor*.
    C. The word *library* should be spelled *libery*.
    D. The word *neither* should be changed to *either*.

18.____

19. The report would have been typed correctly if the typist cold read the draft. 19._____
    A. This is an example of acceptable writing.
    B. The word *would* should be removed.
    C. The word *have* should be inserted after the word *could*.
    D. The word *correctly* should be changed to *correct*.

20. The supervisor brought the reports and forms to an employees desk. 20._____
    A. This is an example of acceptable writing.
    B. The word *brought* should be changed to *took*.
    C. There should be a comma after the word *reports* and a comma after the word *forms*.
    D. The word *employees* should be spelled *employee's*.

21. It's important for all the office personnel to submit their vacation schedules on time. 21._____
    A. This is an example of acceptable writing.
    B. The word *It's* should be spelled *Its*.
    C. The word *their* should be spelled *they're*.
    D. The word *personnel* should be spelled *personal*.

22. The supervisor wants that all staff members report to the office at 9:00 A.M. 22._____
    A. This is an example of acceptable writing.
    B. The word *that* should be removed and the word *to* should be inserted after the word *members*.
    C. There should be a comma after the word *wants* and a comma after the word *office*.
    D. The word *wants* should be changed to *want* and the word *shall* should be inserted after the word *members*.

23. Every morning the clerk opens the office mail and distributes it. 23._____
    A. This is an example of acceptable writing.
    B. The word *opens* should be changed to *open*.
    C. The word *mail* should be changed to *letters*.
    D. The word *it* should be changed to *them*.

24. The secretary typed more fast on an electric typewriter than on a manual typewriter. 24._____
    A. This is an example of acceptable writing.
    B. The words *more fast* should be changed to *faster*.
    C. There should be a comma after the words *electric typewriter*.
    D. The word *than* should be changed to *then*.

25. The new stenographer needed a desk a typewriter, a chair and a blotter. 25._____
    A. This is an example of acceptable writing.
    B. The word *blotter* should be spelled *blodder*.
    C. The word *stenographer* should begin with a capital letter.
    D. There should be a comma after the word *desk*.

6 (#2)
KEY (CORRECT ANSWERS)

1.	C		11.	B
2.	B		12.	A
3.	A		13.	D
4.	B		14.	B
5.	A		15.	B
6.	D		16.	C
7.	D		17.	D
8.	D		18.	B
9.	C		19.	C
10.	D		20.	D

21. A
22. B
23. A
24. B
25. D

EXAMINATION SECTION
TEST 1

DIRECTIONS: Each question or incomplete statement is followed by several suggested answers or completions. Select the one that BEST answers the question or completes the statement. *PRINT THE LETTER OF THE CORRECT ANSWER IN THE SPACE AT THE RIGHT.*

1. Which of the following is the acceptable format for typing the date line?　　　　　1.____

   A. 12/2/16　　　　　　　　　　　　　B. December 2, 2016
   C. December 2nd, 2016　　　　　　　D. Dec. 2 2016

2. When typing a letter, which of the following is INACCURATE?　　　　　　　　　2.____

   A. If the letter is to be more than one page long, subsequent sheets should be blank, but should match the letterhead sheet in size, color, weight, and texture.
   B. Long quoted material must be centered and single-spaced internally.
   C. Quotation marks must be used when there is long quoted material.
   D. Double spacing is used above and below tables and long quotations to set them off from the rest of the material.

3. Which of the following is INACCURATE?　　　　　　　　　　　　　　　　　　3.____

   A. When an addressee's title in an inside address would overrun the center of a page, it's best to carry part of the title over to another line and to indent it by two spaces.
   B. It is permissible to use ordinal numbers in an inside address.
   C. In addresses involving street numbers under three, the number is written out in full.
   D. In the inside address, suite, apartment or room numbers should be placed on the line after the street address.

4. All of the following are common styles of business letters EXCEPT　　　　　　　4.____

   A. simplified　　　　　　　　　　　　B. block
   C. direct　　　　　　　　　　　　　　D. executive

5. Please select the two choices below that correctly represent how a continuation sheet　5.____
   heading may be typed.

   I. Page 2　　　　　　　　　　　　II. Page 2
   　Mr. Alan Post　　　　　　　　　　Mr. Alan Post
   　June 25, 2016　　　　　　　　　　6-25-16
   III. Mr. Alan Post　　　-2-　　　　　　June 25, 2016
   IV. Mr. Alan Post　　　-2-　　　　　　6-25-16

   The CORRECT answer is:

   A. I, II　　　B. II, III　　　C. I, III　　　D. II, IV

6. Which of the following is INCORRECT? It is　　　　　　　　　　　　　　　　6.____

   A. permissible to abbreviate honorifics in the inside address
   B. permissible to abbreviate company or organizational names, departmental designations, or organizational titles in the inside address

C. permissible to use abbreviations in the inside address if they have been used on the printed letterhead and form part of the official company name
D. sometimes permissible to omit the colon after the salutation

7. Which of the following is INCORRECT?

   A. The subject line of a letter gives the main idea of the message as succinctly as possible.
   B. If a letter contains an enclosure, there should be a notation indicating this.
   C. Important enclosures ought to be listed numerically and described.
   D. An enclosure notation should be typed flush with the right margin.

7.____

8. Which of the following is INACCURATE about inside addresses?

   A. An intraoffice or intracompany mail stop number such as DA 3C 61B is put after the organization or company name with at least two spaces intervening.
   B. Words such as *Avenue* should not be abbreviated.
   C. With the exception of runovers, the inside address should not be more than five full lines.
   D. The inside address includes the recipient's courtesy or honorific title and his or her full name on line one; the recipient's title on the next line; the recipient's official organizational affiliation on the next line; the street address on the penultimate line; and the city, state, and zip code on the last line.

8.____

9. Which of the following is an INCORRECT example of how to copy recipients when using copy notation?

   A. cc: Martin A.Sheen
   B. cc: Ms. Connors
          Ms. Grogan
          Ms. Reynolds
   C. CC: Martin A. Sheen
   D. cc: Mr. Right
          Mr. Wrong
          Mr. Perfect

9.____

10. When typing a memo, all of the following are true EXCEPT

    A. it is permissible to use an abbreviation like 1/1/16
    B. the subject line should be underlined
    C. titles such as *Mr.* or *Dr.* are usually not used on the *To* line
    D. unless the memo is very short, paragraphs should be single-spaced and double spacing should be used to separate the paragraphs from each other

10.____

11. When typing a letter, which of the following is INACCURATE?

    A. Paragraphs in business letters are usually single-spaced, with double spacing separating them from each other.
    B. Margin settings used on subsequent sheets should match those used on the letterhead sheet.
    C. If the message contains an enumerated list, it is best to block and center the listed material by five or six more spaces, right and left.
    D. A quotation of more than three typed lines must be single-spaced and centered on the page.

11.____

12. A letter that is to be signed by Hazel Alice Putney, but written by Mary Jane Roberts, and typed by Alice Carol Bell would CORRECTLY bear the following set of initials:

    A. HAP:MJR:acb
    B. HAP:MJR:ab
    C. HAP:mjr:acb
    D. HAP:mjr:ab

13. Which of the following is INCORRECT?

    A. My dear Dr. Jones:
    B. Dear Accounting Department:
    C. Dear Dr. Jones:
    D. Dear Mr. Al Lee, Esq.:

14. Which of the following is INCORRECT?

    A. Bcc stands for blind copy or blind courtesy copy.
    B. When a blind copy is used, the notation bcc appears only on the original.
    C. When a blind copy is used, the notation may appear in the top left corner of the letterhead sheet.
    D. If following a letter style that uses indented paragraphs, the postscript should be indented in exactly the same manner.

15. All of the following are true of the complimentary close EXCEPT

    A. it is typed two lines beneath the last line of the message
    B. when using a minimal punctuation system, you may omit the comma in the complimentary close if you have used a colon in the salutation
    C. where the complimentary close is placed may vary
    D. the first word of the complimentary close is capitalized

16. When typing a letter, which of the following is INACCURATE?

    A. Tables should be centered.
    B. If the letter is to be more than one page long, at least three lines of the message itself should be carried over.
    C. The message begins two lines below the salutation in almost all letter styles.
    D. Triple spacing should be used above and below lists to set them off from the rest of the letter.

17. Which one of the following is INCORRECT?

    A. When used, special mailing instructions should be indicated on both the envelope and the letter itself.
    B. Depending upon the length of the message and the available space, special mailing instructions are usually typed flush left, about four spaces below the date line and about two lines above the first line of the inside address.
    C. Certification, registration, special delivery, and overseas air mail are all considered special mailing instructions.
    D. Special mailing instructions should not be typed in capital letters.

18. Which of the following is INCORRECT?

    A. When a letter is intended to be personal or confidential, these instructions are typewritten in capital letters on the envelope and on the letter itself.

B. When a letter is intended to be personal or confidential, these instructions are typewritten in capital letters on the envelope, but not on the letter.
C. A letter marked PERSONAL is an eyes-only communication for the recipient.
D. A letter marked CONFIDENTIAL means that the recipient and any other authorized person may open and read it.

19. All of the following are true in regard to copy notation EXCEPT

    A. when included in a letter, a copy notation should be typed flush with the left margin, two lines below the signature block or two lines below any preceding notation
    B. copy notation should appear after writer/typist initials and/or enclosure notations, if these are used
    C. the copy recipient's full name and address should be indicated
    D. if more than one individual is to be copied, recipients should be listed in alphabetical order according to full name or initials

20. When addressing envelopes, which of the following is INACCURATE?

    A. When both street address and box number are used, the destination of the letter should be placed on the line just above the city, state, and zip code line.
    B. Special mailing instructions are typed in capital letters below the postage.
    C. Special handling instructions should be typed in capital letters and underlined.
    D. The address should be single-spaced.

21. All of the following should be capitalized EXCEPT the

    A. first word of a direct quotation
    B. first word in the continuation of a split, single-sentence quotation
    C. names of organizations
    D. names of places and geographic districts, regions, divisions, and locales

22. All of the following are true about capitalization EXCEPT

    A. words indicating direction and regions are capitalized
    B. the names of rivers, seas, lakes, mountains, and oceans are capitalized
    C. the names of nationalities, tribes, languages, and races are capitalized
    D. civil, military, corporate, royal and noble, honorary, and religious titles are capitalized when they precede a name

23. All of the following are true about capitalization EXCEPT

    A. key words in the titles of musical, dramatic, artistic, and literary works are capitalized as are the first and last words
    B. the first word of the salutation and of the complimentary close of a letter is capitalized
    C. abbreviations and acronyms are not capitalized
    D. the days of the week, months of the year, holidays, and holy days are capitalized

24. All of the following are true EXCEPT

    A. an apostrophe indicates the omission of letters in contractions
    B. an apostrophe indicates the possessive case of singular and plural nouns

C. an apostrophe should not be used to indicate the omission of figures in dates
D. ellipses are used to indicate the omission of words or sentences within quoted material

25. All of the following are true EXCEPT

    A. brackets may be used to enclose words or passages in quotations to indicate the insertion of material written by someone other than the original writer
    B. brackets may be used to enclose material that is inserted within material already in parentheses
    C. a dash, rather than a colon, should be used to introduce a list
    D. a colon may be used to introduce a long quotation

26. All of the following are true EXCEPT a(n)

    A. comma may be used to set off short quotations and sayings
    B. apostrophe is often used to represent the word *per*
    C. dash may be used to indicate a sudden change or break in continuity
    D. dash may be used to set apart an emphatic or defining phrase

27. All of the following are true EXCEPT

    A. a hyphen may be used as a substitute for the word *to* between figures or words
    B. parentheses are used to enclose material that is not an essential part of the sentence and that, if not included, would not change its meaning
    C. single quotation marks are used to enclose quotations within quotations
    D. semicolons and colons are put inside closing quotation marks

28. All of the following are true EXCEPT

    A. commas and periods should be put inside closing quotation marks
    B. for dramatic effect, a semicolon may be used instead of a comma to signal longer pauses
    C. a semicolon is used to set off city and state in geographic names
    D. italics are used to represent the titles of magazines and newspapers

29. According to standard rules for typing, two spaces are left after a

    A. closing parenthesis   B. comma
    C. number   D. colon

30. All of the following are true EXCEPT

    A. rounding out large numbers is often acceptable
    B. it is best to use numerical figures to express specific hours, measures, dates, page numbers, coordinates, and addresses
    C. when a sentence begins with a number, it is best to use numerical figures rather than to spell the number out
    D. when two or more numbers appear in one sentence, it is best to spell them out consistently or use numerical figures consistently, regardless of the size of the numbers

31. All of the following are true about word division EXCEPT
    A. words should not be divided on a single letter
    B. it is acceptable to carry over two-letter endings
    C. the final word in a paragraph should not be divided
    D. words in headings should not be divided

32. All of the following are true of word division EXCEPT
    A. it is preferable to divide words of three or more syllables after the consonant
    B. it is best to avoid breaking words on more than two consecutive lines
    C. words should be divided according to pronunciation
    D. two-syllable words are divided at the end of the first syllable

33. All of the following are true of word division EXCEPT
    A. words with short prefixes should be divided after the prefix
    B. prefixes and combining forms of more than one syllable should be divided after the first syllable
    C. the following word endings are not divided: -gion, -gious, -sial, -sion, -tial, -tion, -tious, -ceous, -cial, -cient, -cion, -cious, and -geous
    D. words ending in -er should not be divided if the division could only occur on the -er form

34. All of the following are true about word division EXCEPT
    A. words should be divided so that the part of the word left at the end of the line will suggest the word
    B. abbreviations should not be divided
    C. the suffixes -able and -ible are usually divided instead of being carried over intact to the next line
    D. when the addition of -ed, -est, -er, or a similar ending causes the doubling of a final consonant, the added consonant is carried over

35. All of the following are true of word division EXCEPT
    A. words with doubled consonants are usually divided between those consonants
    B. it is permissible to divide contractions
    C. words of one syllable should not be split
    D. it is best to try to avoid divisions that add a hyphen to an already hyphenated word

36. All of the following are true of word division EXCEPT
    A. dividing proper names should be avoided wherever possible
    B. two consonants, preceded and followed by a vowel, are divided after the first consonant
    C. even though two adjoining vowels are sounded separately, it is best not to divide between the two vowels
    D. it is best not to divide the month and day when typing dates, but the year may be carried over to the next line

37. Which of the following four statements are CORRECT? It would be acceptable to divide the word
    I. *organization* after the first *a* in the word
    II. *recommend* after the first *m*
    III. *interface* between the *r* and the *f*
    IV. *development* between the *e* and the *l*
    The CORRECT answer is:

    A. I only
    B. II, III
    C. II only
    D. I, II, III

38. Which of the following is divided INCORRECTLY?

    A. usu-ally
    B. call-ing
    C. pro-blem
    D. micro-computer

39. Which of the following is divided INCORRECTLY?

    A. imag-inary
    B. commun-ity
    C. manage-able
    D. commun-ion

40. Which of the following is divided INCORRECTLY?

    A. spa-ghetti
    B. retro-spective
    C. proof-reader
    D. fix-ed

41. Which of the following is divided INCORRECTLY?

    A. Mr. Han-rahan
    B. control-lable
    C. pro-jectile
    D. proj-ect

42. Which of the following is divided INCORRECTLY?

    A. prom-ise
    B. han-dling
    C. have-n't
    D. pro-duce

43. Which of the following is divided INCORRECTLY?

    A. ship-ped
    B. audi-ble
    C. hypo-crite
    D. refer-ring

44. Which of the following is divided INCORRECTLY?

    A. particu-lar
    B. spac-ious
    C. chang-ing
    D. capac-ity

45. There is a critical need to develop the ability to control the mind, especailly the ability to stop repeating negative thoughts. Often, when we must swallow our anger, we are left running an enless tape of thoughts. We can't stop thinking about what the person said and what we should have said in response. To combat this tendency, it is helpful to practice witnessing our thoughts. If we can remain detached from them, we won't fuel them, and they will just run out of gas. As we watch them, we also learn a lot about ourselves. The catch here is not to judge them. Judging may lead to selfblaming, blaming others, excuses, rationalizations, and other thoughts that just add fuel. Another technique is is substituting positive thoughts for negative ones.

It is difficult to do this in the "heat of the moment". With practice, however, its possible to train the mind to do what we want it to do and to contain what we want it to contain. A mind is like a garden – we can weed it, or we can let it grow wild.
The above paragraph contains a number of typographical errors.
How many lines in this paragraph contain typographical errors?

A. 5 B. 6 C. 8 D. 9

KEY (CORRECT ANSWERS)

1. B	11. D	21. B	31. B	41. A
2. C	12. A	22. A	32. A	42. A
3. D	13. D	23. C	33. B	43. A
4. C	14. B	24. C	34. C	44. B
5. C	15. B	25. C	35. B	45. C
6. B	16. D	26. B	36. C	
7. D	17. D	27. D	37. B	
8. B	18. B	28. C	38. C	
9. D	19. C	29. D	39. B	
10. B	20. C	30. C	40. D	

TEST 2

DIRECTIONS: Each sentence may or may not contain problems in capitalization or punctuation. If there is an error, select the number of the underlined part that must be changed to make the sentence correct. If the sentence has no error, select choice E. <u>No sentence contains more than one error.</u>

1. Is the choice for <u>P</u>resident of the company<u>_George Dawson_</u> or Marilyn Kappel<u>?</u> <u>No error</u>
                  A   B   C   D   E

2. "To tell you the truth<u>_,_</u> I was really <u>disappointed_that</u> our <u>F</u>all percentages did not show more sales growth<u>_,_</u>" remarked the bookkeeper. <u>No error</u>
                           A   B   C   D   E

3. Bruce gave his <u>U</u>ncle clear directions to go <u>s</u>outh on Maplewood Drive<u>_,_</u> turn left at the intersection with Birch Lane, and then proceed for two miles until he reached Columbia <u>C</u>ounty. <u>No error</u>
      A   B   C
   D   E

4. Janet hopes to transfer to a <u>c</u>ollege in the <u>e</u>ast <u>_</u>during her <u>j</u>unior year. <u>No error</u>
                               A   B C   D   E

5. The <u>D</u>eclaration <u>o</u>f Independence states<u>_</u> that we have the right to the pursuit of <u>H</u>appiness, but it doesn't guarantee that we'll ever find it. <u>No error</u>
       A   B   C
   D   E

6. We campaigned hard for the <u>m</u>ayor<u>_,_</u> but <u>we'</u>re still not sure if he'll win against <u>S</u>enator Frankovich. <u>No error</u>
                                    A B   C   D
   E

7. Mr. <u>Butler'_s</u> <u>F</u>ord was parked right behind <u>our's</u> on Atlantic <u>A</u>venue. <u>No error</u>
          A   B   C   D   E

8. "I respect your <u>opinion_,</u> but I cannot agree with <u>it_.</u>" commented my <u>g</u>randmother. <u>No error</u>
   A   B   C   D
   E

9. My friends, of course, were surprised when when I did so well on the Math section
      A   B   C   D
   of the test. No error
                    E

10. Dr. Vogel and Senator Rydell decided that the meeting would be held on February 6,
         A   B   C
    in Ithaca, New York. No error
         D   E

11. "Frank, do you understand what we're telling you?" asked the doctor. No error
          A   B   C   D   E

12. When I asked my daughter what she knew about politics, she claimed she
                             A   B   C
    knew nothing. No error
                    D   E

13. "If you went to my high school, dad, you'd see things differently," snapped Sean.
            A   A   B   C   D
    No error
        E

14. In Carlos' third year of high school, he took geometry, psychology, french, and chemis-
        A   B   B   C   D
    try. No error
              E

15. "When you enter the building," the guard instructed us, "turn left down the long, wind-
                                   A   B   C   D
    ing corridor." No error
                       E

16. We hope to spend a weekend in the Catskill Mountains in the spring, and we'd like to
                                                             A   B   C   D
    go to Florida in January. No error
                                         E

17. A clerk in the department of Justice asked Carol and me if we were there on business or
         A   B   C
    just sight- seeing. . No error
                            D   E

18. Jamie joined a cult, Harry's in a rock band, and Carol-Ann is studying chinese literature
                A   B   C

    at the University of Southern California. No error
          D   E

    18.____

19. Parker Flash asked if my band had ever played at the
                      A

    Purple Turnip, a club in Orinoco Hills. No error
     B   C   D   E

    19.____

20. "The gift of the Magi" is a short story by O'Henry that deals with the sad ironies of life.
        A B C D

    No error
      E

    20.____

21. Darwin's theory was developed, as a result of his trip to the Galapagos Islands.
         A B   C   D

    No error
      E

    21.____

22. Is 10 Downing street the address of Sherlock Holmes or the British Prime Minister?
          A   B   C   D

    No error
      E

    22.____

23. While President Johnson was in Office, his Great Society program passed a great deal
            A   B   C   D

    of important legislation. No error
                              E

    23.____

24. If, as the American Industrial Health Council's study says, one out of every five can-
      A   B   C

    cers today is caused by the workplace, it is a tragic indictment of what is happening
                                  D

    there. No error
           E

    24.____

25. According to the Articles of Confederation, Congress could issue money, but it could
                             A   B   C

    not prevent States from issuing their own money. No error
               D   E

    25.____

4 (#2)

26. "I'd really like to know <u>whos</u> going to be shoveling the driveway this <u>winter,</u>" said
         A   B   C   D

    Laverne. <u>No error</u>
              E

27. According to Carl <u>Jung</u> the <u>Swiss</u> psychologist<u>,</u> playing with fantasy is the <u>key</u> to cre-
                      A   B   C   D

    ativity. <u>No error</u>
              E

28. <u>Don't</u> you find it odd that people would prefer jumping off the Golden Gate <u>bridge</u> to
      A   B

    jumping off other bridges in the <u>area</u><u>?</u> <u>No error</u>
                                      C   D   E

29. While driving through the <u>South,</u> we saw many of the sites of famous Civil <u>war</u> <u>battles</u>.
                               A   B   C   D

    <u>No error</u>
     E

30. Although I have always valued my <u>Grandmother's</u> <u>china</u>, I prefer her collection
                                      A   B   C

    of <u>South</u> American art. <u>No error</u>
        D   E

KEY (CORRECT ANSWERS)

1.	A	16.	E
2.	C	17.	B
3.	A	18.	C
4.	B	19.	C
5.	D	20.	A
6.	E	21.	C
7.	C	22.	B
8.	E	23.	B
9.	D	24.	D
10.	E	25.	D
11.	A	26.	B
12.	B	27.	A
13.	C	28.	B
14.	D	29.	C
15.	E	30.	A

EXAMINATION SECTION
TEST 1

DIRECTIONS: Each question or incomplete statement is followed by several suggested answers or completions. Select the one that BEST answers the question or completes the statement. *PRINT THE LETTER OF THE CORRECT ANSWER IN THE SPACE AT THE RIGHT.*

1. Shortcut keys can be used for 1.____
   - A. navigation
   - B. software
   - C. formatting text
   - D. all of the above

2. A basic keyboard has _____ types of keys. 2.____
   - A. 4
   - B. 6
   - C. 3
   - D. none of the above

3. Which combination of keys is used to switch among opened programs? 3.____
   - A. Ctrl+Tab
   - B. Alt+Tab+Del
   - C. Shift+Alt
   - D. Both A and B

4. To insert hyperlink for selected text, which shortcut key is used? 4.____
   - A. Ctrl+P
   - B. Ctrl+O
   - C. Ctrl+K
   - D. All of the above

5. Pressing the Ctrl and Home keys together clears the screen and sends the cursor to the 5.____
   - A. top of the document or page
   - B. previous page
   - C. next page
   - D. header of the document

6. Which keys are used to open the Start menu in Microsoft Windows? 6.____
   - A. Windows
   - B. Ctrl+Esc
   - C. Ctrl+Tab
   - D. Both A and B

7. The separate keys for letters, numbers and special characters are known as 7.____
   - A. character keys
   - B. special
   - C. functional
   - D. hot keys

8. Which of the following keys perform customized functions for different software? 8.____
   - A. Special
   - B. Functional
   - C. Character
   - D. None of the above

9. To lock or log off Windows, which combination of keys is used? 9.____
   - A. Windows + L
   - B. Windows + M
   - C. Windows + S
   - D. All of the above

10. A dialogue box is opened when _____ is pressed together.
    A. Windows + R   B. Windows + O
    C. Ctrl + O   D. Ctrl + P

11. This symbol (-) on a keyboard is known as a
    A. dash   B. hyphen
    C. minus   D. slash

12. This symbol (') on a keyboard is known as a(n)
    A. apostrophe   B. semicolon
    C. comma   D. ampersand

13. Three periods (...) written in a sentence are called a(n)
    A. full stop   B. dash
    C. ellipsis   D. em dash

14. Which of the following are known as angle brackets?
    A. ()   B. {}
    C. <>   D. all of the above

15. The forward slash (/) is commonly found on the same key as the
    A. exclamation point   B. period
    C. comma   D. question mark

16. Special characters are typed by pressing numeric keys along with the _____ key.
    A. Alt   B. Ctrl
    C. Shift   D. all of the above

17. To type an open and closed parentheses, you would press 9 and 0 while holding the _____ key.
    A. Shift   B. Ctrl
    C. Tab   D. command

18. Which combination of keys is required to display the dollar sign ($)?
    A. Shift + 4   B. Ctrl + 4
    C. Alt + 4   D. Both A and B

19. In standard keyboarding, the pointer fingers are positioned on the __ and __ keys.
    A. F, J   B. G, J
    C. D, K   D. S, L

20. Which of the following words will usually be typed with the left hand only?
    A. Fire   B. Free
    C. True   D. Tired

21. Which of the following symbols can be typed without the use of the Shift key?
    A. Pound sign   B. Percent sign
    C. Semicolon   D. Colon

22. The _____ currency symbol is displayed when Alt+0128 is pressed. 22.____
    A. dollar   B. pound
    C. Euro   D. none of the above

23. Alt+0149 is pressed to display a _____ symbol. 23.____
    A. •   B. -
    C. ;   D. $

24. The special character for copyright is denoted by 24.____
    A. ©   B. @
    C. ¥   D. both A and B

25. Alt+0174 is a key combination to display the special character for 25.____
    A. registered trademark   B. copyright
    C. both A and B   D. none of the above

KEY (CORRECT ANSWERS)

1.	D		11.	B
2.	A		12.	A
3.	A		13.	C
4.	C		14.	C
5.	A		15.	D
6.	D		16.	A
7.	A		17.	A
8.	B		18.	D
9.	A		19.	A
10.	A		20.	B

21. C
22. C
23. A
24. A
25. A

TEST 2

DIRECTIONS: Each question or incomplete statement is followed by several suggested answers or completions. Select the one that BEST answers the question or completes the statement. *PRINT THE LETTER OF THE CORRECT ANSWER IN THE SPACE AT THE RIGHT.*

1. Common control keys are
   - A. Home
   - B. Esc
   - C. Delete
   - D. all of the above

   1.____

2. The numeric keypad is useful for all of the following EXCEPT
   - A. business environment
   - B. data entry
   - C. accounting
   - D. web navigation

   2.____

3. **In the keyboard, mechanical key switches include the**
   - A. **rubber dome**
   - B. **metal contact**
   - C. **foam element**
   - D. **all of the** above

   3.____

4. To create a shortcut of the selected item, which key combination is required?
   - A. Ctrl + Shift
   - B. Ctrl + Alt
   - C. Alt + Shift
   - D. All of the above

   4.____

5. To search a file or folder, the _____ key is the correct option.
   - A. F4
   - B. F11
   - C. F3
   - D. none of the above

   5.____

6. Properties for the selected item can be seen by pressing
   - A. Alt + Enter
   - B. Alt + F4
   - C. Alt + O
   - D. all of the above

   6.____

7. The shortcut menu for the selected item is displayed when _____ are pressed together.
   - A. Shift + Alt
   - B. Shift + F10
   - C. both A and B
   - D. none of the above

   7.____

8. The Ctrl+Shift+Tab combination is used to switch between opened programs in the _____ direction.
   - A. left
   - B. right
   - C. up
   - D. down

   8.____

9. Alt + F4 closes all opened windows to show the desktop, whereas _____ shows the desktop without closing any window.
   - A. Alt + O
   - B. Windows + D
   - C. Alt + Shift
   - D. none of the above

   9.____

10. If the Shift key is pressed five times, it will switch on or off the
 A. filter keys
 B. toggle keys
 C. sticky keys
 D. all of the above

11. The Ctrl+Windows+F key combination works for searching
 A. files
 B. folders
 C. computers
 D. all of the above

12. _____ is an easy way to open *My Computer*.
 A. Windows + E
 B. Windows + O
 C. Both A and B
 D. All of the above

13. (™) is a special character which is displayed as a result of pressing
 A. Alt+0153
 B. Alt+018
 C. Alt+010
 D. none of the above

14. Alt+0163 is used to show _____ currency.
 A. $
 B. £
 C. £
 D. none of the above

15. The ~ symbol is known as a
 A. tilde
 B. hyphen
 C. both A and B
 D. none of the above

16. Isolated sentences that are grammatically independent but have closely connected meanings are joined by using a
 A. colon
 B. comma
 C. semicolon
 D. all of the above

17. The inverted exclamation is shown by typing
 A. Alt+0161
 B. Alt+173
 C. none of the above
 D. both A and B

18. Which one of the following is a currency symbol?
 A. ¤
 B. ¡
 C. ~
 D. none of the above

19. Alt+58 displays the character
 A. "
 B. :
 C. ,
 D. none of the above

20. The logical not sign is denoted by
 A. ¬
 B. ¯
 C. both A and B
 D. none of the above

21. The ¼ (one quarter) special character is displayed when _____ are pressed.
    A. Alt+172
    B. Alt+0188
    C. both A and B
    D. none of the above

    21.____

22. The ¯ symbol is known as a
    A. macron
    B. hyphen
    C. dash
    D. all of the above

    22.____

23. Alt+19 is used to display
    A. ¡
    B. ‼
    C. &
    D. all of the above

    23.____

24. For capital letters, which one of the following works well?
    A. Alt+65 to Alt+90
    B. Shift + alphabets
    C. None of the above
    D. Both A and B

    24.____

25. The special character ¶ is shown when _____ is pressed.
    A. Alt+Tab
    B. Alt+20
    C. Alt+0120
    D. all of the above

    25.____

KEY (CORRECT ANSWERS)

1.	D		11.	C
2.	D		12.	A
3.	D		13.	A
4.	A		14.	B
5.	C		15.	A
6.	A		16.	C
7.	B		17.	D
8.	A		18.	A
9.	B		19.	B
10.	C		20.	D

21.	C
22.	A
23.	B
24.	D
25.	B

TEST 3

DIRECTIONS: Each question or incomplete statement is followed by several suggested answers or completions. Select the one that BEST answers the question or completes the statement. *PRINT THE LETTER OF THE CORRECT ANSWER IN THE SPACE AT THE RIGHT.*

1. Which one of the following key combinations is used to open a new tab in the browser?
   A. Ctrl+Tab   B. Ctrl+O
   C. Ctrl+T   D. All of the above   1._____

2. Snapshot is taken when _____ is pressed together.   2._____
   A. Ctrl+Alt+S   B. Ctrl+Shift+S
   C. Ctrl+Shift+C   D. none of the above

3. Ctrl+Shift+Esc opens the   3._____
   A. task manager   B. control panel
   C. menu   D. none of the above

4. Which command is useful when a magnifier is required for zoom out? 4._____
   A. Windows+-   B. Windows-+
   C. Both A and B   D. None of the above

5. _____ makes all Windows transparent so the desktop could be seen. 5._____
   A. Windows+Alt   B. Windows+Shift
   C. Windows+Space   D. All of the above

6. Which key combination brings all gadgets on top and the forefront? 6._____
   A. Windows+G   B. Windows+O
   C. Windows+P   D. All of the above

7. _____ displays a preview thumbnail of running applications in the Windows taskbar one by one without mouse over. 7._____
   A. Shift+T   B. Windows+T
   C. Windows+P   D. All of the above

8. Windows+X opens windows   8._____
   A. mobility center B. help center
   C. both A and B   D. all of the above

9. Windows+Shift+T cycles _____ in the taskbar.   9._____
   A. backward   B. forward
   C. both A and B   D. all of the above

10. The Windows+U key combination opens   10._____
    A. the control panel   B. ease of access
    C. ease of access center   D. all of the above

11. Which type of keys are included in the basic keyboard? 11.____
    A. Control keys   B. Function keys
    C. Navigation keys   D. All of the above

12. Rarely used keys on the keyboard are 12.____
    A. PrtScn   B. Scroll
    C. Pause   D. all of the above

13. _____ displays Windows help and support center. 13.____
    A. Shift+F1   B. Windows+F1
    C. Alt+F1   D. All of the above

14. When working with the help viewer, which key combination opens the table of contents? 14.____
    A. Alt+T   B. Alt+C
    C. Alt+O   D. All of the above

15. _____ displays the Option menu. 15.____
    A. F10   B. F2
    C. F11   D. None of the above

16. Alt+Home, when pressed together in the browser, opens up 16.____
    A. Menu   B. Start page
    C. none of the above   D. all of the above

17. Alt+A opens the _____ support page in the Help viewer. 17.____
    A. technical   B. customer
    C. help   D. all of the above

18. Fn+key is a combination for some symbols recognized by 18.____
    A. Windows   B. kernel
    C. operating system   D. both A and B

19. The Shift+Tab combination mostly helps out the _____ specialist. 19.____
    A. computer   B. data entry
    C. graphic   D. none of the above

20. Fn+F5 pressed together results in 20.____
    A. brightness down   B. brightness up
    C. close programs   D. none of the above

21. Which of the following keys are concerned with volume? 21.____
    A. Fn+F11   B. Fn+F12
    C. Fn+F10   D. All of the above

22. Which key combination closes the open window within the existing active window in Microsoft Windows?
    A. Shift+F4
    B. Alt+F4
    C. Ctrl+F4
    D. All of the above

23. _____ in Windows renames a highlighted icon, file, or folder in all types of Windows.
    A. F2
    B. F5
    C. F4
    D. None of the above

24. _____ will transform letters from upper to lower case or capitalize each word in Microsoft Word.
    A. Shift+F5
    B. Shift+F3
    C. None of the above
    D. Both A and B

25. In Microsoft Windows, F5 performs which of the following functions?
    A. Refresh pages in browser
    B. Show slideshow in Power Point
    C. Find and replace
    D. All of the above

KEY (CORRECT ANSWERS)

1.	C	11.	D
2.	B	12.	D
3.	A	13.	B
4.	A	14.	B
5.	C	15.	A
6.	A	16.	B
7.	B	17.	B
8.	A	18.	B
9.	A	19.	B
10.	C	20.	A
21.	D		
22.	C		
23.	A		
24.	B		
25.	D		

TEST 4

DIRECTIONS: Each question or incomplete statement is followed by several suggested answers or completions. Select the one that BEST answers the question or completes the statement. *PRINT THE LETTER OF THE CORRECT ANSWER IN THE SPACE AT THE RIGHT.*

1. Alt+double click displays the properties of the
   A. program
   B. selected item
   C. none of the above
   D. both A and B

   1.____

2. F1 frequently displays
   A. Windows help
   B. Menu
   C. tool bar
   D. all of the above

   2.____

3. _____ opens a shortcut menu for the selected item.
   A. Alt+F10
   B. Shift+F10
   C. Both A and B
   D. None of the above

   3.____

4. Ctrl+Esc and _____ do the same thing.
   A. Alt key
   B. Windows key
   C. Fn key
   D. Shift+Esc

   4.____

5. Press and hold down the _____ key while inserting a CD to avoid the automatic run function.
   A. Windows
   B. Alt
   C. Shift
   D. all of the above

   5.____

6. _____ closes the current multiple document interface (MDI) window.
   A. Alt+F4
   B. Ctrl+F4
   C. Shift+F4
   D. All of the above

   6.____

7. _____ switches between multiple windows in the same program.
   A. Alt+F6
   B. Alt+F8
   C. Alt+Shift
   D. None of the above

   7.____

8. Left Alt+left Shift + Num Lock will turn on and off
   A. filter keys
   B. mouse keys
   C. both A and B
   D. none of the above

   8.____

9. Windows+M and Windows+D _____ all opened programs.
   A. maximize
   B. minimize
   C. close
   D. none of the above

   9.____

10. _____ moves focus from start to the quick launch toolbar to the system tray.
    A. Ctrl+Tab+Windows
    B. Ctrl+Windows+Tab
    C. Windows+Tab+Alt
    D. All of the above

    10.____

11. _____ is equivalent to the Cancel command.
    A. Esc
    B. Alt+F4
    C. Alt+Space
    D. All of the above

    11._____

12. _____ opens firebug or brower debug tool.
    A. Alt+F12
    B. F12
    C. Shift+F12
    D. All of the above

    12._____

13. _____ access hidden recovery partitions in Dell and Lenovo computers.
    A. Shift+Alt
    B. F11
    C. Alt
    D. None of the above

    13._____

14. Which functional key is accessed to go in hidden recovery partition in HP and Sony computers?
    A. Fn+F10
    B. F10
    C. Shift+F10
    D. All of the above

    14._____

15. Which one of the following is used to enter in CMOS setup?
    A. F10
    B. Fn+F10
    C. None of the above
    D. Both A and B

    15._____

16. In Microsoft Outlook, which key is used to send and receive email?
    A. Ctrl+S
    B. Fn+F9
    C. F9
    D. All of the above

    16._____

17. Windows safe mode is accessed through
    A. F10
    B. F8
    C. Fn+F10
    D. none of the above

    17._____

18. _____ shows a thumbnail image for all workspaces in Mac OS.
    A. F5
    B. F9
    C. F8
    D. None of the above

    18._____

19. F8 is used to access Windows recovery system in _____ computers.
    A. Dell
    B. some
    C. Sony
    D. none of the above

    19._____

20. In Microsoft programs, spell check and grammar check is performed by
    A. F7
    B. Fn+F7
    C. both A and B
    D. none of the above

    20._____

21. _____ opens to another open Microsoft Word document.
    A. Shift+F6
    B. Ctrl+Shift+F6
    C. Ctrl+Shift+F4
    D. Ctrl+Shift+F5

    21._____

22. In Firefox browser, _____ open clear data windows to quickly clear private data.
    A. Ctrl+Shift+Delete
    B. Shift+Delete
    C. Ctrl+Delete
    D. all of the above

22._____

23. Ctrl+J open up download windows in
    A. Firefox
    B. Chrome
    C. both A and B
    D. none of the above

23._____

24. _____ in Windows 8 opens the Start screen.
    A. Alt+S
    B. Ctrl+Esc
    C. Ctrl+S
    D. Both A and B

24._____

25. In all versions of Windows, _____ starts find or search at the Windows desktop.
    A. Ctrl+F3
    B. F3
    C. Alt+F3
    D. all of the above

25._____

KEY (CORRECT ANSWERS)

1.	B		11.	A
2.	A		12.	B
3.	B		13.	B
4.	B		14.	B
5.	C		15.	A
6.	A		16.	C
7.	A		17.	B
8.	B		18.	C
9.	B		19.	B
10.	B		20.	A

21.	B
22.	A
23.	C
24.	B
25.	B

RECORD KEEPING
EXAMINATION SECTION
TEST 1

DIRECTIONS: Each question or incomplete statement is followed by several suggested answers or completions. Select the one that BEST answers the question or completes the statement. *PRINT THE LETTER OF THE CORRECT ANSWER IN THE SPACE AT THE RIGHT.*

Questions 1-7.

DIRECTIONS: In answering Questions 1 through 7, use the following master list. For each question, determine where the name would fit on the master list. Each answer choice indicates right before or after the name in the answer choice.

   Aaron, Jane
   Armstead, Brendan
   Bailey, Charles
   Dent, Ricardo
   Grant, Mark
   Mars, Justin
   Methieu, Justine
   Parker, Cathy
   Sampson, Suzy
   Thomas, Heather

1. Schmidt, William
 A. Right before Cathy Parker
 B. Right after Heather Thomas
 C. Right after Suzy Sampson
 D. Right before Ricardo Dent

2. Asanti, Kendall
 A. Right before Jane Aaron
 B. Right after Charles Bailey
 C. Right before Justine Methieu
 D. Right after Brendan Armstead

3. O'Brien, Daniel
 A. Right after Justine Methieu
 B. Right before Jane Aaron
 C. Right after Mark Grant
 D. Right before Suzy Sampson

4. Marrow, Alison
 A. Right before Cathy Parker
 B. Right before Justin Mars
 C. Right before Mark Grant
 D. Right after Heather Thomas

5. Grantt, Marissa
 A. Right before Mark Grant
 B. Right after Mark Grant
 C. Right after Justin Mars
 D. Right before Suzy Sampson

1.____

2.____

3.____

4.____

5.____

2 (#1)

6. Thompson, Heath
   A. Right after Justin Mars
   B. Right before Suzy Sampson
   C. Right after Heather Thomas
   D. Right before Cathy Parker

6.____

DIRECTIONS: Before answering Question 7, add in all of the names from Questions 1 through 6. Then fit the name in alphabetical order based on the new list.

7. Francisco, Mildred
   A. Right before Mark Grant
   B. Right after Marissa Grantt
   C. Right before Alison Marrow
   D. Right after Kendall Asanti

7.____

Questions 8-10.

DIRECTIONS: In answering Questions 8 through 10, compare each pair of names and addresses. Indicate whether they are the same or different in any way.

8. William H. Pratt, J.D.   William H. Pratt, J.D.
   Attourney at Law   Attorney at Law
   A. No differences
   B. 1 difference
   C. 2 differences
   D. 3 differences

8.____

9. 1303 Theater Drive,; Apt. 3-B   1330 Theatre Drive,; Apt. 3-B
   A. No differences
   B. 1 difference
   C. 2 differences
   D. 3 differences

9.____

10. Petersdorff, Briana and Mary   Petersdorff, Briana and Mary
    A. No differences
    B. 1 difference
    C. 2 differences
    D. 3 differences

10.____

11. Which of the following words, if any, are misspelled?
    A. Affordable
    B. Circumstansial
    C. Legalese
    D. None of the above

11.____

Questions 12-13.

DIRECTIONS: Questions 12 and 13 are to be answered on the basis of the following table.

Standardized Test Results for High School Students in District #1230

	English	Math	Science	Reading
High School 1	21	22	15	18
High School 2	12	16	13	15
High School 3	16	18	21	17
High School 4	19	14	15	16

The scores for each high school in the district were averaged out and listed for each subject tested. Scores of 0-10 are significantly below College Readiness Standards. 11-15 are below College Readiness, 16-20 meet College Readiness, and 21-25 are above College Readiness.

12. If the high schools need to meet or exceed in at least half the categories in order to NOT be considered "at risk," which schools are considered "at risk"?
    A. High School 2
    B. High School 3
    C. High School 4
    D. Both A and C

13. What percentage of subjects did the district as a whole meet or exceed College Readiness standards?
    A. 25%   B. 50%   C. 75%   D. 100%

Questions 14-15.

DIRECTIONS: Questions 14 and 15 are to be answered on the basis of the following information.

You have seven employees working as a part of your team: Austin, Emily, Jeremy, Christina, Martin, Harriet, and Steve. You have just sent an e-mail informing them that there will be a mandatory training session next week. To ensure that work still gets done, you are offering the training twice during the week: once on Tuesday and also on Thursday. This way half the employees will still be working while the other half attend the training. The only other issue is that Jeremy doesn't work on Tuesdays and Harriet doesn't work on Thursdays due to compressed work schedules.

14. Which of the following is a possible attendance roster for the first training session?
    A. Emily, Jeremy, Steve
    B. Steve, Christina, Harriet
    C. Harriet, Jeremy, Austin
    D. Steve, Martin, Jeremy

15. If Harriet, Christina, and Steve attend the training session on Tuesday, which of the following is a possible roster for Thursday's training session?
    A. Jeremy, Emily, and Austin
    B. Emily, Martin, and Harriet
    C. Austin, Christina, and Emily
    D. Jeremy, Emily, and Steve

Questions 16-20.

DIRECTIONS: In answering Questions 16 through 20, you will be given a word and will need to choose the answer choice that is MOST similar or different to the word.

16. Which word means the SAME as *annual*?
    A. Monthly   B. Usually   C. Yearly   D. Constantly

17. Which word means the SAME as *effort*?
    A. Energy   B. Equate   C. Cherish   D. Commence

18. Which word means the OPPOSITE of *forlorn*?
    A. Neglected   B. Lethargy   C. Optimistic   D. Astonished

19. Which word means the SAME as *risk*?
    A. Admire   B. Hazard   C. Limit   D. Hesitant

4 (#1)

20. Which word means the OPPOSITE of *translucent*? 20.____
    A. Opaque   B. Transparent   C. Luminous   D. Introverted

21. Last year, Jamie's annual salary was $50,000. Her boss called her today 21.____
    to inform her that she would receive a 20% raise for the upcoming year. How
    much more money will Jamie receive next year?
    A. $60,000   B. $10,000   C. $1,000   D. $51,000

22. You and a co-worker work for a temp hiring agency as part of their office 22.____
    staff. You both are given 6 days off per month. How many days off are you
    and your co-worker given in a year?
    A. 24   B. 72   C. 144   D. 48

23. If Margot makes $34,000 per year and she works 40 hours per week for 23.____
    all 52 weeks, what is her hourly rate?
    A. $16.34/hour   B. $17.00/hour   C. $15.54/hour   D. $13.23/hour

24. How many dimes are there in $175.00? 24.____
    A. 175   B. 1,750   C. 3,500   D. 17,500

25. If Janey is three times as old as Emily, and Emily is 3, how old is Janey? 25.____
    A. 6   B. 9   C. 12   D. 15

KEY (CORRECT ANSWERS)

1. C   11. B
2. D   12. A
3. A   13. D
4. B   14. B
5. B   15. A

6. C   16. C
7. A   17. A
8. B   18. C
9. C   19. B
10. A   20. A

21. B
22. C
23. A
24. B
25. B

TEST 2

DIRECTIONS: Each question or incomplete statement is followed by several suggested answers or completions. Select the one that BEST answers the question or completes the statement. *PRINT THE LETTER OF THE CORRECT ANSWER IN THE SPACE AT THE RIGHT.*

Questions 1-6.

DIRECTIONS: Questions 1 through 6 are to be answered on the basis of the following information.

item	name of item to be ordered
quantity	minimum number that can be ordered
beginning amount	amount in stock at start of month
amount received	amount receiving during month
ending amount	amount in stock at end of month
amount used	amount used during month
amount to order	will need at least as much of each item as used in the previous month
unit price	cost of each unit of an item
total price	total price for the order

Item	Quantity	Beginning	Received	Ending	Amount Used	Amount to Order	Unit Price	Total Price
Pens	10	22	10	8	24	20	$0.11	$2.20
Spiral notebooks	8	30	13	12			$0.25	
Binder clips	2 boxes	3 boxes	1 box	1 box			$1.79	
Sticky notes	3 packs	12 packs	4 packs	2 packs			$1.29	
Dry erase markers	1 pack (dozen)	34 markers	8 markers	40 markers			$16.49	
Ink cartridges (printer)	1 cartridge	3 cartridges	1 cartridge	2 cartridges			$79.99	
Folders	10 folders	25 folders	15 folders	10 folders			$1.08	

1. How many packs of sticky notes were used during the month? 1.____
   A. 16   B. 10   C. 12   D. 14

2. How many folders need to be ordered for next month? 2.____
   A. 15   B. 20   C. 30   D. 40

3. What is the total price of notebooks that you will need to order? 3.____
   A. $6.00   B. $0.25   C. $4.50   D. $2.75

4. Which of the following will you spend the second most money on? 4.____
   A. Ink cartridges   B. Dry erase markers
   C. Sticky notes   D. Binder clips

5. How many packs of dry erase markers should you order? 5.____
   A. 1   B. 8   C. 12   D. 0

6. What will be the total price of the file folders you order?   6.____
   A. $20.16   B. $21.60   C. $10.80   D. $4.32

Questions 7-11.

DIRECTIONS: Questions 7 through 11 are to be answered on the basis of the following table.

Number of Car Accidents, By Location and Cause, for 2014						
	Location 1		Location 2		Location 3	
Cause	Number	Percent	Number	Percent	Number	Percent
Severe Weather	10		25		30	
Excessive Speeding	20	40	5		10	
Impaired Driving	15		15	25	8	
Miscellaneous	5		15		2	4
TOTALS	50	100	60	100	50	100

7. Which of the following is the third highest cause of accidents for all three locations?   7.____
   A. Severe Weather
   B. Impaired Driving
   C. Miscellaneous
   D. Excessive Speeding

8. The average number of Severe Weather accidents per week at Location 3 for the year (52 weeks) was MOST NEARLY   8.____
   A. 0.57   B. 30   C. 1   D. 1.25

9. Which location had the LARGEST percentage of accidents caused by Impaired Driving?   9.____
   A. 1   B. 2   C. 3   D. Both A and B

10. If one-third of the accidents at all three locations resulted in at least one fatality, what is the LEAST amount of deaths caused by accidents last year?   10.____
    A. 60   B. 106   C. 66   D. 53

11. What is the percentage of accidents caused by miscellaneous means from all three locations in 2014?   11.____
    A. 5%   B. 10%   C. 13%   D. 25%

12. How many pairs of the following groups of letters are exactly alike?   12.____
    ACDOBJ   ACDBOJ
    HEWBWR   HEWRWB
    DEERVS   DEERVS
    BRFQSX   BRFQSX
    WEYRVB   WEYRVB
    SPQRZA   SQRPZA

    A. 2   B. 3   C. 4   D. 5

Questions 13-19.

DIRECTIONS: Questions 13 through 19 are to be answered on the basis of the following information.

In 2012, the most current information on the American population was finished. The information was compiled by 200 volunteers in each of the 50 states. The territory of Puerto Rico, a sovereign of the United States, had 25 people assigned to compile data. In February of 2010, volunteers in each state and sovereign began collecting information. In Puerto Rico, data collection finished by January 31st, 2011, while work in the United States was completed on June 30, 2012. Each volunteer gathered data on the population of their state or sovereign. When the information was compiled, volunteers sent reports to the nation's capital, Washington, D.C. Each volunteer worked 20 hours per month and put together 10 reports per month. After the data was compiled in total, 50 people reviewed the data and worked from January 2012 to December 2012.

13. How many reports were generated from February 2010 to April 2010 in Illinois and Ohio?
    A. 3,000   B. 6,000   C. 12,000   D. 15,000

14. How many volunteers in total collected population data in January 2012?
    A. 10,000   B. 2,000   C. 225   D. 200

15. How many reports were put together in May 2012?
    A. 2,000   B. 50,000   C. 100,000   D. 100,250

16. How many hours did the Puerto Rican volunteers work in the fall (September-November)?
    A. 60   B. 500   C. 1,500   D. 0

17. How many workers were compiling or reviewing data in July 2012?
    A. 25   B. 50   C. 200   D. 250

18. What was the total amount of hours worked by Nevada volunteers in July 2010?
    A. 500   B. 4,000   C. 4,500   D. 5,000

19. How many reviewers worked in January 2013?
    A. 75   B. 50   C. 0   D. 25

20. John has to file 10 documents per shelf. How many documents would it take for John to fill 40 shelves?
    A. 40   B. 400   C. 4,500   D. 5,000

21. Jill wants to travel from New York City to Los Angeles by bike, which is approximately 2,772 miles. How many miles per day would Jill need to average if she wanted to complete the trip in 4 weeks?
    A. 100   B. 89   C. 99   D. 94

4 (#2)

22. If there are 24 CPU's and only 7 monitors, how many more monitors do you need to have the same amount of monitors as CPU's?
    A. Not enough information
    B. 17
    C. 31
    D. 0

    22._____

23. If Gerry works 5 days a week and 8 hours each day, and John works 3 days a week and 10 hours each day, how many more hours per year will Gerry work than John?
    A. They work the same amount of hours.
    B. 450
    C. 520
    D. 832

    23._____

24. Jimmy gets transferred to a new office. The new office has 25 employees, but only 16 are there due to a blizzard. How many coworkers was Jimmy able to meet on his first day?
    A. 16
    B. 25
    C. 9
    D. 7

    24._____

25. If you do a fundraiser for charities in your area and raise $500 total, how much would you give to each charity if you were donating equal amounts to 3 of them?
    A. $250.00
    B. $167.77
    C. $50.00
    D. $111.11

    25._____

KEY (CORRECT ANSWERS)

1.	D		11.	C
2.	B		12.	B
3.	A		13.	C
4.	C		14.	A
5.	D		15.	C
6.	B		16.	C
7.	D		17.	B
8.	A		18.	B
9.	A		19.	C
10.	D		20.	B

21.	C
22.	B
23.	C
24.	A
25.	B

TEST 3

DIRECTIONS: Each question or incomplete statement is followed by several suggested answers or completions. Select the one that BEST answers the question or completes the statement. *PRINT THE LETTER OF THE CORRECT ANSWER IN THE SPACE AT THE RIGHT.*

Questions 1-3.

DIRECTIONS: In answering Questions 1 through 3, choose the correctly spelled word.

1. A. allusion B. alusion C. allusien D. allution 1.____

2. A. altitude B. alltitude C. atlitude D. altlitude 2.____

3. A. althogh B. allthough C. althrough D. although 3.____

Questions 4-9.

DIRECTIONS: In answering Questions 4 through 9, choose the answer that BEST completes the analogy.

4. Odometer is to mileage as compass is to 4.____
   A. speed B. needle C. hiking D. direction

5. Marathon is to race as hibernation is to 5.____
   A. winter B. dream C. sleep D. bear

6. Cup is to coffee as bowl is to 6.____
   A. dish B. spoon C. food D. soup

7. Flow is to river as stagnant is to 7.____
   A. pool B. rain C. stream D. canal

8. Paw is to cat as hoof is to 8.____
   A. lamb B. horse C. lion D. elephant

9. Architect is to building as sculptor is to 9.____
   A. museum B. chisel C. stone D. statue

Questions 10-14.

DIRECTIONS: Questions 10 through 14 are to be answered on the basis of the following graph.

Population of Carroll City Broken Down by Age and Gender (in Thousands)			
Age	Female	Male	Total
Under 15	60	60	120
15-23		22	
24-33		20	44
34-43	13	18	31
44-53	20		67
64 and Over	65	65	130
TOTAL	230	232	462

10. How many people in the city are between the ages of 15-23?
    A. 70   B. 46,000   C. 70,000   D. 225,000

11. Approximately what percentage of the total population of the city was female aged 24-33?
    A. 10%   B. 5%   C. 15%   D. 25%

12. If 33% of the males have a job and 55% of females don't have a job, which of the following statements is TRUE?
    A. Males have approximately 2,600 more jobs than females.
    B. Females have approximately 49,000 more jobs than males.
    C. Females have approximately 26,000 more jobs than males.
    D. None of the above statements are true.

13. How many females between the ages of 15-23 live in Carroll City?
    A. 67,000   B. 24,000   C. 48,000   D. 91,000

14. Assume all males 44-53 living in Carroll City are employed. If two-thirds of males age 44-53 work jobs outside of Carroll City, how many work within city limits?
    A. 31,333
    B. 15,667
    C. 47,000
    D. Cannot answer the question with the information provided

Questions 15-16.

DIRECTIONS: Questions 15 and 16 are labeled as shown. Alphabetize them for filing. Choose the answer that correctly shows the order.

15. (1) AED
    (2) OOS
    (3) FOA
    (4) DOM
    (5) COB

    A. 2-5-4-3-2   B. 1-4-5-2-3   C. 1-5-4-2-3   D. 1-5-4-3-2

16. Alphabetize the names of the people. Last names are given last.
    (1) Lindsey Jamestown
    (2) Jane Alberta
    (3) Ally Jamestown
    (4) Allison Johnston
    (5) Lyle Moreno

    A. 2-1-3-4-5   B. 3-4-2-1-5   C. 2-3-1-4-5   D. 4-3-2-1-5

17. Which of the following words is misspelled?
    A. disgust
    B. whisper
    C. locale
    D. none of the above

Questions 18-21.

DIRECTIONS: Questions 18 through 21 are to be answered on the basis of the following list of employees.

Robertson, Aaron
Bacon, Gina
Jerimiah, Trace
Gillette, Stanley
Jacks, Sharon

18. Which employee name would come in third in alphabetized list?
    A. Robertson, Aaron
    B. Jerimiah, Trace
    C. Gillette, Stanley
    D. Jacks, Sharon

19. Which employee's first name starts with the letter in the alphabet that is five letters after the first letter of their last name?
    A. Jerimiah, Trace
    B. Bacon, Gina
    C. Jacks, Sharon
    D. Gillette, Stanley

20. How many employees have last names that are exactly five letters long?
    A. 1   B. 2   C. 3   D. 4

21. How many of the employees have either a first or last name that starts with the letter "G"?

   A. 1 B. 2 C. 4 D. 5

21.____

Questions 22-25.

DIRECTIONS: Questions 22 through 25 are to be answered on the basis of the following chart.

Bicycle Sales (Model #34JA32)							
Country	May	June	July	August	September	October	Total
Germany	34	47	45	54	56	60	296
Britain	40	44	36	47	47	46	260
Ireland	37	32	32	32	34	33	200
Portugal	14	14	14	16	17	14	89
Italy	29	29	28	31	29	31	177
Belgium	22	24	24	26	25	23	144
Total	176	198	179	206	208	207	1166

22. What percentage of the overall total was sold to the German importer?

   A. 25.3% B. 22% C. 24.1% D. 23%

22.____

23. What percentage of the overall total was sold in September?

   A. 24.1% B. 25.6% C. 17.9% D. 24.6%

23.____

24. What is the average number of units per month imported into Belgium over the first four months shown?

   A. 26 B. 20 C. 24 D. 31

24.____

25. If you look at the three smallest importers, what is their total import percentage?

   A. 35.1% B. 37.1% C. 40% D. 28%

25.____

KEY (CORRECT ANSWERS)

1.	A		11.	B
2.	A		12.	C
3.	D		13.	C
4.	D		14.	B
5.	C		15.	D
6.	D		16.	C
7.	A		17.	D
8.	B		18.	D
9.	D		19.	B
10.	C		20.	B

21. B
22. A
23. C
24. C
25. A

TEST 4

DIRECTIONS: Each question or incomplete statement is followed by several suggested answers or completions. Select the one that BEST answers the question or completes the statement. *PRINT THE LETTER OF THE CORRECT ANSWER IN THE SPACE AT THE RIGHT.*

Questions 1-6.

DIRECTIONS: In answering Questions 1 through 6, choose the sentence that represents the BEST example of English grammar.

1. A. Joey and me want to go on a vacation next week.
    B. Gary told Jim he would need to take some time off.
    C. If turning six years old, Jim's uncle would teach Spanish to him.
    D. Fax a copy of your resume to Ms. Perez and me.

    1.____

2. A. Jerry stood in line for almost two hours.
    B. The reaction to my engagement was less exciting than I thought it would be.
    C. Carlos and me have done great work on this project.
    D. Two parts of the speech needs to be revised before tomorrow.

    2.____

3. A. Arriving home, the alarm was tripped.
    B. Jonny is regarded as a stand up guy, a responsible parent, and he doesn't give up until a task is finished.
    C. Each employee must submit a drug test each month.
    D. One of the documents was incinerated in the explosion.

    3.____

4. A. As soon as my parents get home, I told them I finished all of my chores.
    B. I asked my teacher to send me my missing work, check my absences, and how did I do on my test.
    C. Matt attempted to keep it concealed from Jenny and me.
    D. If Mary or him cannot get work done on time, I will have to split them up.

    4.____

5. A. Driving to work, the traffic report warned him of an accident on Highway 47.
    B. Jimmy has performed well this season.
    C. Since finishing her degree, several job offers have been given to Cam.
    D. Our boss is creating unstable conditions for we employees.

    5.____

6. A. The thief was described as a tall man with a wiry mustache weighing approximately 150 pounds.
    B. She gave Patrick and I some more time to finish our work.
    C. One of the books that he ordered was damaged in shipping.
    D. While talking on the rotary phone, the car Jim was driving skidded off the road.

    6.____

Questions 7-9.

DIRECTIONS: Questions 7 through 9 are to be answered on the basis of the following graph.

Ice Lake Frozen Flight (2002-2013)		
Year	Number of Participants	Temperature (Fahrenheit)
2002	22	4°
2003	50	33°
2004	69	18°
2005	104	22°
2006	108	24°
2007	288	33°
2008	173	9°
2009	598	39°
2010	698	26°
2011	696	30°
2012	777	28°
2013	578	32°

7. Which two year span had the LARGEST difference between temperatures? 7.____
   A. 2002 and 2003
   B. 2011 and 2012
   C. 2008 and 2009
   D. 2003 and 2004

8. How many total people participated in the years after the temperature reached at least 29°? 8.____
   A. 2,295   B. 1,717   C. 2,210   D. 4,543

9. In 2007, the event saw 288 participants, while in 2008 that number dropped to 173. Which of the following reasons BEST explains the drop in participants? 9.____
   A. The event had not been going on that long and people didn't know about it.
   B. The lake water wasn't cold enough to have people jump in.
   C. The temperature was too cold for many people who would have normally participated.
   D. None of the above reasons explain the drop in participants.

10. In the following list of numbers, how many times does 4 come just after 2 when 2 comes just after an odd number? 10.____
    2365247653898632488572486392424
    A. 2   B. 3   C. 4   D. 5

11. Which choice below lists the letter that is as far after B as S is after N in the alphabet? 11.____
    A. G   B. H   C. I   D. J

Questions 12-15.

DIRECTIONS: Questions 12 through 15 are to be answered on the basis of the following directory and list of changes.

Directory		
Name	Emp. Type	Position
Julie Taylor	Warehouse	Packer
James King	Office	Administrative Assistant
John Williams	Office	Salesperson
Ray Moore	Warehouse	Maintenance
Kathleen Byrne	Warehouse	Supervisor
Amy Jones	Office	Salesperson
Paul Jonas	Office	Salesperson
Lisa Wong	Warehouse	Loader
Eugene Lee	Office	Accountant
Bruce Lavine	Office	Manager
Adam Gates	Warehouse	Packer
Will Suter	Warehouse	Packer
Gary Lorper	Office	Accountant
Jon Adams	Office	Salesperson
Susannah Harper	Office	Salesperson

Directory Updates:
- Employee e-mail addresses will adhere to the following guidelines: lastnamefirstname@apexindustries.com (ex. Susannah Harper is harpersusannah@apexindustries.com). Currently, employees in the warehouse share one e-mail, distribution@apexindustries.com.
- The "Loader" position will now be referred to as "Specialist I"
- Adam Gates has accepted a Supervisor position within the Warehouse and is no longer a Packer. All warehouse employees report to the two Supervisors and all office employees report to the Manager.

12. Amy Jones tried to send an e-mail to Adam Gates, but it wouldn't send. Which of the following offers the BEST explanation?
    A. Amy put Adam's first name first and then his last name.
    B. Adam doesn't check his e-mail, so he wouldn't know if he received the e-mail or not.
    C. Adam does not have his own e-mail.
    D. Office employees are not allowed to send e-mails to each other.

12.____

13. How many Packers currently work for Apex Industries?
    A. 2 B. 3 C. 4 D. 5

13.____

14. What position does Lisa Wong currently hold?
    A. Specialist I   B. Secretary
    C. Administrative Assistant   D. Loader

14.____

15. If an employee wanted to contact the office manager, which of the following e-mails should the e-mail be sent to? 15.____
    A. officemanager@apexindustries.com
    B. brucelavine@apexindustries.com
    C. lavinebruce@apexindustries.com
    D. distribution@apexindustries.com

Questions 16-19.

DIRECTIONS: In answering Questions 16 through 19, compare the three names, numbers or addresses.

16. Smiley Yarnell   Smiley Yarnel   Smily Yarnell   16.____
    A. All three are exactly alike.
    B. The first and second are exactly alike.
    C. The second and third are exactly alike.
    D. All three are different.

17. 1583 Theater Drive   1583 Theater Drive   1583 Theatre Drive   17.____
    A. All three are exactly alike.
    B. The first and second are exactly alike.
    C. The second and third are exactly alike.
    D. All three are different.

18. 3341893212   3341893212   3341893212   18.____
    A. All three are exactly alike.
    B. The first and second are exactly alike.
    C. The second and third are exactly alike.
    D. All three are different.

19. Douglass Watkins   Douglas Watkins   Douglass Watkins   19.____
    A. All three are exactly alike.
    B. The first and third are exactly alike.
    C. The second and third are exactly alike.
    D. All three are different.

Questions 20-24.

DIRECTIONS: In answering Questions 20 through 24, you will be presented with a word. Choose the synonym that BEST represents the word in question.

20. Flexible   20.____
    A. delicate   B. inflammable   C. strong   D. pliable

21. Alternative   21.____
    A. choice   B. moderate   C. lazy   D. value

22. Corroborate
    A. examine   B. explain   C. verify   D. explain

23. Respiration
    A. recovery   B. breathing   C. sweating   D. selfish

24. Negligent
    A. lazy   B. moderate   C. hopeless   D. lax

25. Plumber is to Wrench as Painter is to
    A. pipe   B. shop   C. hammer   D. brush

KEY (CORRECT ANSWERS)

1.	D	11.	A
2.	A	12.	C
3.	D	13.	A
4.	C	14.	A
5.	B	15.	C
6.	C	16.	D
7.	C	17.	B
8.	B	18.	A
9.	C	19.	B
10.	C	20.	D

21. A
22. C
23. B
24. D
25. D

EXAMINATION SECTION
TEST 1

DIRECTIONS: Each question or incomplete statement is followed by several suggested answers or completions. Select the one that BEST answers the question or completes the statement. *PRINT THE LETTER OF THE CORRECT ANSWER IN THE SPACE AT THE RIGHT.*

1. Suppose that you are requested to transmit to the stenographers in your bureau an order curtailing certain privileges that they have been enjoying. You anticipate that your staff may resent curtailment of such privileges. Of the following, the BEST action for you to take is to

    A. impress upon your staff that an order is an order and must be obeyed
    B. attempt to explain to your staff the probable reasons for curtailing their privileges
    C. excuse the curtailment of privileges by saying that the welfare of the staff was evidently not considered
    D. warn your staff that violation of an order may be considered sufficient cause for immediate dismissal

    1.____

2. The supervisor should set a good example.
Of the following, the CHIEF implication of the above statement is that the supervisor should

    A. behave as he expects his workers to behave
    B. know as much about the work as his workers do
    C. keep his workers informed of what he is doing
    D. keep ahead of his workers

    2.____

3. Of the following, the LEAST desirable procedure for the competent supervisor to follow is to

    A. organize his work before taking responsibility for helping others with theirs
    B. avoid schedules and routines when he is busy
    C. be flexible in planning and carrying out his responsibilities
    D. secure the support of his staff in organizing the total job of the unit

    3.____

4. Evaluation helps the worker by increasing his security.
Of the following, the BEST justification for this statement is that

    A. security and growth depend upon knowledge by the worker of the agency's evaluation
    B. knowledge of his evaluation by agency and supervisor will stimulate the worker to better performance
    C. evaluation enables the supervisor and worker to determine the reasons for the worker's strengths and weaknesses
    D. the supervisor and worker together can usually recognize and deal with any worker's insecurity

    4.____

5. A supervisor may encourage his subordinates to make suggestions by

    A. keeping a record of the number of suggestions an employee makes
    B. providing a suggestion box

    5.____

C. outlining a list of possible suggestions
D. giving credit to a subordinate whose suggestion has been accepted and used

6. If you were required to give service ratings to employees under your supervision, you should consider as MOST important during the current period the

   A. personal characteristics and salary and grade of an employee
   B. length of service and the volume of work performed
   C. previous service rating given him
   D. personal characteristics and the quality of work of an employee

7. A supervisor must consider many factors in evaluating a worker whom he has supervised for a considerable time. In evaluating the capacity of such a worker to use independent judgment, the one of the following to which the supervisor should generally give MOST consideration is the worker's

   A. capacity to establish good relationships with people (clients and colleagues)
   B. educational background
   C. emotional stability
   D. the quality and judgment shown by the investigator in previous work situations known to the supervisor

8. Experts in the field of personnel relations feel that it is generally a bad practice for subordinate employees to become aware of pending or contemplated changes in policy or organizational set-up via the "grapevine" CHIEFLY because

   A. evidence that one or more responsible officials have proved untrustworthy will undermine confidence in the agency
   B. the information disseminated by this method is seldom entirely accurate and generally spreads needless unrest among the subordinate staff
   C. the subordinate staff may conclude that the administration feels the staff cannot be trusted with the true information
   D. the subordinate staff may conclude that the administration lacks the courage to make an unpopular announcement through official channels

9. Assume that a supervisor praises his subordinates for satisfactory aspects of their work only when he is about to criticize them for unsatisfactory aspects of their work. Such a practice is UNDESIRABLE primarily because

   A. his subordinates may expect to be praised for their work even if it is unsatisfactory
   B. praising his subordinates for some aspects of their work while criticizing other aspects will weaken the effects of the criticisms
   C. his subordinates would be more receptive to criticism if it were followed by praise
   D. his subordinates may come to disregard praise and wait for criticism to be given

10. The one of the following which would be the BEST reason for an agency to eliminate a procedure for obtaining and recording certain information is that

    A. it is no longer legally required to obtain the information
    B. there is an advantage in obtaining the information
    C. the information could be compiled on the basis of other information available
    D. the information obtained is sometimes incorrect

11. In determining the type and number of records to be kept in an agency, it is important to recognize that records are of value PRIMARILY as

    A. raw material to be used in statistical analysis
    B. sources of information about the agency's activities
    C. by-products of the activities carried on by the agency
    D. data for evaluating the effectiveness of the agency

11.____

12. Assume that you are a supervisor. One of the workers under your supervision is careless about the routine aspects of his work.
    Of the following, the action MOST likely to develop in this worker a better attitude toward job routines is to demonstrate that

    A. it is just as easy to do his job the right way
    B. organization of his job will leave more time for field work
    C. the routine part of the job is essential to performing a good piece of work
    D. job routines are a responsibility of the worker

12.____

13. A supervisor can MOST effectively secure necessary improvement in a worker's office work by

    A. encouraging the worker to keep abreast of his work
    B. relating the routine part of his job to the total job to be done
    C. helping the worker to establish a good system for covering his office work and holding him to it
    D. informing the worker that he will be required to organize his work more efficiently

13.____

14. A supervisor should offer criticism in such a manner that the criticism is helpful and not overwhelming.
    Of the following, the LEAST valid inference that can be drawn on the basis of the above statement is that a supervisor should

    A. demonstrate that the criticism is partial and not total
    B. give criticism in such a way that it does not undermine the worker's self-confidence
    C. keep his relationships with the worker objective
    D. keep criticism directed towards general work performance

14.____

15. The one of the following areas in which a worker may LEAST reasonably expect direct assistance from the supervisor is in

    A. building up rapport with all clients
    B. gaining insight into the unmet needs of clients
    C. developing an understanding of community resources
    D. interpreting agency policies and procedures

15.____

16. You are informed that a worker under your supervision has submitted a letter complaining of unfair service rating. Of the following, the MOST valid assumption for you to make concerning this worker is that he should be

    A. more adequately supervised in the future
    B. called in for a supervisory conference
    C. given a transfer to some other unit where he may be more happy
    D. given no more consideration than any other inefficient worker

16.____

17. Assume that you are a supervisor. You find that a somewhat bewildered worker, newly appointed to the department, hesitates to ask questions for fear of showing his ignorance and jeopardizing his position.
    Of the following, the BEST procedure for you to follow is to

    A. try to discover the reason for his evident fear of authority
    B. tell him that when he is in doubt about a procedure or a policy he should consult his fellow workers
    C. develop with the worker a plan for more frequent supervisory conferences
    D. explain why each staff member is eager to give him available information that will help him do a good job

18. In order to teach an employee to develop an objective approach, the BEST action for the supervisor to take is to help the worker to

    A. develop a sincere interest in his job
    B. understand the varied responsibilities that are an integral part of his job
    C. differentiate clearly between himself as a friend and as an employee
    D. find satisfaction in his work

19. Of the following, the MOST effective method of helping a newly appointed employee adjust to his new job is to

    A. assure him that with experience his uncertain attitudes will be replaced by a professional approach
    B. help him, by accepting him as he is, to have confidence in his ability to handle the job
    C. help him to be on guard against the development of punitive attitudes
    D. help him to recognize the mutability of the agency's policies and procedures

20. Suppose that, as a supervisor, you have scheduled an individual conference with an experienced employee under your supervision.
    Of the following, the BEST plan of action for this conference is to

    A. discuss the work that the employee is most interested in
    B. plan with the employee to cover any problems that are difficult for him
    C. advise the employee that the conference is his to do with as he sees fit
    D. spot check the employee's work in advance and select those areas for discussion in which the employee has done poor work

21. Of the following, the CHIEF function of a supervisor should be to

    A. assist in the planning of new policies and the evaluation of existing ones
    B. promote congenial relationships among members of the staff
    C. achieve optimum functioning of each unit and each worker
    D. promote the smooth functioning of job routines

22. The competent supervisor must realize the importance of planning.
    Of the following, the aspect of planning which is LEAST appropriately considered a responsibility of the supervisor is

    A. long-range planning for the proper functioning of his unit
    B. planning to take care of peak and slack periods
    C. planning to cover agency policies in group conferences

D. long-range planning to develop community resources

23. The one of the following objectives which should be of LEAST concern to the supervisor in the performance of his duties is to   23._____

    A. help the worker to make friends with all of his fellow employees
    B. be impartial and fair to all members of the staff
    C. stimulate the worker's growth on the job
    D. meet the needs of the individual employee

24. The one of the following which is LEAST properly considered a direct responsibility of the supervisor is   24._____

    A. liaison between the staff and the administrator
    B. interpreting administrative orders and procedures to the employee
    C. training new employees
    D. maintaining staff morale at a high level

25. If an employee shows excessive submission which indicates a need for dependence on the supervisor in handling an assignment, it would be MOST advisable for the supervisor to   25._____

    A. indicate firmly that the employee-supervisor relationship does not call for submission
    B. define areas of responsibility of employee and of superior
    C. recognize the employee's need to be sustained and supported and help him by making decisions for him
    D. encourage the employee to do his best to overcome his handicap

KEY (CORRECT ANSWERS)

1.	B	11.	B
2.	A	12.	D
3.	B	13.	B
4.	C	14.	D
5.	D	15.	A
6.	D	16.	B
7.	D	17.	C
8.	B	18.	C
9.	D	19.	B
10.	C	20.	B

21.	C
22.	D
23.	A
24.	A
25.	B

TEST 2

DIRECTIONS: Each question or incomplete statement is followed by several suggested answers or completions. Select the one that BEST answers the question or completes the statement. *PRINT THE LETTER OF THE CORRECT ANSWER IN THE SPACE AT THE RIGHT.*

1. Assume that, as a supervisor, you are conducting a group conference.
   Of the following, the BEST procedure for you to follow in order to stimulate group discussion is to

   A. permit the active participation of all members
   B. direct the discussion to an acceptable conclusion
   C. resolve conflicts of opinion among members of the group
   D. present a question for discussion on which the group members have some knowledge or experience

2. Suppose that, as a new supervisor, you wish to inform the staff under your supervision of your methods of operation. Of the following, the BEST procedure for you to follow is to

   A. advise the staff that they will learn gradually from experience
   B. inform each employee in an individual conference
   C. call a group conference for this purpose
   D. distribute a written memorandum among all members of the staff

3. The MOST constructive and effective method of correcting an employee who has made a mistake is, in general, to

   A. explain that his evaluation is related to his errors
   B. point out immediately where he erred and tell him how it should have been done
   C. show him how to readjust his methods so as to avoid similar errors in the future
   D. try to discover by an indirect method why the error was made

4. The MOST effective method for the supervisor to follow in order to obtain the cooperation of an employee under his supervision is, wherever possible, to

   A. maintain a careful record of performance in order to keep the employee on his toes
   B. give the employee recognition in order to promote greater effort and give him more satisfaction in his work
   C. try to gain the employee's cooperation for the good of the service
   D. advise the employee that his advancement on the job depends on his cooperation

5. Of the following, the MOST appropriate initial course for an employee to take when he is unable to clarify a policy with his supervisor is to

   A. bring up the problem at the next group conference
   B. discuss the policy immediately with his fellow employees
   C. accept the supervisor's interpretation as final
   D. determine what responsibility he has for putting the policy into effect

6. Good administration allows for different treatment of different workers.
   Of the following, the CHIEF implication of this quotation is that

A. it would be unfair for the supervisor not to treat all staff members alike
B. fear of favoritism tends to undermine staff morale
C. best results are obtained by individualization within the limits of fair treatment
D. difficult problems call for a different kind of approach

7. The MOST effective and appropriate method of building efficiency and morale in a group of employees is, in general,

   A. by stressing the economic motive
   B. through use of the authority inherent in the position
   C. by a friendly approach to all
   D. by a discipline that is fair but strict

8. Of the following, the LEAST valid basis for the assignment of work to an employee is the

   A. kind of service to be rendered
   B. experience and training of the employee
   C. health and capacity of the employee
   D. racial composition of the community where the office is located

9. The CHIEF justification for staff education, consisting of in-service training, lies in its contribution to

   A. improvement in the quality of work performed
   B. recruitment of a better type of employee
   C. employee morale accruing from a feeling of growth on the job
   D. the satisfaction that the employee gets on his job

10. Suppose that you are a supervisor. An employee no longer with your department requests you, as his former supervisor, to write a letter recommending him for a position with a private organization.
    Of the following, the BEST procedure for you to follow is to include in the letter only information that

    A. will help the applicant get the job
    B. is clear, factual, and substantiated
    C. is known to you personally
    D. can readily be corroborated by personal interview

11. Of the following, the MOST important item on which to base the efficiency evaluation of an employee under your supervision is

    A. the nature of the relationship that he has built up with his fellow employees
    B. how he gets along with his supervisors
    C. his personal habits and skills
    D. the effectiveness of his control over his work

12. According to generally accepted personnel practice, the MOST effective method of building morale in a new employee is to

    A. exercise caution in praising the employee, lest he become overconfident
    B. give sincere and frank commendation whenever possible, in order to stimulate interest and effort

C. praise the employee highly even for mediocre performance so that he will be stimulated to do better
D. warn the employee frequently that he cannot hope to succeed unless he puts forth his best effort

13. Errors made by newly appointed employees often follow a predictable pattern. The one of the following errors likely to have LEAST serious consequences is the tendency of a new employee to

    A. discuss problems that are outside his province with the client
    B. persuade the client to accept the worker's solution of a problem
    C. be too strict in carrying out departmental policy and procedure
    D. depend upon the use of authority due to his inexperience and lack of skill in working with people

14. The MOST effective way for a supervisor to break down a worker's defensive stand against supervisory guidance is to

    A. come to an understanding with him on the mutual responsibilities involved in the job of the employee and supervisor
    B. tell him he must feel free to express his opinions and to discuss basic problems
    C. show him how to develop toward greater objectivity, sensitivity, and understanding
    D. advise him that it is necessary to carry out agency policy and procedures in order to do a good job

15. Of the following, the LEAST essential function of the supervisor who is conducting a group conference should be to

    A. keep attention focused on the purpose of the conference
    B. encourage discussion of controversial points
    C. make certain that all possible viewpoints are discussed
    D. be thoroughly prepared in advance

16. When conducting a group conference, the supervisor should be LEAST concerned with

    A. providing an opportunity for the free interchange of ideas
    B. imparting knowledge and understanding of case work
    C. leading the discussion toward a planned goal
    D. pointing out where individual workers have erred in work practice

17. If the participants in a group conference are unable to agree on the proper application of a concept to the work of a department, the MOST suitable temporary procedure for the supervisor to follow is to

    A. suggest that each member think the subject through before the next meeting
    B. tell the group to examine their differences for possible conflicts with present policies
    C. suggest that practices can be changed because of new conditions
    D. state the acceptable practice in the agency and whether deviations from such practice can be permitted

18. If an employee is to participate constructively in any group discussion, it is MOST important that he have

    A. advance notice of the agenda for the meeting
    B. long experience in the department
    C. knowledge and experience in the particular work
    D. the ability to assume a leadership role

19. Of the following, the MOST important principle for the supervisor to follow when conducting a group discussion is that he should

    A. move the discussion toward acceptance by the group of a particular point of view
    B. express his ideas clearly and succinctly
    C. lead the group to accept the authority inherent in his position
    D. contribute to the discussion from his knowledge and experience

20. The one of the following which is considered LEAST important as a purpose of the group conference is to

    A. provide for a free exchange of ideas among the members of the group
    B. evaluate work methods and procedures in order to protect the members from individual criticism
    C. provide an opportunity to interpret procedures and work practices
    D. pool the experience of the group members for the benefit of all

21. In order for the evaluation conference to stimulate MOST effectively the employee's professional growth on the job, it should

    A. start him thinking, about his present status with the department
    B. show him the necessity for taking stock of his total performance
    C. give him a sense of direction in relation to his future development
    D. give him a better perspective on the work in his department

22. The development of good public relations in the area for which the supervisor is responsible should be considered by the supervisor as

    A. not his responsibility as he is primarily responsible for his employees' services
    B. dependent upon him as he is in the best position to interpret the department to the community
    C. not important to the adequate functioning of the department
    D. a part of his method of carrying out his job responsibility, as what his employees do affect the community

23. Of the following, the MOST valuable and desirable trait in a supervisor is a(n)

    A. ability to get the best work out of his men
    B. ability to inspire his men with the desire to "get ahead in the world"
    C. persuasive manner of speech
    D. tall and commanding appearance

24. The supervisor who is MOST suitable for the general practical needs of a department is the one who gets

   A. a great deal of satisfactory work done although usually handicapped by constant bickering among fellow employees
   B. a great deal of satisfactory work done because of his ability to do a large amount of it himself
   C. less work done than the other supervisors but has unusually high quality work production standards
   D. more than an average amount of satisfactory work done because of the cooperative way in which the employees work for him

25. A supervisor has been transferred to a new section.
    The BEST way for him to get cooperation from his employees would be to

   A. ask the (general manager)(chief) to give him strong support
   B. explain his policy firmly so that the employees cannot blame him for any mistakes made
   C. note the troublemakers and have them transferred out
   D. show his men that he not only is interested in getting work done but also has their welfare in mind

KEY (CORRECT ANSWERS)

1. D		11. D	
2. C		12. B	
3. C		13. C	
4. B		14. A	
5. D		15. B	
6. C		16. D	
7. D		17. D	
8. D		18. A	
9. A		19. D	
10. B		20. B	

21. C
22. D
23. A
24. D
25. D

TEST 3

DIRECTIONS: Each question or incomplete statement is followed by several suggested answers or completions. Select the one that BEST answers the question or completes the statement. *PRINT THE LETTER OF THE CORRECT ANSWER IN THE SPACE AT THE RIGHT.*

1. Jones and Smith, who work together, do slightly more than an average amount of work for two men together. But you find that Jones does most of the work while Smith does less than he should.
   To correct this situation, the BEST thing for you as supervisor to do would be to

   A. assign work to Smith for which he must be personally responsible
   B. make a complaint to the bureau chief about Smith but praise Jones
   C. point out to Jones that he does most of the work and that he should urge Smith to do more
   D. require Smith to do more whenever the work of both men together falls below the expected average

   1._____

2. You have given a new employee detailed instructions on how he should do a job. When you return a little later, you find that the employee was afraid to start the job because he did not completely understand your instructions.
   In this situation, it would be BEST for you to

   A. assign the man to a job where less intelligence is needed
   B. explain again, illustrating if possible how the job is to be done
   C. explain again and recommend him for dropping at the end of probation if he does not understand
   D. make the man explain why he did not at least start the job

   2._____

3. An employee does very good work but has trouble getting to work on time.
   To get him to come on time, the supervisor should

   A. bring him up on charges to stop the lateness once and for all
   B. have him report to the general manager every time he is late
   C. talk over the problem with him to find its cause and possible solution
   D. threaten to transfer him if he cannot get to work early

   3._____

4. As supervisor, you observe that an employee keeps making mistakes.
   Of the following, the BEST thing for you to do would be to

   A. make no mention of these mistakes as they gradually disappear with experience
   B. point the mistakes out to the employee in front of the other employees so all may learn from them
   C. talk to the employee privately about these mistakes and show her how to avoid them
   D. try to transfer this employee out in exchange for an employee who can do the work

   4._____

5. Proper action by the supervisor could MOST probably prevent work delays in his section caused by

   A. a large number of employees quitting their jobs in the department
   B. the daily assignments of the employees not being properly planned

   5._____

C. the inexperience of new employees transferred into his section
D. unexpected delays in processing

6. If, after careful thought, you have definitely decided that one of your employees should be disciplined, it is MOST important for you to realize that

   A. discipline is the best tool for leading workers
   B. discipline should be severe in order to get the best results
   C. the discipline should be delayed so that its full force can be felt
   D. the employee should know why she is being disciplined

7. A knowledge of the experience and abilities of the men working under him is MOST useful to a supervisor in

   A. deciding what type of discipline to exercise when necessary
   B. finding the cause of minor errors in the assignments
   C. making proper work assignments
   D. making vacation schedules

8. A supervisor will be able to train his employees better if he is familiar with basic principles of learning.
   Which one of the following statements about the learning process is MOST correct?

   A. An employee who learns one job quickly will learn any other job quickly.
   B. Emphasizing correct things done by the employee usually gives him an incentive to improve.
   C. Great importance placed on an employee's mistakes is the best way to help him to get rid of them.
   D. It is very hard to teach new methods to middle-aged or older employees.

9. Several experienced employees have resigned. You have decided to arrange for permanent transfers of other experienced employees in your section to fill their jobs, leaving only jobs that new inexperienced employees can fill easily.
   For you, the supervisor, to talk this over with the employees who will be affected by the move would be

   A. *bad;* it would show weakness and wavering by you
   B. *bad;* transfers should be made on the basis of efficiency
   C. *good;* it will help you get better cooperation from the employees involved
   D. *good;* transfers should be made on the basis of seniority

10. An employee under your supervision does much less work than he is capable of.
    What should be your FIRST step in an effort to improve his performance?

    A. Discovering why he is not working up to his full capacity
    B. Going over his mistakes and shortcomings with him to reduce them
    C. Pointing out to him that the quality of his work is below standard
    D. Showing him that the other men produce much more than he does

11. The FIRST thing a supervisor does when he assigns an employee to a new job is to find out what the employee already knows about the job.
    This practice is

A. *good;* mainly because the employees may know more than the supervisor about the job
B. *good;* mainly because this information will help the supervisor in instructing the employee
C. *poor;* mainly because since it is a new job, the employee cannot be expected to know anything
D. *poor;* mainly because the supervisor should first find out how the employee will feel toward the job

12. Your superior has assigned to you a task which, in your opinion, should not be performed at this stage of the operation.
In this situation, it would be BEST for you to

    A. carry out the assignment since your superior is responsible
    B. refuse to carry out the assignment
    C. talk it over with the employees under you to see if they think as you do
    D. talk the matter over with your superior right away

12.____

13. It is important for a supervisor to take prompt action upon requests from subordinates MAINLY because

    A. delays in making decisions mean that they must then be made on the basis of facts which can no longer be up-to-date
    B. favorable action on such requests is more likely to result when a decision is made quickly
    C. it is an indication that the supervisor has his work well-organized
    D. promptness in such matters helps maintain good employee morale

13.____

14. As a supervisor, you realize that your superior, when under pressure, has a habit of giving you oral orders which are not always clear and also lack sufficient detail. The BEST procedure for you to follow in such situations would be to

    A. obtain clarification by requesting needed details at the time you receive such orders
    B. consider past orders of a similar nature to determine the probable intent of your superior
    C. frequently consult your superior during the course of the job in order to secure the required details to complete the job
    D. request your superior to put all his orders to you in writing

14.____

15. Some supervisors have their subordinates meet with them in group discussion of troublesome problems.
The MAIN advantage of such group discussions as a supervisory tool is that they can be directed toward the

    A. appraisal of the personalities involved
    B. development of new policies and regulations
    C. circulation of new material and information
    D. pooling of experience in the solution of common problems

15.____

16. The PRINCIPAL disadvantage of using form letters to reply to written complaints made by the public is that such form letters

16.____

A. tend to make any investigation of the original complaint rather superficial
B. are limited by their design to handle only a few possible situations that could give rise to complaints
C. lack the desirable element of the personal touch for the recipient
D. tend to lose their effectiveness by quickly becoming obsolete

17. With respect to standard employee grievance procedure, it would be MOST correct to state that

    A. the Commissioner of Labor is the highest ranking official, excepting the judge, who can be involved in a particular grievance
    B. the person with the grievance has the right to be represented by virtually anyone he chooses
    C. the one having the grievance (the grievant) can be represented by the majority organization only if he is a member thereof
    D. time limits are not set concerning adjudication in order to insure the fullest consideration of the particular grievance

18. In order for a supervisor to employ the system of democratic leadership in his supervision, it would generally be BEST for him to

    A. allow his subordinates to assist in deciding on methods of work performance and job assignments but only in those areas where decisions have not been made on higher administrative levels
    B. allow his subordinates to decide how to do the required work, interposing his authority when work is not completed on schedule or is improperly completed
    C. attempt to make assignments of work to individuals only of the type which they enjoy doing
    D. maintain control over the job assignments and work production but allow the subordinates to select methods of work and internal conditions of work at democratically conducted staff conferences

19. In an office in which supervision has been considered quite effective, it has become necessary to press for above-normal production for a limited period to achieve a required goal.
    The one of the following which is a LEAST likely result of this pressure is that

    A. there will be more "gripings" by employees
    B. some workers will do both more and better work than has been normal for them
    C. there will be an enhanced feeling of group unity
    D. there will be increased absenteeism

20. It is the practice of some supervisors, when they believe that it would be desirable for a subordinate to take a particular action in a case, to inform the subordinate of this in the form of a suggestion rather than in the form of a direct order. In general, this method of getting a subordinate to take the desired action is

    A. *inadvisable;* it may create in the mind of the subordinate the impression that the supervisor is uncertain about the efficacy of his plan and is trying to avoid whatever responsibility he may have in resolving the case
    B. *advisable;* it provides the subordinate with the maximum opportunity to use his own judgment in handling the case

C. *inadvisable;* it provides the subordinate with no clear-cut direction and, therefore, is likely to leave him with a feeling of uncertainty and frustration
D. *advisable;* it presents the supervisor's view in a manner which will be most likely to evoke the subordinate's cooperation

21. At a group training conference conducted by a supervisor, one of the employees asks a question which is only partially related to the subject under discussion. He believes that the question was asked to embarrass him since he recently reprimanded the employees for inattention to his work. Under these circumstances, it would generally be BEST for the assistant supervisor to

    A. pointedly ignore the question and the questioner and go on to other matters
    B. request the questioner to remain after the group session, at which time the question and the questioner's attitude will be considered
    C. state that he does not know the answer and ask for a volunteer to give a brief answer, brief because the question is only partially relevant
    D. tell the questioner that the question is not pertinent, show wherein it is not pertinent, and state that the time of the group should not be wasted on it

22. The one of the following circumstances when it would generally be MOST proper for a supervisor to do a job himself rather than to train a subordinate to do the job is when it is

    A. a job which the supervisor enjoys doing and does well
    B. not a very time-consuming job but an important one
    C. difficult to train another to do the job yet is not difficult for the supervisor to do
    D. unlikely that this or any similar job will have to be done again at any future time

23. Effective training of subordinates requires that the supervisor understand certain facts about learning and forgetting processes.
    Among these is the fact that people generally

    A. both learn and forget at a relatively constant rate and this rate is dependent upon their general intellectual capacity
    B. forget what they learned at a much greater rate during the first day than during subsequent periods
    C. learn at a relatively constant rate except for periods of assimilation when the quantity of retained learning decreases while information is becoming firmly fixed in the mind
    D. learn very slowly at first when introduced to a new topic, after which there is a great increase in the rate of learning

24. It has been suggested that a subordinate who likes his supervisor will tend to do better work than one who does not. According to the MOST widely-held current theories of supervision, this suggestion is a

    A. *bad one;* since personal relationships tend to interfere with proper professional relationships
    B. *bad one;* since the strongest motivating factors are fear and uncertainty
    C. *good one;* since liking one's supervisor is a motivating factor for good work performance
    D. *good one;* since liking one's supervisor is the most important factor in employee performance

25. A supervisor is supervising an employee who is very soon to complete his six months' probationary period. The supervisor finds him to be slow, to make many errors, to do work poorly, to be antagonistic toward the supervisor, and to be disliked by most of his co-workers. The supervisor is aware that he is the sole support of his wife and two children. He has never been late or absent during his service with the department. If he is terminated, there will be a considerable delay before a replacement for him arrives.
It would generally be BEST for the supervisor to recommend that this employee be

    A. transferred to work with another supervisor and other staff members with whom he may get along better
    B. retained but be very closely supervised until his work shows marked improvement
    C. retained since his services are needed with the expectation that he be terminated at some later date when a replacement is readily available
    D. terminated

25. ____

KEY (CORRECT ANSWERS)

1.	A		11.	B
2.	B		12.	D
3.	C		13.	D
4.	C		14.	A
5.	B		15.	D
6.	D		16.	C
7.	C		17.	B
8.	B		18.	A
9.	C		19.	D
10.	A		20.	D

21. C
22. D
23. B
24. C
25. D

SAMPLE QUESTIONS
TEST 1
ENGLISH USAGE

DIRECTIONS: Many jobs require an employee to communicate, verbally and/or in writing, in accordance with the principles of correct English usage. The questions on this test measure these abilities by testing your knowledge of grammar, punctuation, and sentence structure. In the following questions, choose the sentence that represents the BEST English usage. *PRINT THE LETTER OF THE CORRECT ANSWER IN THE SPACE AT THE RIGHT.*

1. A. Of the two runners, John is the worst.
   B. Of the two runner, John is the better.
   C. John is the worst of the two runners.
   D. John is the best of the two runners.

   1._____

2. A. We seldom ever receive this type of request anymore.
   B. Neither of the employees are doing what is expected of him.
   C. Each of these regulations apply to your case.
   D. I have enclosed a copy of the file you requested.

   2._____

KEY (CORRECT ANSWERS)

1. The correct answer is B. The correct way to write Option A is "Of the two runners, John is worse." The correct way to write Option C is "John is the worse of the two runners." The correct way to write Option D is "John is the better of the two runners."

2. The correct answer is D. The correct way to write Option A is "We seldom receive this type of request." The correct way to write Option B is "Neither of the employees is doing what is expected of him." The correct way to write Option C is "Each of these regulations applies to your case."

TEST 2

FOLLOWING DIRECTIONS

DIRECTIONS: The ability to follow directions is very important for many jobs. These types of questions measure the ability to follow directions by giving a set of rules, which must be followed in answering the questions. *PRINT THE LETTER OF THE CORRECT ANSWER IN THE SPACE AT THE RIGHT.*

RULES

The three types of storage are regular, warehouse, and special. Listed below are the rules for deciding which type of storage to use.

- Regular or warehouse storage should be used for items that do not need special handling.
- Special storage should be used for items that need special handling.
- Warehouse storage should be used for items weighing over 200 pounds.
- Regular storage should be used for items weighing under 200 pounds.
- Special storage should always be used for storing hazardous materials.

Codes:
  1 – Special
  2 – Warehouse
  3 - Regular

1. What type of storage would be used for equipment weighing 350 pounds? 1.____
   A. Special   B. Warehouse   C. Regular

2. What type of storage would be used for a fifty-pound box of dynamite? 2.____
   A. Special   B. Warehouse   C. Regular

3. What type of storage would be used for a five-gallon drum needing refrigeration? 3.____
   A. Special   B. Warehouse   C. Regular

4. What type of storage would be used for machinery weighing 175 pounds? 4.____
   A. Special   B. Warehouse   C. Regular

5. What type of storage would be used for a cement truck used for parts? 5.____
   A. Special   B. Warehouse   C. Regular

KEY (CORRECT ANSWERS)

1. The correct answer is B, Warehouse, because according to the third rule, warehouse storage should be used for items weighing over 200 pounds.

2. The correct answer is A, Special, because the last rule states that special storage should always be used for storing hazardous materials.

3. The correct answer is A, Special, because the item needs the special handling of refrigeration.

4. The correct answer is C, Regular, because the item weighs less than 200 pounds.

5. The correct answer is B, Warehouse, because a cement truck weighs more than 200 pounds.

ENGLISH GRAMMAR AND USAGE
EXAMINATION SECTION
TEST 1

DIRECTIONS: In the passages that follow, certain words and phrases are underlined and numbered. In each question, you will find alternatives for each underlined part. You are to choose the one that BEST expresses the idea, makes the statement appropriate for standard written English, or is worded MOST consistently with the style and tone of the passage as a whole. Choose the alternative you consider BEST and write the letter in the space at the right. If you think the original version is BEST, choose NO CHANGE. Read each passage through once before you begin to answer the questions that accompany it. You cannot determine most answers without reading several sentences beyond the phrase in question. Be sure that you have read far enough ahead each time you choose an alternative.

Questions 1-14.

DIRECTIONS: Questions 1 through 14 are based on the following passage.

Modern filmmaking <u>had began</u> in Paris in 1895 with the work of the Lumiere brothers.
                                1
Using their <u>invention, the Cinématographe,</u> the Lumières were able to photograph, print,
              2
and project moving pictures onto a screen. Their films showed <u>actual occurrences. A</u> train
                                                                        3
approaching a station, people a factory, workers demolishing a wall.

These early films had neither plot nor sound. But another Frenchman, Georges Méliès,

soon incorporated plot lines <u>into</u> his films. And with his attempts to draw upon the potential of
                              4
film to create fantasy <u>worlds</u>. Méliès also <u>was an early pioneer from</u> special film effects. Edwin
                         5   6
Porter, an American filmmaker, took Méliès emphasis on narrative one step further. Believing

<u>that, continuity of shots</u> was of primary importance in filmmaking, Porter connected
        7
<u>images to present,</u> a sustained action. His GREAT TRAIN ROBBERY of 1903 opened a new
        8
era in film.

<u>Because</u> film was still considered <u>as</u> low entertainment in early twentieth century America,
    9   10
it was on its way to becoming a respected art form. Beginning in 1908, the American director

D.W. Griffith discovered and explored techniques to make film a more expressive medium.

2 (#1)

With his technical contributions, as well as his attempts to develop the intellectual and moral
                                    11
potential of film, Griffith helped build a solid foundation for the industry.

Thirty years after the Lumière brothers' first show, sound had yet been added to the
 12   13
movies. Finally, in 1927, Hollywood produced its first *talkie*, THE JAZZ SINGER. With sound,

modern film coming of age.
              14

1. A. NO CHANGE   B. begun   1._____
    C. began   D. had some beginnings

2. A. NO CHANGE   B. invention—the Cinématographe   2._____
    C. invention, the Cinématgraphe—   D. invention, the Cinématographe

3. A. NO CHANGE   B. actually occurrences, a   3._____
    C. actually occurrences—a   D. actual occurrences: a

4. A. NO CHANGE   B. about   4._____
    C. with   D. to

5. A. NO CHANGE   B. worlds   5._____
    C. worlds' and   D. worlds and

6. A. NO CHANGE   B. pioneered   6._____
    C. pioneered the beginnings of   D. pioneered the early beginnings of

7. A. NO CHANGE   B. that continuity of shots   7._____
    C. that, continuity of shots,   D. that continuity of shots

8. A. NO CHANGE   B. images to present   8._____
    C. that, continuity of shots   D. that continuity of shots

9. A. NO CHANGE   9._____
    B. (Begin new paragraph) in view of the fact that
    C. (Begin new paragraph) Although
    D. Do NOT begin new paragraph) Since

10. A. NO CHANGE   B. as if it were   10._____
    C. like it was   D. OMIT the underlined portion

11. A. NO CHANGE   B. similar to   11._____
    C. similar with   D. like with

3 (#1)

12. A. NO CHANGE
    B. (Begin new paragraph) Consequently, thirty
    C. (Do NOT begin new paragraph) Therefore, thirty
    D. (Do NOT begin new paragraph) As a consequence, thirty

12.____

13. A. NO CHANGE
    B. (Begin new paragraph) Consequently, thirty
    C. (No NOT begin new paragraph) Therefore, thirty
    D. (Do NOT begin new paragraph As a consequence, thirty

13.____

14. A. NO CHANGE   B. comes
    C. came   D. had came

14.____

Questions 15-22.

DIRECTIONS: Questions 15 through 22 are based on the following passage.

One of the most awesome forces in nature is the tsunami, or tidal wave. A tsunami—the word is Japanese for harbor wave, can generate the destructive power of many atomic bombs.
                                    15

Tsunamis usually appear in a series of four or five waves about fifteen minutes apart.
    16
They begin deep in the ocean, gather remarkable speed as they travel, and cover great instances. The wave triggered by the explosion of Krakatoa in 1883 circled the world in three days.

Tsunamis being known to sink large ships at sea, they are most dangerous when they
    17
reach land. Close to shore, an oncoming tsunami is forced upward and skyward, perhaps as
                                                                    18
high as 100 feet. This combination of height and speed accounts for the tsunami's great power.

That *tsunami* is a Japanese word is no accident, due to the fact that no nation
                                                    19
frequently has been so visited by giant waves as Japan. Tsunamis reach that country regularly,
    20   21
and with devastating consequences. One Japanese tsunami flattened several towns in

1896, also killed 27,000 people. The 2011 tsunami caused similar loss of life as well as untold
        22
damage from nuclear radiation.

149

15. A. NO CHANGE
    B. tsunami, the word is Japanese for harbor wave—
    C. tsunami—the word is Japanese for harbor wave—
    D. tsunami—the word being Japanese for harbor wave,

16. A. NO CHANGE
    B. (Begin new paragraph) Consequently, tsunamis
    C. (Do NOT begin new paragraph) Tsunamis consequently
    D. (Do NOT begin new paragraph) Yet, tsunamis

17. A. NO CHANGE   B. Because tsunamis have been
    C. Although tsunamis have been   D. Tsunamis have been

18. A. NO CHANGE   B. upward to the sky,
    C. upward in the sky   D. upward,

19. A. NO CHANGE
    B. when one takes into consideration the fact that
    C. seeing as how
    D. for

20. A. NO CHANGE   B. (Place after *has*)
    C. (Place after *so*)   D. (Place after *visited*)

21. A. NO CHANGE   B. Moreover, tsunamis
    C. However, tsunamis   D. Because tsunamis

22. A. NO CHANGE   B. 1896 and killed 27,000 people
    C. 1896 and killing 27,000 people   D. 1896, and 27,000 people as well

Questions 23-33.

DIRECTIONS: Questions 23 through 33 are based on the following passage.

I was <u>married one</u> August on a farm in Maine. The <u>ceremony, itself, taking</u> place in an
            23   24
arbor of pine boughs <u>we had built and constructed</u> in the yard next to the house. On the morning
                              25
of the wedding day, we parked the tractors behind the shed, <u>have tied</u> the dogs to an oak tree to
                                                                  26
keep them from chasing the guests, and put the cows out to pasture. <u>Thus</u> we had thought of
                                                                        27
everything, it seemed. we had forgotten how interested a cow can be in what is going on

<u>around them.</u> During the ceremony, my sister <u>(who has taken several years of lessons)</u> was to
    28   29
play a flute solo. We were all listening intently when she <u>had began</u> to play. As the first notes
                                                                30
reached us, we were surprised to hear a bass line under the flute's treble melody. Looking

around, the source was quickly discovered. There was Star, my pet Guernsey, her head hanging
                31
over the pasture fence, mooing along with the delicate strains of Bach.

   Star took our laughter as being like a compliment, and we took her contribution that way,
                            32
too. It was a sign of approval—the kind you would find only at a farm wedding.

23. A. NO CHANGE   B. married, one   23.____
    C. married on an   D. married, in an

24. A. NO CHANGE   B. ceremony itself taking   24.____
    C. ceremony itself took   D. ceremony, itself took

25. A. NO CHANGE   25.____
    B. which had been built and constructed
    C. we had built and constructed it
    D. we had built

26. A. NO CHANGE   B. tie   26.____
    C. tied   D. tying

27. A. NO CHANGE   27.____
    B. (Do NOT begin new paragraph) And
    C. (Begin new paragraph) But
    D. (Begin new paragraph (Moreover,

28. A. NO CHANGE   B. around her   28.____
    C. in her own vicinity   D. in their immediate area

29. A. NO CHANGE   29.____
    B. (whom has taken many years of lessons)
    C. (who has been trained in music)
    D. OMIT the underlined portion

30. A. NO CHANGE   B. begun   30.____
    C. began   D. would begin

31. A. NO CHANGE   31.____
    B. the discovery of the source was quick
    C. the discovery of the source was quickly made.
    D. we quickly discovered the source.

32. A. NO CHANGE   A. as   32.____
    C. just as   D. as if

33. A. NO CHANGE   B. Yet it was
    C. But it was   D. Being

Questions 34-42.

DIRECTIONS: Questions 34 through 42 are based on the following passage,

Riding a bicycle in Great Britain is not the same as riding a bicycle in the United States. Americans bicycling in Britain will find some basic fundamental differences in the rules of the
                                                                                       34
road and in the attitudes of motorists.

Probably most difficult for the American cyclist is adjusting with British traffic patterns.
  35   36
Knowing that traffic in Britain moves on the left-hand side of the road, bicycling once there is the
    37   38
mirror image of what it is in the United States.

The problem of adjusting to traffic patterns is somewhat lessened, however by the respect
                                                                         39
with which British motorists treat bicyclists. A cyclist in a traffic circle, for example, is given the same right-of-way with the driver of any other vehicle. However, the cyclist is expected to obey
                     40
the rules of the road. This difference in the American and British attitudes toward bicyclists may
                        41
stem from differing attitudes toward the bicycle itself. Whereas Americans frequently view bicycles as toys, but the British treat them primarily as vehicles.
              42

34. A. NO CHANGE   B. basic and fundamental   34._____
    C. basically fundamental D. basic

35. A. NO CHANGE   B. Even so, probably   35._____
    C. Therefore, probably   D. As a result, probably

36. A. NO CHANGE   B. upon   36._____
    C. on   D. to

37. A. NO CHANGE   B. Seeing that traffic   37._____
    C. Because traffic   D. Traffic

38. A. NO CHANGE   B. once you are   38._____
    C. once one is   D. OMIT the underlined portion

39. A. NO CHANGE   B. also,   39.___
    C. moreover,   D. therefore,

40. A. NO CHANGE   B. as   40.___
    C. as if   D. as with

41. A. NO CHANGE   41.___
    B. difference in the American and British attitudes toward bicyclists
    C. difference, in the American and British attitudes toward bicyclists
    D. difference in the American, and British, attitudes toward bicyclists

42. A. NO CHANGE   B. toy;   42.___
    C. toys,   D. toys; but

Questions 43-51.

DIRECTIONS: Questions 43 through 51 are based on the following passage.

People have always believed that supernatural powers <u>tend toward some influence on</u>
                                                                    43
lives for good or for ill. Superstition originated with the idea that individuals <u>could in turn,</u> exert
                                                                                         44
influence <u>at</u> spirits. Certain superstitions are <u>so deeply embedded</u> in our culture that intelligent
          45   46
people sometimes act in accordance with them.

One common superstitious act is knocking on wood after boasting of good fortune. People once believed that gods inhabited trees and, therefore, were present in the wood used to build houses. Fearing that speaking of good luck within the gods' hearing might anger <u>them, people</u>
                                                                                                  47
knocked on wood to deafen the gods and avoid their displeasure.

Another superstitious <u>custom and practice</u> is throwing salt over the left shoulder.
                                48
<u>Considering</u> salt was once considered sacred, people thought that spilling it brought bad
    49
luck. Since right and left represented good and evil, the believers used their right hands, which symbolized good, to throw a pinch of salt over their left shoulders into the eyes of the evil gods.
<u>Because of this</u>, people attempted to avert misfortune.
      50
Without realizing the origin of superstitions, many people exhibit superstitious behavior.

<u>Others avoid</u> walking under ladders and stepping on cracks in sidewalks, without having any
      51
idea why they are doing so.

43. A. NO CHANGE
     C. tend to influence on
     C. can influence
     D. are having some influence on

44. A. NO CHANGE.
     C. could, in turn
     B. could, turning
     D. could, in turn,

45. A. NO CHANGE
     C. toward
     C. of
     D. on

46. A. NO CHANGE
     C. deepest embedded
     B. deepest embedded
     D. embedded deepest

47. A. NO CHANGE
     C. them: some people
     B. them; some people
     D. them, they

48. A. NO CHANGE
     C   traditional custom
     B. Custom
     D. customary habit

49. A. NO CHANGE
     C. Because
     B. Although
     D. Keeping in mind that

50. A. NO CHANGE
     C. Consequently
     B. As a result of this,
     D. In this way,

51. A. NO CHANGE
     C. Avoiding
     B. Often avoiding
     D. They avoid

Questions 52-66.

DIRECTIONS: Questions 52 through 65 are based on the following passage.

In the 1920s, the Y.M.C.A. sponsored one of the first programs <u>in order to promote</u>
                                                                        52
more enlightened public opinion on racial matters; the organization started special university

classes <u>in which</u> young people could study race relations. Among the guest speakers invited to
        53
conduct the sessions, one of the most popular was George Washington Carver, the scientist

from Tuskegee Institute.

   As a student, Carver himself had been active in the Y.M.C.A. <u>He shared</u> its evangelical
                                                                      54
and educational philosophy. However, in <u>1923,</u> the Y.M.C.A. arranged <u>Carver's first initial</u>
                                         55   56
speaking tour, the scientist accepted with apprehension. He was to speak at several white

colleges, most of whose students had never seen, let alone heard, an educated black man.

9 (#1)

Although Carver's appearances <u>did sometimes</u> cause occasional <u>controversy, but</u>
                                  57   58
his quiet dedication prevailed, and his humor quickly won over his audiences. <u>Nevertheless, for</u>
                                                                                        59
the next decade, Carver toured the Northeast, Midwest, and South under Y.M.C.A.

<u>sponsorship. Speaking</u> at places never before open to blacks. On these tours Carver
          60
befriended thousands of students, many of <u>whom</u> subsequently corresponded with his
                                             61
<u>afterwards</u>. The <u>tours, unfortunately were</u> not without discomfort for Carver. There were
    62   63
the indignities of *Jim Crow* accommodations and racial insults from strangers. <u>As a result,</u>
                                                                                    64
the scientist's enthusiasm never faltered. <u>Avoiding any discussion of</u> the political and social
                                                      65
aspects of racial injustice; instead, Carver conducted his whole life as an indirect attack <u>to</u>
                                                                                              66
prejudice. This, as much as his science, is his legacy to humankind.

52. A. NO CHANGE   B. to promote   52.____
    C. for the promoting of what is   D. for the promotion of what are

53. A. NO CHANGE   C. from which   53.____
    C. that   D. by which

54. A. NO CHANGE   B. Sharing.   54.____
    C. Having Shared   D. Because He Shared

55. A. NO CHANGE   B. 1923   55.____
    C. 1923, and   D. 1923, when

56. A. NO CHANGE   B. Carvers' first, initial   56.____
    C. Carvers first initial D. Carver's first

57. A. NO CHANGE   B. sometimes did   57.____
    C. did   D. OMIT the underlined portion

58. A. NO CHANGE   B. controversy and   58.____
    C. controversy   D. controversy, however

59. A. NO CHANGE   B. However, for   59.____
    C. However, from   D. For

60. A. NO CHANGE   B. sponsorship and spoke   60.____
    C. sponsorship; and spoke D. sponsorship, and speaking

155

61. A. NO CHANGE   B. who
    C. them   D. those

62. A. NO CHANGE
    B. later
    C. sometimes later.
    D. OMIT the underlined portion and end the sentence with a period

63. A. NO CHANGE   B. tours, unfortunately, were
    C. tours unfortunately, were   D. tours, unfortunately, are

64. A. NO CHANGE   B. So
    C. But   D. Therefore,

65. A. NO CHANGE   B. He avoided discussing
    C. Having avoided discussing D. Upon avoiding the discussion of

66. A. NO CHANGE   B. over
    C. on   D. of

Questions 67-75.

DIRECTIONS: Questions 67 through 75 are based on the following passage.

Shooting rapids is not the only way to experience the thrill of canoeing. An ordinary-
                                                                          67
looking stream, innocent of rocks and white water, can provide adventure, as long as it has

three essential features; a swift current, close banks, and has plenty of twists and turns.
                68   69
A powerful current causes tension, for canoeists know they will have only seconds for
70
executing the maneuvers necessary to prevent crashing into the threes lining the narrow

streams banks. Of course, the narrowness, itself, being crucial in creating the tension. On a
71   72
broad stream, canoeists can pause frequently, catch their breath, and get their bearings.

However to a narrow stream, where every minute you run the risk of being knocked down by a
        73   74
low-hanging tree limb, they be constantly alert. Yet even the fast current and close banks would

be manageable if the stream were fairly straight. The expenditure of energy required to paddle

furiously, first on one side of the canoe and then on the other, wearies both the nerves as well
                                                                          75
as the body.

11 (#1)

67. A. NO CHANGE
    C. Many finding that an
    B. They say that for adventure an
    D. The old saying that an
    67._____

68. A. NO CHANGE
    C. features,
    B. features
    D. features; these being
    68._____

69. A. NO CHANGE
    C. with
    B. there must be
    D. OMIT the underlined portion
    69._____

70. A. NO CHANGE
    C. Therefore, a
    B. Thus, a
    D. Furthermore, a
    70._____

71. A. NO CHANGE
    C. streams bank's
    B. stream's banks.
    D. banks of the streams
    71._____

72. A. NO CHANGE
    C. narrowness itself is
    B. narrowness, itself is
    D. narrowness in itself being
    72._____

73. A. NO CHANGE
    C. on
    B. near
    D. with
    73._____

74. A. NO CHANGE
    C. one runs
    B. the canoer runs
    D. they run
    74._____

75. A. NO CHANGE
    B. the nerves as well as the body
    C. the nerves, also, as well as the body
    D. not only the body but also the nerves as well
    75._____

KEY (CORRECT ANSWERS)

1.	C	21.	A	41.	A	61.	A
2.	A	22.	B	42.	C	62.	D
3.	D	23.	A	43.	B	63.	B
4.	A	24.	C	44.	C	64.	C
5.	B	25.	D	45.	D	65.	B
6.	B	26.	C	46.	A	66.	C
7.	D	27.	C	47.	A	67.	A
8.	B	28.	B	48.	B	68.	B
9.	C	29.	D	49.	C	69.	D
10.	D	30.	C	50.	D	70.	A
11.	A	31.	D	51.	D	71.	B
12.	A	32.	B	52.	B	72.	C
13.	B	33.	A	53.	A	73.	C
14.	C	34.	D	54.	A	74.	D
15.	C	35.	A	55.	D	75.	B
16.	A	36.	D	56.	D		
17.	C	37.	C	57.	C		
18.	D	38.	D	58.	C		
19.	D	39.	A	59.	D		
20.	C	40.	B	60.	B		

EXAMINATION SECTION
TEST 1

DIRECTIONS: Each question or incomplete statement is followed by several suggested answers or completions. Select the one that BEST answers the question or completes the statement.

Questions 1-17.

DIRECTIONS: In each of the following groups of sentences, there are three sentences which are correct and one which is incorrect because it contains an error in grammar, usage, diction, or punctuation. Indicate the letter of the INCORRECT sentence.

1. A. The business was organized under the name of Allen & Co.
   B. The price of admission was two dollars.
   C. The news was brought to Mr. Walters.
   D. There are less slips to be checked today than there were yesterday.

2. A. He only wants you to go with him; consequently I would be in the way.
   B. Whom do you think I saw on my way to lunch today?
   C. I am very much pleased with the work you are doing in my office.
   D. I think he is better than anyone else in his class.

3. A. I do not believe in his going so far away from home.
   B. She dresses exactly like her sister does.
   C. Neither Flora nor I are going to the movies tonight.
   D. The reason for my lateness is that the train was derailed.

4. A. I cannot understand its being on the bottom shelf because I remember putting it on the top shelf.
   B. If you do not agree with the statement above, please put a check next to it.
   C. We were both chosen to represent the association.
   D. The doctor assured us that she would not have to be operated.

5. A. Near the desk stand three chairs.
   B. How many crates of oranges were delivered?
   C. Where's your coat and hat?
   D. Either you or your mother is wrong.

6. A. She attacked the proposal with bitter words.
   B. Last year our team beat your team.
   C. The careless child spilled some milk on the table cloth.
   D. For three weeks last summer, Molly stood with her aunt.

7. A. Don't blame me for it.
   B. I have met but four.
   C. Loan me five dollars.
   D. May I leave early tonight?

8. A. It's time you knew how to divide by two numbers.
    B. Are you sure the bell has rung?
    C. Whose going to prepare the luncheon?
    D. Will it be all right if you are called at ten o'clock?

9. A. He had a wide knowledge of birds.
    B. New Orleans is further from Seattle than from Camden.
    C. Keats's poetry is characterized by rich imagery.
    D. He objected to several things—the cost, the gaudiness, and the congestion.

10. A. There was, in the first place, no indication that a crime had been committed.
    B. She is taller than any other member of the class.
    C. She decided to leave the book lay on the table.
    D. Haven't you any film in stock at this time?

11. A. Why do you still object to him coming with us to the party?
    B. If I were you, I should wait for them.
    C. If I were ten years older, I should like this kind of job.
    D. I shall go if you desire it.

12. A. Swimming in the pool, the water looked green.
    B. His speech is so precise as to seem affected.
    C. I would like to go overseas.
    D. We read each other's letters.

13. A. It must be here somewhere.
    B. The reason is that there is no bread.
    C. Of all other cities, New York is the largest.
    D. The sand was very warm at the beach.

14. A. If he were wealthy, he would build a hospital for the poor.
    B. I shall insist that he obey you.
    C. They saw that it was him.
    D. What kind of cactus is this one?

15. A. Because they had been trained for emergencies, the assault did not catch them by surprise.
    B. They divided the loot between the four of them in proportion to their efforts.
    C. The number of strikes is gradually diminishing.
    D. Between acts we went out to the lobby for a brief chat.

16. A. Through a ruse, the prisoners affected their escape from the concentration camp.
    B. Constant esposure to danger has affected his mind.
    C. Her affected airs served to alienate her from her friends.
    D. Her vivacity was an affectation.

17. A. It is difficult to recollect what life was like before the war.
    B. Will each of the pupils please hand their home work in?
    C. There are fewer serious mistakes in this pamphlet than I had thought.
    D. "Leave Her to Heaven" is the title of a novel by Ben Ames Williams.

Questions 18-25.

DIRECTIONS: Each of Questions 18 through 25 consists of three sentences lettered A, B, and C. In each of these questions, one of the sentences may contain an error in grammar, sentence structure, or punctuation, or all three sentences may be correct. If one of the sentences in a question contains an error in grammar, sentence structure, or punctuation, write in the space at the right the letter preceding the sentence which contains the error. If all three sentences are correct, write the letter D.

18. A. Mr. Smith appears to be less competent than I in performing these duties. 18.____
    B. The supervisor spoke to the employee, who had made the error, but did not reprimand him.
    C. When he found the book lying on the table, he immediately notified the owner.

19. A. Being locked in the desk, we were certain that the papers would not be taken. 19.____
    B. It wasn't I who dictated the telegram; I believe it was Eleanor.
    C. You should interview whoever comes to the office today.

20. A. The clerk was instructed to set the machine on the table before summoning the manager. 20.____
    B. He said that he was not familiar with those kind of activities.
    C. A box of pencils, in addition to erasers and blotters, was included in the shipment of supplies.

21. A. The supervisor remarked, "Assigning an employee to the proper type of work is not always easy." 21.____
    B. The employer found that each of the applicants were qualified to perform the duties of the position.
    C. Any competent student is permitted to take this course if he obtains the consent of the instructor.

22. A. The prize was awarded to the employee whom the judges believed to be most deserving. 22.____
    B. Since the instructor believes this book is the better of the two, he is recommending it for use in the school.
    C. It was obvious to the employees that the completion of the task by the scheduled date would require their working overtime.

23. A. These reports have been typed by employees who are trained by a capable supervisor. 23.____
    B. This employee is as old, if not older, than any other employee in the department.
    C. Running rapidly down the street, the messenger soon reached the office.

24. A. It is believed, that if these terms are accepted, the building can be constructed at a reasonable cost. 24.____
    B. The typists are seated in the large office; the stenographers, in the small office.
    C. Either the operators or the machines are at fault.

25. A. Mr. Jones, who is the head of the agency, will come today to discuss the plans for the new training program.
    B. The reason the report is not finished is that the supply of paper is exhausted.
    C. It is now obvious that neither of the two employees is able to handle this type of assignment.

25._____

KEY (CORRECT ANSWERS)

1.	D	11.	A
2.	A	12.	A
3.	B	13.	C
4.	D	14.	C
5.	C	15.	B
6.	D	16.	A
7.	C	17.	B
8.	C	18.	B
9.	B	19.	A
10.	C	20.	B

21. B
22. D
23. B
24. A
25. D

TEST 2

DIRECTIONS: In each of the following groups of sentences, one sentence is incorrect because it includes an error in grammar, usage, sentence structure, diction, capitalization, or punctuation. Indicate the INCORRECT sentence in each group.

1. A. We shall have to leave it to the jury to make a determination of the facts.
   B. His precision resulted in a nice discrimination between their relative merits.
   C. Green vegetables are healthy foods.
   D. We shall attempt to ascertain whether there has been any tampering with the lock.

   1.____

2. A. Have you made any definitive plans which may be applied to budget preparation?
   B. We planned on taking a walking trip through the mountains.
   C. I would much rather he had called me after we had taken the trip.
   D. Do you believe that he has a predisposition toward that kind of response?

   2.____

3. A. He carried out the orders with great dispatch but with little effect.
   B. The cook's overbearing manner overawed his employer.
   C. All of us shall partake of the benefits of exercise.
   D. Miss Smith made less errors than the other typists.

   3.____

4. A. I believe that we are liable to have good weather tomorrow.
   B. From what I could see, I thought he acted like the others.
   C. Perpetual motion is an idea which is not unthinkable.
   D. Many of us taxpayers are displeased with the service.

   4.____

5. A. She was incredulous when I told her the incredible tale.
   B. She was told that the symptoms would disappear within a week.
   C. If possible, I should like to sit in front of the very tall couple.
   D. Punish whomever disobeys our commands.

   5.____

6. A. The men were trapped inside the cave for four days.
   B. The man seated in back of me was talking throughout the play.
   C. He told me that he doesn't know whether he will be able to visit us.
   D. Please bring me the pair of scissors from the table.

   6.____

7. A. He was charged with having committed many larcenous acts.
   B. Material wealth is certainly not something to be dismissed cavalierly.
   C. He is one of those people who do everything promptly.
   D. I hope to be able to retaliate for the assistance you have given me.

   7.____

8. A. Have you noted the unusual phenomena to be seen in that portion of the heavens?
   B. The data is as accurate as it is possible to make it.
   C. The enormity of the crime was such that we could not comprehend it.
   D. The collection of monies from some clients was long overdue.

   8.____

9. A. What you are doing is not really different than what I had suggested.
   B. The enormousness of the animal was enough to make her gasp.
   C. The judge brought in a decision which aroused antagonism in the community.
   D. I asked the monitor to take the papers to the principal.

   9.____

10. A. He talks as if he were tired.
    B. He amended his declaration to include additional income.
    C. I know that he would have succeeded if he had tried.
    D. Whom does Mrs. Jones think wrote the play?

    10._____

11. A. The stone made a very angry bruise on his forearm.
    B. He said to me: "I'm very mad at you."
    C. In all likelihood, we shall be unable to go to the fair.
    D. He would have liked to go to the theatre with us.

    11._____

12. A. The lawyers tried to settle the case out of court.
    B. "Get out of my life!" she cried.
    C. Walking down the road, the lake comes into view.
    D. The loan which I received from the bank helped me to keep the business going.

    12._____

13. A. I shall go with you providing that we return home early.
    B. He has been providing us with excellent baked goods for many years.
    C. It has been proved, to my satisfaction, to be correct.
    D. Whether we go or not is for you to decide.

    13._____

14. A. He does not seem able to present a logical and convincing argument.
    B. Each of the goaltenders was trying to protect his respective cage.
    C. He said, "I shall go there directly."
    D. The reason he was late was on account of the delay in transportation.

    14._____

15. A. Her mien revealed her abhorrence of his actions.
    B. She used a great deal of rope so it would not come apart.
    C. After he had lived among them, he found much to admire in their way of life.
    D. He waited patiently for the fish to snatch at the bait.

    15._____

16. A. As a result of constant exposure to the elements, he took sick and required medical attention.
    B. Although the automobile is very old, we think it can still be used for a long trip.
    C. He purchased all the supplies she requested with one exception.
    D. He has repeated the story so frequently that I think he has begun to believe it.

    16._____

17. A. It is the noise made by the crickets that you hear.
    B. She told us that she would be at home on Sunday.
    C. She said, "If I'm not there on time, don't wait on me."
    D. Please try to maintain a cheerful disposition under any and all provocations.

    17._____

18. A. Who is the tallest boy in the class?
    B. Where shall I look to find a similar kind of stone?
    C. The horse took the jumps with a great deal of ease.
    D. He is as good, if not better than, any other jumper in the country.

    18._____

19. A. Which of the two machines would be the most practical?
    B. All of us are entitled to a reply if we are to determine whether you should remain as a member of the club.
    C. Everyone who was listening got to his feet and applauded.
    D. There was no indication from his actions that he knew he was wrong.

    19._____

20. A. I beg leave to call upon you in case of emergency. 20.____
    B. Do not deter me from carrying out the demands of my office.
    C. Please see me irregardless of the time of day.
    D. The intrepid captain shouted: "Into the fray!"

21. A. The teacher asked me whether she could lend the book from me. 21.____
    B. You are not permitted to enter the public address system control room while an announcement is being made.
    C. The mother announced loudly that she was going to the district office to find out whether we could refuse to accept her daughter.
    D. It was my opinion that the salesman arrived at a most inopportune time to demonstrate his machine.

22. A. Perhaps we can eliminate any possibility of a misunderstanding by placing a special notice on the bulletin board. 22.____
    B. The heavy snow storm caused a noticeable drop in student attendance.
    C. We received two different relays, due to the fact that both the district office and the division office sent out separate notices.
    D. Nevertheless, I urge you to prepare for the regular examination by taking the required courses.

23. A. By rotating the secretaries' tasks, we should be able to train the entire office staff in all duties. 23.____
    B. The boy who had fallen told me that he felt alright, so that I didn't make out an accident report.
    C. The flowers that the secretary had brought added a delightful touch of color to the office.
    D. We shall have to work fast to complete the task before the deadline.

24. A. The telephone caller said that he was the boy's father, but his voice sounded immature. 24.____
    B. There are very few situations which would require that we close the office and send the staff home early.
    C. Although a packing slip accompanied the package, we had not received an invoice.
    D. The parent claimed that the child had been in school, but the roll book indicated that the boy had been absent from school.

25. A. Needless to say, I could not grant the parent her request to see the teacher immediately since the teacher was teaching a class. 25.____
    B. The small boy entered the office crying bitterly, and he refused to tell me the cause of his tears.
    C. In describing her son, the mother told me that he was smaller than any boy in his class.
    D. By holding teachers' checks until after lunch, you prevent many teachers from getting to the bank.

KEY (CORRECT ANSWERS)

1.	C	11.	B
2.	B	12.	C
3.	D	13.	A
4.	A	14.	D
5.	D	15.	B
6.	B	16.	A
7.	D	17.	C
8.	B	18.	D
9.	A	19.	A
10.	D	20.	C

21. A
22. C
23. B
24. D
25. C

———

TEST 3

DIRECTIONS: In each of the following groups of sentences, one of the four sentences contains one or more errors in grammar, sentence structure, English usage, or diction. Select the INCORRECT sentence in each case.

1. A. Protest as much as you like, I shall stick to my plan to the bitter end.
   B. It took two men to lift the refrigerator off of the truck.
   C. The dancer, with her company, her orchestra, and her manager, occupies the sixth floor.
   D. When one has worked with his hands he has really earned his keep.

   1.____

2. A. The large number of crises among African governments indicate the difficulty of transition to independence.
   B. No sooner had the final bell rung than there was a mad scramble toward the door.
   C. Being as helpful as he could, the traffic policeman offered to send for a mechanic.
   D. They climbed higher that they might reach the little souvenir shop.

   2.____

3. A. That angry retort of Father's came after long provocation.
   B. The frankness of the book presented a difficult problem as far as advertising it.
   C. It is the glory of Yale that she has many famous men to select from.
   D. The stars of the team were the following: Jones, center Smith, end; and Harris, quarterback.

   3.____

4. A. Next year we shall nominate whomever we please.
   B. The story is so well told that anything but the author's desired effect is impossible.
   C. My Oldsmobile has a Mercury motor, which makes it hard to shift gears.
   D. He is one of those people who believe in existentialist ideas.

   4.____

5. A. After my previous experiences, I never expect to come this far again.
   B. I like my present work as preparing the way to my future occupation.
   C. To sit and smoke and think and dream was his idea of gratification.
   D. The snowball of knowledge sweeps relentlessly on, stamping additional rivets into the body of science.

   5.____

6. A. The student racked his brains back and forth over the algebra problem.
   B. It must be conceded that all the young men adapted themselves to the new regulations.
   C. Formal talks were held between the three great powers in an effort to achieve disarmament.
   D. The librarian felt bad about the damaged encyclopedia.

   6.____

7. A. The policeman wanted to know if the driver of the car had a license.
   B. Not many of these churches are less than thirty years old.
   C. The athlete failed to break his unofficial world decathlon record by a narrow margin.
   D. How different things appear in Washington than in London.

   7.____

8.
   A. The agenda for the next meeting contains several highly important topics.
   B. Stemming from the prelate's remarks was the inference that all was not well at the council.
   C. Because the weight of majority opinion is so great is no reason why a dissenter should remain silent.
   D. The general dominating the conference, there was no danger of chaos erupting.

   8.____

9.
   A. Our company, which has thousands of employees, rates Jones one of its best men.
   B. That wars go on may be considered somewhat of an inherited curse for posterity to bear.
   C. Either Italian dressing or mayonnaise goes well with lettuce hearts.
   D. Granted that he had the best intentions, his conduct was not above reproach.

   9.____

10.
    A. There are two "i's" and two "e's" in privilege.
    B. There is no use in Harry's brother saying anything about the situation.
    C. I, not you, am to blame for the condition of this desk.
    D. By relentless logic the group was lead to accept the statements of the eloquent stranger.

    10.____

11.
    A. "It is one of those cars that go faster than 90 miles an hour," said the salesman.
    B. Elementary school children are not the only ones who are tardy; it is also true of high school and college students.
    C. My handsome brother who is in college writes that he is "having a wonderful time"; he is, however, not doing too well scholastically.
    D. A number of clerks were drinking coffee during the coffee break; the number of cups they drank was unbelievable.

    11.____

12.
    A. He asked what had caused the accident. She replied that she did not know since she had not been present when it had occurred.
    B. The new party headed by Prime Minister Wilson advocated government for the people, not by the people.
    C. Five hundred yards of cloth are sufficient to do the work satisfactorily, and I plan to work continually until I finish.
    D. She thought it would be all right for her to do the work in advance of the due date owing to the fact that none of the machines was being used by others.

    12.____

13.
    A. "Oh! please stop that," he said; but when he looked up, they were nowhere to be seen.
    B. The president of the company often told us workers of his experiences as a penniless, untrained beginner forty years ago.
    C. The family showed its approval of the plan and decided to leave for Detroit, Michigan, on May 18th, or, if delay was unavoidable, on May 25th.
    D. "I'm not buying," he said, "it's too expensive.

    13.____

14.
    A. We expect in the next decade to more than hold our own in our race to the moon.
    B. The teachers who have been considering the annual promotion plan today gave their report to the principal.
    C. You are likely to find him sitting beside the brook in the park.
    D. I shall have eaten by the time we go if my plans proceed according to schedule.

    14.____

15. A. If you must know – of course, however, this is a secret – Billy just asked to borrow my car. 15.____
    B. The job is over with, and neither my wife nor my children will ever persuade me to do it again.
    C. You ought not to have said what you said, and I suggest that you apologize at once.
    D. His friends had begun to understand how much he had done for the organization, but then they seemed to forget everything.

16. A. Unlike Bill and me, Ted looks really good in a stylish suit. 16.____
    B. They have good teachers in our high schools; therefore, I plan to become a high school teacher.
    C. Do you remember the name of the book? the author? the copyright date? the name of the publisher? of the editor?
    D. The secretary and treasurer of the firm intends to hold a meeting with his president within a week or two.

17. A. Foreign films may be interesting, but I do not see them often. I usually prefer listening to music. 17.____
    B. Court reporting has always fascinated me, but last spring I went to a lecture by a famous reporter. Then I made up my mind to be a reporter.
    C. Haven't I asked you a hundred times to take the damaged typewriter to the repair shop which is in the store next to Jones's Candy Store?
    D. Your typewriter should be kept absolutely clean and should be dusted as soon as you have completed your day's work.

18. A. The salesmen felt very pleased when they heard the manager say that their sales for the month of July, August, and September were much higher than that for the same months the previous year. 18.____
    B. Four hundred dollars is too much to pay for these typewriters; I therefore suggest that you do some additional shopping before you make a final decision.
    C. John said that he had swum around the lake three times and that he was now eligible for his swimming certificate.
    D. I recently read "Trade Winds" in The Saturday Review.

19. A. Neither being sufficiently prepared for it, both brothers had to apply for additional training at the technical school. 19.____
    B. The question was laid before them, and after weeks of argument it was still unsettled.
    C. If all goes satisfactorily – and why shouldn't it? – we shall be in Europe before the middle of May
    D. In his first year he was only an office boy, and in his fifth year he was president of the company.

20. A. Of all my friends he is the one on whom I can most surely depend. 20.____
    B. We value the Constitution because of it's guarantees to freedom.
    C. The audience was deeply stirred by the actor's performance.
    D. Give the book to whoever comes into the room first.

21. A. Everything was in order: the paper rules, the pencils sharpened, the chairs placed.
    B. Neither John nor Peter were able to attend the reception.
    C. In April the streets which had been damaged by cold weather were repaired by the workmen.
    D. You may lend my book to the pupil who you think will enjoy it most.

    21.____

22. A. He fidgeted, like most children do, while the grown-ups were discussing the problem.
    B. I won't go unless you go with me.
    C. Sitting beside the charred ruins of his cabin, the frontiersman told us the story of the attack.
    D. Certainly there can be no objection to the boys' working on a volunteer basis.

    22.____

23. A. The congregation was dismissed.
    B. The congregation were deeply moved by the sermon.
    C. What kind of an automobile is that?
    D. His explanation and mine agree.

    23.____

24. A. There is no danger of him being elected.
    B. There is no doubt of his election.
    C. John and he are to be the speakers.
    D. John and she are to be the speakers.

    24.____

25. A. Them that honor me I will honor.
    B. They that believe in me shall be rewarded.
    C. Who did you see at the meeting?
    D. Whom are you writing to?

    25.____

KEY (CORRECT ANSWERS)

1. B
2. A
3. B
4. C
5. D

6. A
7. C
8. C
9. B
10. D

11. B
12. B
13. D
14. D
15. B

16. B
17. B
18. A
19. A
20. B

21. B
22. A
23. C
24. A
25. C

SPELLING

EXAMINATION SECTION

TEST 1

DIRECTIONS: In each of the following tests in this part, select the letter of the one MISSPELLED word in each of the following groups of words. *PRINT THE LETTER OF THE CORRECT ANSWER IN THE SPACE AT THE RIGHT.*

1. A. grateful   B. fundimental   C. census   D. analysis   1._____
2. A. installment   B. retrieve   C. concede   D. dissapear   2._____
3. A. accidentaly   B. dismissal   C. conscientious D. indelible   3._____
4. A. perceive   B. carreer   C. anticipate   D. acquire   4._____
5. A. facillity   B. reimburse   C. assortment   D. guidance   5._____
6. A. plentiful   B. across   C. advantagous   D. similar   6._____
7. A. omission   B. pamphlet   C. guarrantee   D. repel   7._____
8. A. maintenance   B. always   C. liable   D. anouncement   8._____
9. A. exaggerate   B. sieze   C. condemn   D. commit   9._____
10. A. pospone   B. altogether   C. grievance   D. excessive   10._____
11. A. banana   B. trafic   C. spectacle   D. boundary   11._____
12. A. commentator   B. abbreviation   C. battaries   D. monastery   12._____
13. A. practically   B. advise   C. pursuade   D. laboratory   13._____
14. A. fatigueing   B. invincible   C. strenuous   D. ceiling   14._____
15. A. propeller   B. reverence   C. piecemeal   D. underneth   15._____
16. A. annonymous   B. envelope   C. transit   D. variable   16._____
17. A. petroleum   B. bigoted   C. meager   D. resistence   17._____

2 (#1)

18. A. permissible   B. indictment   C. fundemental   D. nowadays   18.____
19. A. thief   B. bargin   C. nuisance   D. vacant   19.____
20. A. technique   B. vengeance   C. aquatic   D. heighth   20.____

KEY (CORRECT ANSWERS)

1. B. fundamental
2. D. disappear
3. A. accidentally
4. B. career
5. A. facility

6. C. advantageous
7. C. guarantee
8. D. announcement
9. B. seize
10. A. postpone

11. B. traffic
12. C. batteries
13. C. persuade
14. A. fatiguing
15. D. underneath

16. A. anonymous
17. D. resistance
18. C. fundamental
19. B. bargain
20. D. height

TEST 2

DIRECTIONS: In each of the following tests in this part, select the letter of the one MISSPELLED word in each of the following groups of words. *PRINT THE LETTER OF THE CORRECT ANSWER IN THE SPACE AT THE RIGHT.*

1. A. apparent   B. superintendent   C. relieve   D. calendar   1.____
2. A. foreign   B. negotiate   C. typical   D. disipline 2.____
3. A. posponed   B. argument   C. susceptible   D. deficit   3.____
4. A. preferred B. column   C. peculiar D. equiped   4.____
5. A. exaggerate B. disatisfied   C. repetition D. already   5.____
6. A. livelihood B. physician   C. obsticle D. strategy   6.____
7. A. courageous B. ommission   C. ridiculous D. awkward   7.____
8. A. sincerely B. abundance   C. negligable D. elementary 8.____
9. A. obsolete   B. mischievous   C. enumerate D. atheletic 9.____
10. A. fiscel   B. beneficiary   C. concede   D. translate 10.____
11. A. segregate B. excessivly   C. territory D. obstacle   11.____
12. A. unnecessary B. monopolys   C. harmonious D. privilege 12.____
13. A. sinthetic B. intellectual   C. gracious D. archaic   13.____
14. A. beneficial B. fulfill   C. sarcastic D. disolve   14.____
15. A. umbrella B. sentimental   C. inefficent D. psychiatrist 15.____
16. A. noticable B. knapsack   C. librarian D. meant   16.____
17. A. conference B. upheaval   C. vulger   D. odor   17.____
18. A. surmount B. pentagon   C. calorie   D. inumerable 18.____
19. A. classifiable B. moisturize   C. monitor   D. assesment 19.____
20. A. thermastat B. corrupting   C. approach D. thinness   20.____

KEY (CORRECT ANSWERS)

1. C. relieve
2. D. discipline
3. A. postponed
4. D. equipped
5. B. dissatisfied

6. C. obstacle
7. B. omission
8. C. negligible
9. D. athletic
10. A. fiscal

11. B. excessively
12. B. monopolies
13. A. synthetic
14. D. dissolve
15. C. inefficient

16. A. noticeable
17. C. vulgar
18. D. innumerable
19. D. assessment
20. A. thermostat

TEST 3

DIRECTIONS: In each of the following tests in this part, select the letter of the one MISSPELLED word in each of the following groups of words. *PRINT THE LETTER OF THE CORRECT ANSWER IN THE SPACE AT THE RIGHT.*

1. A. typical   B. descend   C. summarize   D. continuel   1.____
2. A. courageous   B. recomend   C. omission   D. eliminate   2.____
3. A. compliment   B. illuminate   C. auxilary   D. installation   3.____
4. A. preliminary   B. aquainted   C. syllable   D. analysis   4.____
5. A. accustomed   B. negligible   C. interupted   D. bulletin   5.____
6. A. summoned   B. managment   C. mechanism   D. sequence   6.____
7. A. commitee   B. surprise   C. noticeable   D. emphasize   7.____
8. A. occurrance   B. likely   C. accumulate   D. grievance   8.____
9. A. obstacle   B. particuliar   C. baggage   D. fascinating   9.____
10. A. innumerable   B. seize   C. applicant   D. dictionery   10.____
11. A. monkeys   B. rigid   C. unnatural   D. roomate   11.____
12. A. surveying   B. figurative   C. famous   D. curiosety   12.____
13. A. rodeo   B. inconcievable   C. calendar   D. magnificence   13.____
14. A. handicaped   B. glacier   C. defiance   D. emperor   14.____
15. A. schedule   B. scrawl   C. seclusion   D. sissors   15.____
16. A. tissues   B. tomatos   C. tyrants   D. tragedies   16.____
17. A. casette   B. graceful   C. penicillin   D. probably   17.____
18. A. gnawed   B. microphone   C. clinicle   D. batch   18.____
19. A. amateur   B. altitude   C. laborer   D. expence   19.____
20. A. mandate   B. flexable   C. despise   D. verify   20.____

KEY (CORRECT ANSWERS)

1. D. continual
2. B. recommend
3. C. auxiliary
4. B. acquainted
5. C. interrupted

6. B. management
7. A. committee
8. A. occurrence
9. B. particular
10. D. dictionary

11. D. roommate
12. D. curiosity
13. B. inconceivable
14. A. handicapped
15. D. scissors

16. B. tomatoes
17. A. cassette
18. C. clinical
19. D. expense
20. B. flexible

TEST 4

DIRECTIONS: In each of the following tests in this part, select the letter of the one MISSPELLED word in each of the following groups of words. *PRINT THE LETTER OF THE CORRECT ANSWER IN THE SPACE AT THE RIGHT.*

1. A. primery   B. mechanic   C. referred   D. admissible   1._____
2. A. cessation   B. beleif   C. aggressive   D. allowance   2._____
3. A. leisure   B. authentic   C. familiar   D. contemtable   3._____
4. A. volume   B. forty   C. dilemma   D. seldum   4._____
5. A. discrepancy B. aquisition   C. exorbitant   D. lenient   5._____
6. A. simultanous B. penetrate   C. revision   D. conspicuous   6._____
7. A. ilegible   B. gracious   C. profitable   D. obedience   7._____
8. A. manufacturer B. authorize   C. compelling   D. pecular   8._____
9. A. anxious   B. rehearsal   C. handicaped   D. tendency   9._____
10. A. meticulous B. accompaning   C. initiative   D. shelves   10._____
11. A. hammaring   B. insecticide   C. capacity   D. illogical   11._____
12. A. budget   B. luminous   C. aviation   D. lunchon   12._____
13. A. moniter   B. bachelor   C. pleasurable   D. omitted   13._____
14. A. monstrous   B. transistor   C. narrative   D. anziety   14._____
15. A. engagement B. judical   C. pasteurize   D. tried   15._____
16. A. fundimental B. innovation   C. perpendicular D. extravagant   16._____
17. A. bookkeeper B. brutality   C. gymnaseum   D. cemetery   17._____
18. A. sturdily   B. pretentious   C. gourmet   D. enterance   18._____
19. A. resturant   B. tyranny   C. kindergarten   D. ancestry   19._____
20. A. benefit   B. possess   C. speciman   D. noticing   20._____

KEY (CORRECT ANSWERS)

1. A. primary
2. B. belief
3. D. contemptible
4. D. seldom
5. B. acquisition

6. A. simultaneous
7. A. illegible
8. D. peculiar
9. C. handicapped
10. B. accompanying

11. A. hammering
12. D. luncheon
13. A. monitor
14. D. anxiety
15. B. judicial

16. A. fundamental
17. C. gymnasium
18. D. entrance
19. A. restaurant
20. C. specimen

TEST 5

DIRECTIONS: In each of the following tests in this part, select the letter of the one MISSPELLED word in each of the following groups of words. *PRINT THE LETTER OF THE CORRECT ANSWER IN THE SPACE AT THE RIGHT.*

1. A. arguing   B. correspondance   1._____
   C. forfeit   D. dissension

2. A. occasion   B. description   C. prejudice   D. elegible   2._____
3. A. accomodate   B. initiative   C. changeable   D. enroll   3._____
4. A. temporary   B. insistent   C. benificial   D. separate   4._____
5. A. achieve   B. dissappoint   C. unanimous   D. judgment   5._____
6. A. procede   B. publicly   C. sincerity   D. successful   6._____
7. A. deceive   B. goverment   C. preferable   D. repetitive   7._____
8. A. emphasis   B. skillful   C. advisible   D. optimistic   8._____
9. A. tendency   B. rescind   C. crucial   D. noticable   9._____
10. A. privelege   B. abbreviate   C. simplify   D. divisible   10._____
11. A. irresistible B. varius   C. mutual   D. refrigerator   11._____
12. A. amateur   B. distinguish   C. rehearsal   D. poision   12._____
13. A. biased   B. ommission   C. precious   D. coordinate   13._____
14. A. calculated   B. enthusiasm   C. sincerely   D. parashute   14._____
15. A. sentry   B. materials   C. incredable   D. budget   15._____
16. A. chocolate   B. instrument   C. volcanoe   D. shoulder   16._____
17. A. ancestry   B. obscure   C. intention   D. ninty   17._____
18. A. artical   B. bracelet   C. beggar   D. hopeful   18._____
19. A. tournament   B. sponsor   C. perpendiclar   D. dissolve   19._____
20. A. yeild   B. physician   C. greasiest   D. admitting   20._____

KEY (CORRECT ANSWERS)

1. B. correspondence
2. D. eligible
3. A. accommodate
4. C. beneficial
5. B. disappoint

6. A. proceed
7. B. government
8. C. advisable
9. D. noticeable
10. A. privilege

11. B. various
12. D. poison
13. B. omission
14. D. parachute
15. C. incredible

16. C. volcano
17. D. ninety
18. A. article
19. C. perpendicular
20. A. yield

TEST 6

DIRECTIONS: In each of the following tests in this part, select the letter of the one MISSPELLED word in each of the following groups of words. *PRINT THE LETTER OF THE CORRECT ANSWER IN THE SPACE AT THE RIGHT.*

1. A. achievment   B. maintenance   C. questionnaire   D. all are correct   1.____
2. A. prevelant   B. pronunciation C. separate   D. all are correct   2.____
3. A. permissible B. relevant   C. seize   D. all are correct   3.____
4. A. corroborate B. desparate   C. eighth   D. all are correct   4.____
5. A. exceed   B. feasibility   C. psycological   D. all are correct   5.____
6. A. parallel   B. aluminum   C. calendar   D. eigty   6.____
7. A. microbe   B. ancient   C. autograph   D. existance   7.____
8. A. plentiful   B. skillful   C. amoung   D. capsule   8.____
9. A. erupt   B. quanity   C. opinion   D. competent   9.____
10. A. excitement B. discipline   C. luncheon   D. regreting   10.____
11. A. magazine   B. expository   C. imitation   D. permenent   11.____
12. A. ferosious   B. machinery   C. precise   D. magnificent   12.____
13. A. conceive   B. narritive   C. separation   D. management   13.____
14. A. muscular   B. witholding   C. pickle   D. glacier   14.____
15. A. vehicel   B. mismanage   C. correspondence D. dissatisfy   15.____
16. A. sentince   B. bulletin   C. notice   D. definition   16.____
17. A. appointment B. exactly   C. typest   D. light   17.____
18. A. penalty   B. suparvise   C. consider   D. division   18.____
19. A. schedule   B. accurate   C. corect   D. simple   19.____
20. A. suggestion B. installed   C. proper   D. agincy   20.____

KEY (CORRECT ANSWERS)

1. A. achievement
2. B. prevalent
3. D. all are correct
4. B. desperate
5. C. psychological

6. D. eighty
7. D. existence
8. C. among
9. B. quantity
10. D. regretting

11. D. permanent
12. A. ferocious
13. B. narrative
14. B. withholding
15. A. vehicle

16. A. sentence
17. C. typist
18. B. supervise
19. C. correct
20. D. agency

TEST 7

DIRECTIONS: In each of the following tests in this part, select the letter of the one MISSPELLED word in each of the following groups of words. *PRINT THE LETTER OF THE CORRECT ANSWER IN THE SPACE AT THE RIGHT.*

1. A. symtom   B. serum   B. antiseptic   D. aromatic   1.____
2. A. register   B. registrar   C. purser   D. burser   2.____
3. A. athletic   B. tragedy   C. batallion   D. sophomore   3.____
4. A. latent   B. godess   C. aisle   D. whose   4.____
5. A. rhyme   B. rhythm   C. thime   D. thine   5.____
6. A. eighth   B. exaggerate   C. electorial   D. villain   6.____
7. A. statute   B. superintendent   7.____
   C. iresistible   D. colleague
8. A. sieze   B. therefor   C. auxiliary   D. changeable   8.____
9. A. siege   B. knowledge   C. lieutenent   D. weird   9.____
10. A. acquitted   B. polititian   C. professor   D. conqueror   10.____
11. A. changeable   B. chargeable   C. salable   D. useable   11.____
12. A. promissory   B. prisoner   C. excellent   D. tyrrany   12.____
13. A. conspicuous   B. essance   C. comparative   D. brilliant   13.____
14. A. notefying   B. accentuate   C. adhesive   D. primarily   14.____
15. A. exercise   B. sublime   C. stuborn   D. shameful   15.____
16. A. presume   B. transcript   C. strech   D. wizard   16.____
17. A. specify   B. regional   C. arbitrary   D. segragation   17.____
18. A. requirement   B. happiness   C. achievement   D. gentely   18.____
19. A. endurance   B. fusion   C. balloon   D. enormus   19.____
20. A. luckily   B. schedule   C. simplicity   D. sanwich   20.____

183

KEY (CORRECT ANSWERS)

1. A. symptom
2. D. bursar
3. C. battalion
4. B. goddess
5. C. thyme

6. C. electoral
7. C. irresistible
8. A. seize
9. C. lieutenant
10. B. politician

11. D. usable
12. D. tyranny
13. B. essence
14. A. notifying
15. C. stubborn

16. C. stretch
17. D. segregation
18. D. gently
19. D. enormous
20. D. sandwich

TEST 8

DIRECTIONS: In each of the following tests in this part, select the letter of the one MISSPELLED word in each of the following groups of words. *PRINT THE LETTER OF THE CORRECT ANSWER IN THE SPACE AT THE RIGHT.*

1. A. maintain B. maintainance C. sustain D. sustenance 1.____
2. A. portend B. portentious C. pretend D. pretentious 2.____
3. A. prophesize B. prophesies C. farinaceous D. spaceous 3.____
4. A. choose B. chose C. choosen D. chasten 4.____
5. A. censure B. censorious C. pleasure D. pleasurable 5.____
6. A. cover B. coverage C. adder D. adage 6.____
7. A. balloon B. diregible C. direct D. descent 7.____
8. A. whemsy B. crazy C. flimsy D. lazy 8.____
9. A. derision B. pretention C. sustention D. contention 9.____
10. A. question B. questionaire C. legion D. legionary 10.____
11. A. chattle B. cattle C. dismantle D. kindle 11.____
12. A. canal B. cannel C. chanel D. colonel 12.____
13. A. hemorrage B. storage C. manage D. foliage 13.____
14. A. surgeon B. sturgeon C. luncheon D. stancheon 14.____
15. A. diploma B. commission C. dependent D. luminious 15.____
16. A. likelihood B. blizzard C. machanical D. suppress 16.____
17. A. commercial B. releif C. disposal D. endeavor 17.____
18. A. operate B. bronco C. excaping D. grammar 18.____
19. A. orchard B. collar C. embarass D. distant 19.____
20. A. sincerly B. possessive C. weighed D. waist 20.____

KEY (CORRECT ANSWERS)

1. B. maintenance
2. B. portentous
3. D. spacious
4. C. chosen
5. D. pleasurable
6. D. adage
7. B. dirigible
8. A. whimsy
9. B. pretension
10. B. questionnaire
11. A. chattel
12. C. channel
13. A. hemorrhage
14. D. stanchion
15. D. luminous
16. C. mechanical
17. B. relief
18. C. escaping
19. C. embarrass
20. A. sincerely

TEST 9

DIRECTIONS: In each of the following tests in this part, select the letter of the one MISSPELLED word in each of the following groups of words. *PRINT THE LETTER OF THE CORRECT ANSWER IN THE SPACE AT THE RIGHT.*

1. A. statute B. stationary C. staturesque D. stature 1.____
2. A. practicible B. practical C. particle D. reticule 2.____
3. A. plague B. plaque C. ague D. aigrete 3.____
4. A. theology B. idealogy C. psychology D. philology 4.____
5. A. dilema B. stamina C. feminine D. strychnine 5.____
6. A. deceit B. benefit C. grieve D. hienous 6.____
7. A. commensurable B. measurable C. duteable D. salable 7.____
8. A. homogeneous B. heterogeneous C. advantageous D. religeous 8.____
9. A. criticize B. dramatise C. exorcise D. exercise 9.____
10. A. ridiculous B. comparable C. merciful D. cotten 10.____
11. A. antebiotic B. stitches C. pitiful D. sneaky 11.____
12. A. amendment B. candadate C. accountable D. recommendation 12.____
13. A. avocado B. recruit C. tripping D. probally 13.____
14. A. calendar B. desirable C. familar D. vacuum 14.____
15. A. deteriorate B. elligible C. liable D. missile 15.____
16. A. amateur B. competent C. mischeivous D. occasion 16.____
17. A. friendliness B. saleries C. cruelty D. ammunition 17.____
18. A. wholesome B. cieling C. stupidity D. eligible 18.____
19. A. comptroller B. traveled C. accede D. procede 19.____
20. A. Britain B. Brittainica C. conductor D. vendor 20.____

KEY (CORRECT ANSWERS)

1. C. statuesque
2. A. practicable
3. D. aigrette
4. B. ideology
5. A. dilemma

6. D. heinous
7. C. dutiable
8. D. religious
9. B. dramatize
10. D. cotton

11. A. antibiotic
12. B. candidate
13. D. probably
14. C. familiar
15. B. eligible

16. C. mischievous
17. B. salaries
18. B. ceiling
19. D. proceed
20. B. Brittanica

TEST 10

DIRECTIONS: In each of the following tests in this part, select the letter of the one MISSPELLED word in each of the following groups of words. *PRINT THE LETTER OF THE CORRECT ANSWER IN THE SPACE AT THE RIGHT.*

1. A. lengthen B. region C. gases D. inspecter 1.____
2. A. imediately B. forbidden 2.____
   C. complimentary D. aeronautics
3. A. continuous B. paralel C. opposite D. definite 3.____
4. A. Antarctic B. Wednesday C. Febuary D. Hungary 4.____
5. A. transmission B. exposure C. pistol D. customery 5.____
6. A. juvinile B. martyr C. deceive D. collaborate 6.____
7. A. unnecessary B. repetitive C. cancellation D. airey 7.____
8. A. transit B. availible C. objection D. galaxy 8.____
9. A. ineffective B. believeable C. arrangement D. aggravate 9.____
10. A. possession B. progress C. reception D. predjudice 10.____
11. A. congradulate B. percolate C. major D. leisure 11.____
12. A. convenience B. privilige C. emerge D. immerse 12.____
13. A. erasable B. inflammable C. audable D. laudable 13.____
14. A. final B. fines C. finis D. Finish 14.____
15. A. emitted B. representative 15.____
    C. discipline D. insistance
16. A. diphthong B. rarified C. library D. recommend 16.____
17. A. compel B. belligerent C. successful D. sergeant 17.____
18. A. dispatch B. dispise C. dispose D. dispute 18.____
19. A. administrator B. adviser C. diner D. celluler 19.____
20. A. ignite B. ignision C. igneous D. ignited 20.____

KEY (CORRECT ANSWERS)

1. D. inspector
2. A. immediately
3. B. parallel
4. C. February
5. D. customary

6. A. juvenile
7. D. airy
8. B. available
9. B. believable
10. D. prejudice

11. A. congratulate
12. B. privilege
13. C. audible
14. D. Finnish
15. D. insistence

16. B. rarefied
17. D. sergeant
18. B. despise
19. D. cellular
20. B. ignition

TEST 11

DIRECTIONS: In each of the following tests in this part, select the letter of the one MISSPELLED word in each of the following groups of words. *PRINT THE LETTER OF THE CORRECT ANSWER IN THE SPACE AT THE RIGHT.*

1. A. repellent B. secession C. sebaceous D. saxaphone 1._____
2. A. navel B. counteresolution C. marginalia D. perceptible 2._____
3. A. Hammerskjold B. Nehru C. U Thamt D. Krushchev 3._____
4. A. perculate B. periwinkle C. perigee D. retrogression 4._____
5. A. buccaneer B. tobacco C. buffalo D. oscilate 5._____
6. A. siege B. wierd C. seize D. cemetery 6._____
7. A. equaled B. bigoted C. benefited D. kaleideoscope 7._____
8. A. blamable B. bullrush C. questionnaire D. irascible 8._____
9. A. tobogganed B. acquiline C. capillary D. cretonne 9._____
10. A. daguerrotype B. elegiacal C. iridescent D. inchoate 10._____
11. A. bayonet B. braggadocio C. corollary D. connoiseur 11._____
12. A. equinoctial B. fusillade C. fricassee D. potpouri 12._____
13. A. octameter B. impressario C. hyetology D. hieroglyphics 13._____
14. A. innanity B. idyllic C. fylfot D. inimical 14._____
15. A. liquefy B. rarefy C. putrify D. sapphire 15._____
16. A. canonical B. stupified C. millennium D. memorabilia 16._____
17. A. paraphenalia B. odyssey C. onomatopoeia D. osseous 17._____
18. A. peregrinate B. pecadillo C. reptilian D. uxorious 18._____
19. A. pharisaical B. vicissitude C. puissance D. wainright 19._____
20. A. holocaust B. tesselate C. scintilla D. staccato 20._____

KEY (CORRECT ANSWERS)

1. D. saxophone
2. B. counterresolution
3. C. U Thant
4. A. percolate
5. D. oscillate

6. B. weird
7. D. kaleidoscope
8. B. bulrush
9. B. aquiline
10. A. daguerreotype

11. D. connoisseur
12. D. potpourri
13. B. impresario
14. A. inanity
15. C. putrefy

16. B. stupefied
17. A. paraphernalia
18. B. peccadillo
19. D. wainwright
20. B. tessellate

TEST 12

DIRECTIONS: In each of the following tests in this part, select the letter of the one MISSPELLED word in each of the following groups of words. *PRINT THE LETTER OF THE CORRECT ANSWER IN THE SPACE AT THE RIGHT.*

1. A. questionnaire   B. gondoleer   C. chandelier   D. acquiescence   1.____
2. A. surveilance   B. surfeit   C. vaccinate   D. belligerent   2.____
3. A. occassionally   B. recurrence   C. silhouette   D. incessant   3.____
4. A. transferral   B. benefical   C. descendant   D. dependent   4.____
5. A. separately   B. flouresence   C. deterrent   D. parallel   5.____
6. A. acquittal   B. enforceable   C. counterfeit   D. indispensible   6.____
7. A. susceptible   B. accelarate   C. exhilarate   D. accommodation   7.____
8. A. impedimenta   B. collateral   C. liason   D. epistolary   8.____
9. A. inveigle   B. panegyric   C. reservoir   D. manuver   9.____
10. A. synopsis   B. paraphernalia C. affidavit   D. subpoena   10.____
11. A. grosgrain   B. vermilion   C. abbatoir   D. connoiseur   11.____
12. A. gabardine   B. camoflage   C. hemorrhage   D. contraband   12.____
13. A. opprobrious   B. defalcate   C. fiduciery   D. recommendations   13.____
14. A. nebulous   B. necessitate   C. impricate   D. discrepancy   14.____
15. A. discrete   B. condescension C. condign   D. condiment   15.____
16. A. cavalier   B. effigy   C. legitimatly   D. misalliance   16.____
17. A. rheumatism   B. vaporous   C. cannister   D. hallucinations   17.____
18. A. paleonthology   B. octogenarian   C. gradient   D. impingement   18.____
19. A. fusilade   B. fusilage   C. ensilage   D. desiccate   19.____
20. A. rationale   B. raspberry   C. reprobate   D. varigated   20.____

KEY (CORRECT ANSWERS)

1. B. gondolier
2. A. surveillance
3. A. occasionally
4. B. beneficial
5. B. fluorescence

6. D. indispensable
7. B. accelerate
8. C. liaison
9. D. maneuver
10. B. paraphernalia

11. D. connoisseur
12. B. camouflage
13. C. fiduciary
14. C. imprecate
15. B. condescension

16. C. legitimately
17. C. canister
18. A. paleontology
19. A. fusillade
20. D. variegated

400 SPELLING DEMONS

The candidate should overlearn the correct spelling of the words that follow.
TEST YOURSELF.

1. partial
2. therefore
3. usually
4. acknowledgment
5. promptly
6. basis
7. envelope
8. actually
9. parcel post
10. executive
11. credited
12. balance
13. asked
14. material
15. receiving
16. commission
17. academy
18. airplane
19. alley
20. accustom
21. already
22. anxiety
23. audience
24. clothes
25. adviser
26. descend
27. encouraging
28. baseball
29. committee
30. destroy
31. everybody
32. beggar
33. digging
34. exceptional
35. biscuit
36. conscience
37. disappoint
38. disavowal
39. buoyant
40. dissatisfied
41. fascinate
42. course
43. finally
44. cemetery
45. dormitories
46. formally
47. characteristic
48. ecstasy
49. fourth
50. chosen
51. incidentally
52. independence
53. obstacle
54. generally
55. influence
56. manufacturer
57. occurrence
58. grandeur
59. intentionally
60. shown
61. existence
62. arrangement
63. having
64. appreciation
65. almost
66. recommend
67. merely
68. remember
69. suggestions
70. apparently
71. possibly
72. suppose
73. instructions
74. definitely
75. due
76. volume
77. referring
78. basketball
79. considerably
80. writer
81. always
82. assistance
83. absurd
84. aggravate
85. among
86. analogous
87. accumulate
88. ally
89. annual
90. athletic
91. addressed
92. alumnus
93. derived
94. eminent
95. barring
96. desperate
97. competent
98. difference
99. benefited
100. conqueror
101. disappear
102. expense
103. Britannica
104. familiar
105. distribute
106. cylinder
107. forfeit
108. changing
109. deceitful
110. forty
111. chose
112. loose
113. nowadays
114. lying
115. infinite
116. manual
117. occurred
118. grammar
119. intelligence
120. material
121. hoping
122. exceedingly
123. planning
124. secretary
125. affectionately
126. necessarily
127. criticism
128. dearest
129. position
130. handling
131. success
132. merchandise
133. opportunities
134. additional
135. doubt
136. returning
137. affects
138. amateur
139. arising
140. arithmetic
141. all right
142. angle
143. across
144. altogether
145. appropriate

400 SPELLING DEMONS (CONT'D)

146. embarrass
147. baring
148. coming
149. despair
150. especially
151. becoming
152. compelled
153. dictionary
154. excellent
155. believing
156. conquer
157. existence
158. Britain
159. continuous
160. discuss
161. business
162. countries
163. fiery
164. candidate
165. cruelty
166. changeable
167. debater
168. forth
169. choose
170. deferred
171. eliminate
172. noticeable
173. furniture
174. oblige
175. induce
176. maintenance
177. occur
178. governor
179. intellectual
180. cede
181. officers
182. Wednesday
183. pleat
184. acceptable
185. quote
186. society
187. error
188. schedule
189. possible
190. stating
191. always
192. argument
193. accommodate
194. angel
195. ascend
196. acquitted
197. alter
198. appearance
199. awkward
200. barbarous
201. column
202. equipped
203. bearing
204. device
205. beginning
206. conferred
207. dining room
208. exhilarate
209. brilliant
210. considered
211. discipline
212. bureau
213. distinction
214. calendar
215. courtesy
216. doctor
217. foreign
218. dealt
219. eighth
220. fraternity
221. incredulous
222. gallant
223. maintain
224. occasionally
225. government
226. instant
227. marriage
228. o'clock
229. apparently
230. guard
231. although
232. already
233. knowledge
234. library
235. service
236. accepted
237. supply
238. extremely
239. benefit
240. arctic
241. allotted
242. analysis
243. arrival
244. auxiliary
245. balance
246. coarse
247. enemy
248. comparative
249. device
250. exaggerate
251. conceivable
252. begging
253. dilemma
254. exhaust
255. boundaries
256. conscientious
257. dissipate
258. February
259. courteous
260. divine
261. financier
262. drudgery
263. formerly
264. decide
265. effects
266. frantically
267. freshman
268. incidents
269. losing
270. indispensable
271. occasion
272. goddess
273. instance
274. grievous
275. intercede
276. omission
277. hiatus
278. irresistible
279. harass
280. mattress
281. miniature
282. misspelled
283. laboratory
284. murmur
285. parliament
286. hurriedly
287. peaceable
288. Negroes
289. neither
290. immigration
291. literature
292. perseverance
293. supersede
294. shiftless
295. tendency
296. recognize
297. precedents

298. sacrilegious
299. principle
300. soliloquy
301. ophthalmologist
302. cinnamon
303. phlegmatic
304. berserk
305. cellophane
306. xylophone
307. calisthenics
308. inebriate
309. chlorophyll
310. broccoli
311. ecumenical
312. acupuncture
313. deterrent
314. assassin
315. eligible
316. all right
317. infrared
318. antidote
319. impresario
320. beige
321. ellipse
322. bony
323. descendant
324. liaison
325. accommodate
326. despair
327. fallacious
328. caramel
329. forego
330. receipt
331. received
332. believe
333. convenient
334. sufficient
335. literature
336. beginning
337. clothes
338. cooperation
339. ought
340. paid
341. arrange
342. approval
343. beautiful
344. connection
345. certificate
346. disposition
347. grateful
348. finally
349. based
350. stopped
351. exactly
352. least
353. community
354. necessary
355. business
356. probably
357. course
358. remittance
359. their
360. truly
361. enclosed
362. instant
363. whether
364. referred
365. really
366. original
367. separate
368. further
369. catalog
370. forward
371. expect
372. canceled
373. coming
374. inquiry
375. waste
376. definite
377. great
378. courtesy
379. assure
380. sense
381. invoice
382. usual
383. awful
384. college
385. different
386. similar
387. freight
388. cancel
389. weather
390. tomorrow
391. recent
392. guess
393. prior
394. mutual
395. perhaps
396. accept
397. prices
398. semester
399. regret
400. although

SPELLING DIFFICULTIES
WORDS PRESENTING DIFFICULTIES BECAUSE OF THEIR ENDINGS

1. **ENDING IN ABLE**
   - acceptable
   - admirable
   - available
   - charitable
   - desirable
   - excitable
   - formidable
   - imaginable
   - incurable
   - inevitable
   - inextricable
   - intolerable
   - justifiable
   - lovable
   - movable
   - pardonable
   - perishable
   - presumable
   - profitable
   - serviceable
   - suitable
   - transferable
   - unconquerable
   - unconscionable

2. **ENDING IN ANCE**
   - abundance
   - acquaintance
   - annoyance
   - deliverance
   - maintenance
   - repentance
   - resistance
   - resonance
   - significance
   - sustenance

3. **ENDING IN AR**
   - beggar
   - burglar
   - calendar
   - circular
   - familiar
   - grammar
   - peculiar
   - popular
   - similar
   - solar
   - tabular
   - vinegar

4. **ENDING IN ARY**
   - actuary
   - auxiliary
   - dictionary
   - lapidary
   - necessary
   - obituary
   - subsidiary
   - stationary
   - supplementary

5. **ENDING IN ENCE**
   - circumference
   - coherence
   - competence
   - deference
   - excellence
   - obedience
   - opulence
   - reminiscence
   - violence

6. **ENDING IN ER**
   - adviser
   - clothier
   - colander
   - debater
   - defender
   - embroider
   - foreigner
   - laborer
   - provider
   - reciter
   - subscriber
   - trotter

7. **ENDING IN ERY**
   - bribery
   - cemetery
   - delivery
   - flattery
   - monastery
   - stationery
   - thievery

8. **ENDING IN IBLE**
   - accessible
   - admissible
   - discernible
   - infallible
   - indestructible
   - intelligible
   - invisible
   - irresistible
   - ostensible
   - perceptible
   - plausible
   - responsible

9. **ENDING IN OR**
   - creator
   - demeanor
   - distributor
   - editor
   - endeavor
   - governor
   - impostor
   - inventor
   - legislator
   - monitor
   - orator
   - persecutor
   - predecessor
   - protector

spectator
suitor
survivor
ventilator

10. **PLURAL OF WORDS ENDING IN O**
    cameo -cameos   solo -solos
    folio -folios   mango -mangoes
    piano -pianos   potato -potatoes

11. **ADDING TO WORDS ENDING IN C**
    bivouac -bivouacked, bivouacking
    colic   -colicky
    frolic -frolicked, frolicking
    mimic   -mimicked, mimicking
    panic   -panicky
    picnic -picnicked, picnicking

12. **WORDS ENDING IN SILENT E**
    force -forcible, forcing
    love   -lovable, loving
    move   -movable, moving
    shape -shaping
    write -writing
    use   -using, usage

13. **WORDS ENDING IN CE OR GE**
    manage -manageable
    notice -noticeable
    service -serviceable

ABBREVIATIONS AND CONTRACTIONS

Abbreviations are shortened forms for words and phrases in common use. For example, U.S.P.S. = United States Postal Service. Abbreviations always require <u>periods</u>.

Contractions are shortened forms of words produced by the omission of letters (Sec'y - Secretary) or by combination (it's = it is) in order to save space or time. Contractions always require an <u>apostrophe</u> to indicate the missing letters.

Jan.	- January	Mon.	- Monday	A.M. (or a.m.) -	morning
Feb.	- February	Tues.	- Tuesday	P.M. (or p.m.) -	afternoon
Mar.	- March	Wed.	- Wednesday	Mr. -	Mister
Apr.	- April	Thurs.	- Thursday	Mrs. -	Mistress
Jun.	- June	Fri.	- Friday	.St. -	Street
Jul.	- July	Sat.	- Saturday	Ave .-	Avenue
Aug.	- August	Sun.	- Sunday	Blvd. -	Boulevard
Sept.	- September	E.	- East	Rd. -	Road
Oct.	- October	S.	- South	P.S. -	Public School Post Script
Nov.	- November	N.	- North		
Dec.	- December	W.	- West	No. -	Number
Rev.	- Reverend	Co.	- Company	R.N. -	Registered Nurse, or Royal Navy
Dr.	- Doctor	S.S.	- Steamship		
f.o.b.	- free on board	Dept.	- Department	Pres. -	President
Gov.	- Governor	Prin.	- Principal	U.S.A.-	United States of America
Supt.	- Superintendent	Treas.	- Treasurer		
Jr.	- Junior	Sr.	- Senior	C.O.D. -	Cash on Delivery
Gen.	- General	Capt	.-Captain	Sgt .-	Serveant
Cpl.	- Corporal	Pvt.	- Private	A.D .-	Anno Domini (year of our Lord)
B.C.	- Before Christ	chap.	- chapter		
p.	- page	e.g.	- for example	i.e. -	that is
pp.	- pages	viz.	- namely	etc .-	and so forth
Hon	--. Honorable	P.O.	- Post Office	Messrs.-	Gentlemen
oz.	- ounce	masc.	- masculine	R.F.D. -	Rural Free Delivery
lb.	- pound	fern.	- feminine	R.I.P. -	Rest in Peace
yd.	- yard	sing.	- singular	Inc. -	Incorporated
ft.	- foot or feet	pl.	- plural	Ltd -	Limited
in.	- inch	Bros.	- Brothers		

CONTRACTIONS

n't

isn't	= is not	hasn't	= has not	aren't	= are not
wasn't	= was not	hadn't	= had not	won't	= will not
haven't	= have not	didn't	= did not	wouldn't	= would not
don't	= do not	doesn't	= does not	couldn't	= could not
can't	= cannot	shouldn't	= should not		

'm

I'm = I am

've

I've	= I have	we've	= we have	you've	= you have
they've	= they have				

'

ne'er	= never	o'er	= over	e'er	= ever

PHILOSOPHY, PRINCIPLES, PRACTICES, AND TECHNICS OF SUPERVISION, ADMINISTRATION, MANAGEMENT, AND ORGANIZATION

TABLE OF CONTENTS

	Page
MEANING OF SUPERVISION	1
THE OLD AND THE NEW SUPERVISION	1
THE EIGHT (8) BASIC PRINCIPLES OF THE NEW SUPERVISION	1
I. Principle of Responsibility	1
II. Principle of Authority	2
III. Principle of Self-Growth	2
IV. Principle of Individual Worth	2
V. Principle of Creative Leadership	2
VI. Principle of Success and Failure	2
VII. Principle of Science	3
VIII. Principle of Cooperation	3
WHAT IS ADMINISTRATION?	3
I. Practices Commonly Classed as "Supervisory"	3
II. Practices Commonly Classed as "Administrative"	3
III. Practices Commonly Classed as Both "Supervisory" and "Administrative"	4
RESPONSIBILITIES OF THE SUPERVISOR	4
COMPETENCIES OF THE SUPERVISOR	4
THE PROFESSIONAL SUPERVISOR-EMPLOYEE RELATIONSHIP	4
MINI-TEXT IN SUPERVISION, ADMINISTRATION, MANAGEMENT, AND ORGANIZATION	5
I. Brief Highlights	5
A. Levels of Management	6
B. What the Supervisor Must Learn	6
C. A Definition of Supervision	6
D. Elements of the Team Concept	6
E. Principles of Organization	6
F. The Four Important Parts of Every Job	7
G. Principles of Delegation	7
H. Principles of Effective Communications	7
I. Principles of Work Improvement	7
J. Areas of Job Improvement	7
K. Seven Key Points in Making Improvements	8

L.	Corrective Techniques for Job Improvement	8
M.	A Planning Checklist	8
N.	Five Characteristics of Good Directions	9
O.	Types of Directions	9
P.	Controls	9
Q.	Orienting the New Employee	9
R.	Checklist for Orienting New Employees	9
S.	Principles of Learning	10
T.	Causes of Poor Performance	10
U.	Four Major Steps in On-the-Job Instructions	10
V.	Employees Want Five Things	10
W.	Some Don'ts in Regard to Praise	11
X.	How to Gain Your Workers' Confidence	11
Y.	Sources of Employee Problems	11
Z.	The Supervisor's Key to Discipline	11
AA.	Five Important Processes of Management	12
BB.	When the Supervisor Fails to Plan	12
CC.	Fourteen General Principles of Management	12
DD.	Change	12

II. Brief Topical Summaries   13
   A. Who/What is the Supervisor?   13
   B. The Sociology of Work   13
   C. Principles and Practices of Supervision   14
   D. Dynamic Leadership   14
   E. Processes for Solving Problems   15
   F. Training for Results   15
   G. Health, Safety, and Accident Prevention   16
   H. Equal Employment Opportunity   16
   I. Improving Communications   16
   J. Self-Development   17
   K. Teaching and Training   17
      1. The Teaching Process   17
         a. Preparation   17
         b. Presentation   18
         c. Summary   18
         d. Application   18
         e. Evaluation   18
      2. Teaching Methods   18
         a. Lecture   18
         b. Discussion   18
         c. Demonstration   19
         d. Performance   19
         e. Which Method to Use   19

PHILOSOPHY, PRINCIPLES, PRACTICES, AND TECHNICS
OF
SUPERVISION, ADMINISTRATION, MANAGEMENT, AND ORGANIZATION

MEANING OF SUPERVISION

The extension of the democratic philosophy has been accompanied by an extension in the scope of supervision. Modern leaders and supervisors no longer think of supervision in the narrow sense of being confined chiefly to visiting employees, supplying materials, or rating the staff. They regard supervision as being intimately related to all the concerned agencies of society, they speak of the supervisor's function in terms of "growth," rather than the "improvement" of employees.

This modern concept of supervision may be defined as follows: Supervision is leadership and the development of leadership within groups which are cooperatively engaged in inspection, research, training, guidance, and evaluation.

THE OLD AND THE NEW SUPERVISION

TRADITIONAL
1. Inspection
2. Focused on the employee
3. Visitation
4. Random and haphazard
5. Imposed and authoritarian
6. One person usually

MODERN
1. Study and analysis
2. Focused on aims, materials, methods, supervisors, employees, environment
3. Demonstrations, intervisitation, workshops, directed reading, bulletins, etc.
4. Definitely organized and planned (scientific)
5. Cooperative and democratic
6. Many persons involved (creative)

THE EIGHT (8) BASIC PRINCIPLES OF THE NEW SUPERVISION

I. Principle of Responsibility
    Authority to act and responsibility for acting must be joined.
    A. If you give responsibility, give authority.
    B. Define employee duties clearly.
    C. Protect employees from criticism by others.
    D. Recognize the rights as well as obligations of employees.
    E. Achieve the aims of a democratic society insofar as it is possible within the area of your work.
    F. Establish a situation favorable to training and learning.
    G. Accept ultimate responsibility for everything done in your section, unit, office, division, department.
    H. Good administration and good supervision are inseparable.

II. Principle of Authority
The success of the supervisor is measured by the extent to which the power of authority is not used.
   A. Exercise simplicity and informality in supervision
   B. Use the simplest machinery of supervision
   C. If it is good for the organization as a whole, it is probably justified.
   D. Seldom be arbitrary or authoritative.
   E. Do not base your work on the power of position or of personality.
   F. Permit and encourage the free expression of opinions.

III. Principle of Self-Growth
The success of the supervisor is measured by the extent to which, and the speed with which, he is no longer needed.
   A. Base criticism on principles, not on specifics.
   B. Point out higher activities to employees.
   C. Train for self-thinking by employees to meet new situations.
   D. Stimulate initiative, self-reliance, and individual responsibility
   E. Concentrate on stimulating the growth of employees rather than on removing defects.

IV. Principle of Individual Worth
Respect for the individual is a paramount consideration in supervision.
   A. Be human and sympathetic in dealing with employees.
   B. Don't nag about things to be done.
   C. Recognize the individual differences among employees and seek opportunities to permit best expression of each personality.

V. Principle of Creative Leadership
The best supervision is that which is not apparent to the employee.
   A. Stimulate, don't drive employees to creative action.
   B. Emphasize doing good things.
   C. Encourage employees to do what they do best.
   D. Do not be too greatly concerned with details of subject or method.
   E. Do not be concerned exclusively with immediate problems and activities.
   F. Reveal higher activities and make them both desired and maximally possible.
   G. Determine procedures in the light of each situation but see that these are derived from a sound basic philosophy.
   H. Aid, inspire, and lead so as to liberate the creative spirit latent in all good employees.

VI. Principle of Success and Failure
There are no unsuccessful employees, only unsuccessful supervisors who have failed to give proper leadership.
   A. Adapt suggestions to the capacities, attitudes, and prejudices of employees.
   B. Be gradual, be progressive, be persistent.
   C. Help the employee find the general principle; have the employee apply his own problem to the general principle.
   D. Give adequate appreciation for good work and honest effort.
   E. Anticipate employee difficulties and help to prevent them.
   F. Encourage employees to do the desirable things they will do anyway.
   G. Judge your supervision by the results it secures.

VII. Principle of Science
Successful supervision is scientific, objective, and experimental. It is based on facts, not on prejudices.
  A. Be cumulative in results.
  B. Never divorce your suggestions from the goals of training.
  C. Don't be impatient of results.
  D. Keep all matters on a professional, not a personal, level.
  E. Do not be concerned exclusively with immediate problems and activities.
  F. Use objective means of determining achievement and rating where possible.

VIII. Principle of Cooperation
Supervision is a cooperative enterprise between supervisor and employee.
  A. Begin with conditions as they are.
  B. Ask opinions of all involved when formulating policies.
  C. Organization is as good as its weakest link.
  D. Let employees help to determine policies and department programs.
  E. Be approachable and accessible—physically and mentally.
  F. Develop pleasant social relationships.

WHAT IS ADMINISTRATION

Administration is concerned with providing the environment, the material facilities, and the operational procedures that will promote the maximum growth and development of supervisors and employees. (Organization is an aspect and a concomitant of administration.)

There is no sharp line of demarcation between supervision and administration; these functions are intimately interrelated and, often, overlapping. They are complementary activities.

I. Practices Commonly Classed as "Supervisory"
  A. Conducting employees' conferences
  B. Visiting sections, units, offices, divisions, departments
  C. Arranging for demonstrations
  D. Examining plans
  E. Suggesting professional reading
  F. Interpreting bulletins
  G. Recommending in-service training courses
  H. Encouraging experimentation
  I. Appraising employee morale
  J. Providing for intervisitation

II. Practices Commonly Classified as "Administrative"
  A. Management of the office
  B. Arrangement of schedules for extra duties
  C. Assignment of rooms or areas
  D. Distribution of supplies
  E. Keeping records and reports
  F. Care of audio-visual materials
  G. Keeping inventory records
  H. Checking record cards and books

　　　　I.　Programming special activities
　　　　J.　Checking on the attendance and punctuality of employees

　　III.　Practices Commonly Classified as Both "Supervisory" and "Administrative"
　　　　A.　Program construction
　　　　B.　Testing or evaluating outcomes
　　　　C.　Personnel accounting
　　　　D.　Ordering instructional materials

RESPONSIBILITIES OF THE SUPERVISOR

A person employed in a supervisory capacity must constantly be able to improve his own efficiency and ability. He represent the employer to the employees and only continuous self-examination can make him a capable supervisor.

Leadership and training are the supervisor's responsibility. An efficient working unit is one in which the employees work with the supervisor. It is his job to bring out the best in his employees. He must always be relaxed, courteous, and calm in his association with his employees. Their feelings are important, and a harsh attitude does not develop the most efficient employees.

COMPETENCES OF THE SUPERVISOR

　　　I.　Complete knowledge of the duties and responsibilities of his position.
　　　II.　To be able to organize a job, plan ahead, and carry through.
　　　III.　To have self-confidence and initiative.
　　　IV.　To be able to handle the unexpected situation and make quick decisions.
　　　V.　To be able to properly train subordinates in the positions they are best suited for.
　　　VI.　To be able to keep good human relations among his subordinates.
　　　VII.　To be able to keep good human relations between his subordinates and himself and to earn their respect and trust.

THE PROFESSIONAL SUPERVISOR-EMPLOYEE RELATIONSHIP

There are two kinds of efficiency: one kind is only apparent and is produced in organizations through the exercise of mere discipline; this is but a simulation of the second, or true, efficiency which springs from spontaneous cooperation. If you are a manager, no matter how great or small your responsibility, it is your job, in the final analysis, to create and develop this involuntary cooperation among the people whom you supervise. For, no matter how powerful a combination of money, machines, and materials a company may have, this is a dead and sterile thing without a team of willing, thinking, and articulate people to guide it.

The following 21 points are presented as indicative of the exemplary basic relationship that should exist between supervisor and employee:

1. Each person wants to be liked and respected by his fellow employee and wants to be treated with consideration and respect by his superior.
2. The most competent employee will make an error. However, in a unit where good relations exist between the supervisor and his employees, tenseness and fear do not exist. Thus, errors are not hidden or covered up, and the efficiency of a unit is not impaired.

3. Subordinates resent rules, regulations, or orders that are unreasonable or unexplained.
4. Subordinates are quick to resent unfairness, harshness, injustices, and favoritism.
5. An employee will accept responsibility if he knows that he will be complimented for a job well done, and not too harshly chastised for failure; that his supervisor will check the cause of the failure, and, if it was the supervisor's fault, he will assume the blame therefore. If it was the employee's fault, his supervisor will explain the correct method or means of handling the responsibility.
6. An employee wants to receive credit for a suggestion he has made, that is used. If a suggestion cannot be used, the employee is entitled to an explanation. The supervisor should not say "no" and close the subject.
7. Fear and worry slow up a worker's ability. Poor working environment can impair his physical and mental health. A good supervisor avoids forceful methods, threats, and arguments to get a job done.
8. A forceful supervisor is able to train his employees individually and as a team, and is able to motivate them in the proper channels.
9. A mature supervisor is able to properly evaluate his subordinates and to keep them happy and satisfied.
10. A sensitive supervisor will never patronize his subordinates.
11. A worthy supervisor will respect his employees' confidences.
12. Definite and clear-cut responsibilities should be assigned to each executive.
13. Responsibility should always be coupled with corresponding authority.
14. No change should be made in the scope or responsibilities of a position without a definite understanding to that effect on the part of all persons concerned.
15. No executive or employee, occupying a single position in the organization, should be subject to definite orders from more than one source.
16. Orders should never be given to subordinates over the head of a responsible executive. Rather than do this, the officer in question should be supplanted.
17. Criticisms of subordinates should, whoever possible, be made privately, and in no case should a subordinate be criticized in the presence of executives or employees of equal or lower rank.
18. No dispute or difference between executives or employees as to authority or responsibilities should be considered too trivial for prompt and careful adjudication.
19. Promotions, wage changes, and disciplinary action should always be approved by the executive immediately superior to the one directly responsible.
20. No executive or employee should ever be required, or expected, to be at the same time an assistant to, and critic of, another.
21. Any executive whose work is subject to regular inspection should, wherever practicable, be given the assistance and facilities necessary to enable him to maintain an independent check of the quality of his work.

MINI-TEXT IN SUPERVISION, ADMINISTRATION, MANAGEMENT, AND ORGANIZATION

I. Brief Highlights

Listed concisely and sequentially are major headings and important data in the field for quick recall and review.

A. Levels of Management
Any organization of some size has several levels of management. In terms of a ladder, the levels are:

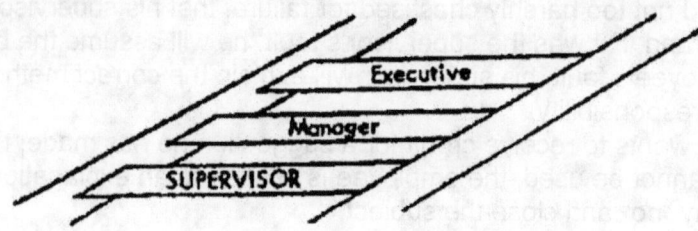

The first level is very important because it is the beginning point of management leadership.

B. What the Supervisor Must Learn
A supervisor must learn to:
1. Deal with people and their differences
2. Get the job done through people
3. Recognize the problems when they exist
4. Overcome obstacles to good performance
5. Evaluate the performance of people
6. Check his own performance in terms of accomplishment

C. A Definition of Supervisor
The term supervisor means any individual having authority, in the interests of the employer, to hire, transfer, suspend, lay-off, recall, promote, discharge, assign, reward, or discipline other employees or responsibility to direct them, or to adjust their grievances, or effectively to recommend such action, if, in connection with the foregoing, exercise of such authority is not of a merely routine or clerical nature but requires the use of independent judgment.

D. Elements of the Team Concept
What is involved in teamwork? The component parts are:
1. Members
2. A leader
3. Goals
4. Plans
5. Cooperation
6. Spirit

E. Principles of Organization
1. A team member must know what his job is.
2. Be sure that the nature and scope of a job are understood.
3. Authority and responsibility should be carefully spelled out.
4. A supervisor should be permitted to make the maximum number of decisions affecting his employees.
5. Employees should report to only one supervisor.
6. A supervisor should direct only as many employees as he can handle effectively.
7. An organization plan should be flexible.

8. Inspection and performance of work should be separate.
9. Organizational problems should receive immediate attention.
10. Assign work in line with ability and experience.

F. The Four Important Parts of Every Job
1. Inherent in every job is the *accountability* for results.
2. A second set of factors in every job is *responsibilities*.
3. Along with duties and responsibilities one must have the *authority* to act within certain limits without obtaining permission to proceed.
4. No job exists in a vacuum. The supervisor is surrounded by key *relationships*.

G. Principles of Delegation
Where work is delegated for the first time, the supervisor should think in terms of these questions:
1. Who is best qualified to do this?
2. Can an employee improve his abilities by doing this?
3. How long should an employee spend on this?
4. Are there any special problems for which he will need guidance?
5. How broad a delegation can I make?

H. Principles of Effective Communications
1. Determine the media.
2. To whom directed?
3. Identification and source authority.
4. Is communication understood?

I. Principles of Work Improvement
1. Most people usually do only the work which is assigned to them.
2. Workers are likely to fit assigned work into the time available to perform it.
3. A good workload usually stimulates output.
4. People usually do their best work when they know that results will be reviewed or inspected.
5. Employees usually feel that someone else is responsible for conditions of work, workplace layout, job methods, type of tools/equipment, and other such factors.
6. Employees are usually defensive about their job security.
7. Employees have natural resistance to change.
8. Employees can support or destroy a supervisor.
9. A supervisor usually earns the respect of his people through his personal example of diligence and efficiency.

J. Areas of Job Improvement
The areas of job improvement are quite numerous, but the most common ones which a supervisor can identify and utilize are:
1. Departmental layout
2. Flow of work
3. Workplace layout
4. Utilization of manpower
5. Work methods
6. Materials handling

7. Utilization
8. Motion economy

K. Seven Key Points in Making Improvements
1. Select the job to be improved
2. Study how it is being done now
3. Question the present method
4. Determine actions to be taken
5. Chart proposed method
6. Get approval and apply
7. Solicit worker participation

L. Corrective Techniques of Job Improvement
Specific Problems
1. Size of workload
2. Inability to meet schedules
3. Strain and fatigue
4. Improper use of men and skills
5. Waste, poor quality, unsafe conditions
6. Bottleneck conditions that hinder output
7. Poor utilization of equipment and machine
8. Efficiency and productivity of labor

General Improvement
1. Departmental layout
2. Flow of work
3. Work plan layout
4. Utilization of manpower
5. Work methods
6. Materials handling
7. Utilization of equipment
8. Motion economy

Corrective Techniques
1. Study with scale model
2. Flow chart study
3. Motion analysis
4. Comparison of units produced to standard allowance
5. Methods analysis
6. Flow chart and equipment study
7. Down time vs. running time
8. Motion analysis

M. A Planning Checklist
1. Objectives
2. Controls
3. Delegations
4. Communications
5. Resources
6. Manpower

7. Equipment
8. Supplies and materials
9. Utilization of time
10. Safety
11. Money
12. Work
13. Timing of improvements

N. Five Characteristics of Good Directions
In order to get results, directions must be:
1. Possible of accomplishment
2. Agreeable with worker interests
3. Related to mission
4. Planned and complete
5. Unmistakably clear

O. Types of Directions
1. Demands or direct orders
2. Requests
3. Suggestion or implication
4. volunteering

P. Controls
A typical listing of the overall areas in which the supervisor should establish controls might be:
1. Manpower
2. Materials
3. Quality of work
4. Quantity of work
5. Time
6. Space
7. Money
8. Methods

Q. Orienting the New Employee
1. Prepare for him
2. Welcome the new employee
3. Orientation for the job
4. Follow-up

R. Checklist for Orienting New Employees   Yes   No
1. Do you appreciate the feelings of new employees
   when they first report for work?   ___   ___
2. Are you aware of the fact that the new employee must
   make a big adjustment to his job?   ___   ___
3. Have you given him good reasons for liking the job and
   the organization?   ___   ___
4. Have you prepared for his first day on the job?   ___   ___
5. Did you welcome him cordially and make him feel needed?   ___   ___

	Yes	No

6. Did you establish rapport with him so that he feels free to talk and discuss matters with you? ___ ___
7. Did you explain his job to him and his relationship to you? ___ ___
8. Does he know that his work will be evaluated periodically on a basis that is fair and objective? ___ ___
9. Did you introduce him to his fellow workers in such a way that they are likely to accept him? ___ ___
10. Does he know what employee benefits he will receive? ___ ___
11. Does he understand the importance of being on the job and what to do if he must leave his duty station? ___ ___
12. Has he been impressed with the importance of accident prevention and safe practice? ___ ___
13. Does he generally know his way around the department? ___ ___
14. Is he under the guidance of a sponsor who will teach the right way of doing things? ___ ___
15. Do you plan to follow-up so that he will continue to adjust successfully to his job? ___ ___

S. Principles of Learning
   1. Motivation
   2. Demonstration or explanation
   3. Practice

T. Causes of Poor Performance
   1. Improper training for job
   2. Wrong tools
   3. Inadequate directions
   4. Lack of supervisory follow-up
   5. Poor communications
   6. Lack of standards of performance
   7. Wrong work habits
   8. Low morale
   9. Other

U. Four Major Steps in On-The-Job Instruction
   1. Prepare the worker
   2. Present the operation
   3. Tryout performance
   4. Follow-up

V. Employees Want Five Things
   1. Security
   2. Opportunity
   3. Recognition
   4. Inclusion
   5. Expression

W. Some Don'ts in Regard to Praise
    1. Don't praise a person for something he hasn't done.
    2. Don't praise a person unless you can be sincere.
    3. Don't be sparing in praise just because your superior withholds it from you.
    4. Don't let too much time elapse between good performance and recognition of it

X. How to Gain Your Workers' Confidence
    Methods of developing confidence include such things as:
    1. Knowing the interests, habits, hobbies of employees
    2. Admitting your own inadequacies
    3. Sharing and telling of confidence in others
    4. Supporting people when they are in trouble
    5. Delegating matters that can be well handled
    6. Being frank and straightforward about problems and working conditions
    7. Encouraging others to bring their problems to you
    8. Taking action on problems which impede worker progress

Y. Sources of Employee Problems
    On-the-job causes might be such things as:
    1. A feeling that favoritism is exercised in assignments
    2. Assignment of overtime
    3. An undue amount of supervision
    4. Changing methods or systems
    5. Stealing of ideas or trade secrets
    6. Lack of interest in job
    7. Threat of reduction in force
    8. Ignorance or lack of communications
    9. Poor equipment
    10. Lack of knowing how supervisor feels toward employee
    11. Shift assignments

    Off-the-job problems might have to do with:
    1. Health
    2. Finances
    3. Housing
    4. Family

Z. The Supervisor's Key to Discipline
    There are several key points about discipline which the supervisor should keep in mind:
    1. Job discipline is one of the disciplines of life and is directed by the supervisor.
    2. It is more important to correct an employee fault than to fix blame for it.
    3. Employee performance is affected by problems both on the job and off.
    4. Sudden or abrupt changes in behavior can be indications of important employee problems.
    5. Problems should be dealt with as soon as possible after they are identified.
    6. The attitude of the supervisor may have more to do with solving problems than the techniques of problem solving.
    7. Correction of employee behavior should be resorted to only after the supervisor is sure that training or counseling will not be helpful.

8. Be sure to document your disciplinary actions.
9. Make sure that you are disciplining on the basis of facts rather than personal feelings.
10. Take each disciplinary step in order, being careful not to make snap judgments, or decisions based on impatience.

AA. Five Important Processes of Management
1. Planning
2. Organizing
3. Scheduling
4. Controlling
5. Motivating

BB. When the Supervisor Fails to Plan
1. Supervisor creates impression of not knowing his job
2. May lead to excessive overtime
3. Job runs itself—supervisor lacks control
4. Deadlines and appointments missed
5. Parts of the work go undone
6. Work interrupted by emergencies
7. Sets a bad example
8. Uneven workload creates peaks and valleys
9. Too much time on minor details at expense of more important tasks

CC. Fourteen General Principles of Management
1. Division of work
2. Authority and responsibility
3. Discipline
4. Unity of command
5. Unity of direction
6. Subordination of individual interest to general interest
7. Remuneration of personnel
8. Centralization
9. Scalar chain
10. Order
11. Equity
12. Stability of tenure of personnel
13. Initiative
14. Esprit de corps

DD. Change

Bringing about change is perhaps attempted more often, and yet less well understood, than anything else the supervisor does. How do people generally react to change? (People tend to resist change that is imposed upon them by other individuals or circumstances.

Change is characteristic of every situation. It is a part of every real endeavor where the efforts of people are concerned.

1. Why do people resist change?
   People may resist change because of:
   a. Fear of the unknown
   b. Implied criticism
   c. Unpleasant experiences in the past
   d. Fear of loss of status
   e. Threat to the ego
   f. Fear of loss of economic stability

2. How can we best overcome the resistance to change?
   In initiating change, take these steps:
   a. Get ready to sell
   b. Identify sources of help
   c. Anticipate objections
   d. Sell benefits
   e. Listen in depth
   f. Follow up

II. Brief Topical Summaries

   A. Who/What is the Supervisor?
      1. The supervisor is often called the "highest level employee and the lowest level manager."
      2. A supervisor is a member of both management and the work group. He acts as a bridge between the two.
      3. Most problems in supervision are in the area of human relations, or people problems.
      4. Employees expect: Respect, opportunity to learn and to advance, and a sense of belonging, and so forth.
      5. Supervisors are responsible for directing people and organizing work. Planning is of paramount importance.
      6. A position description is a set of duties and responsibilities inherent to a given position.
      7. It is important to keep the position description up-to-date and to provide each employee with his own copy.

   B. The Sociology of Work
      1. People are alike in many ways; however, each individual is unique.
      2. The supervisor is challenged in getting to know employee differences. Acquiring skills in evaluating individuals is an asset.
      3. Maintaining meaningful working relationships in the organization is of great importance.
      4. The supervisor has an obligation to help individuals to develop to their fullest potential.
      5. Job rotation on a planned basis helps to build versatility and to maintain interest and enthusiasm in work groups.
      6. Cross training (job rotation) provides backup skills.

7. The supervisor can help reduce tension by maintaining a sense of humor, providing guidance to employees, and by making reasonable and timely decisions. Employees respond favorably to working under reasonably predictable circumstances.
8. Change is characteristic of all managerial behavior. The supervisor must adjust to changes in procedures, new methods, technological changes, and to a number of new and sometimes challenging situations.
9. To overcome the natural tendency for people to resist change, the supervisor should become more skillful in initiating change.

C. Principles and Practices of Supervision
1. Employees should be required to answer to only one superior.
2. A supervisor can effectively direct only a limited number of employees, depending upon the complexity, variety, and proximity of the jobs involved.
3. The organizational chart presents the organization in graphic form. It reflects lines of authority and responsibility as well as interrelationships of units within the organization.
4. Distribution of work can be improved through an analysis using the "Work Distribution Chart."
5. The "Work Distribution Chart" reflects the division of work within a unit in understandable form.
6. When related tasks are given to an employee, he has a better chance of increasing his skills through training.
7. The individual who is given the responsibility for tasks must also be given the appropriate authority to insure adequate results.
8. The supervisor should delegate repetitive, routine work. Preparation of recurring reports, maintaining leave and attendance records are some examples.
9. Good discipline is essential to good task performance. Discipline is reflected in the actions of employees on the job in the absence of supervision.
10. Disciplinary action may have to be taken when the positive aspects of discipline have failed. Reprimand, warning, and suspension are examples of disciplinary action.
11. If a situation calls for a reprimand, be sure it is deserved and remember it is to be done in private.

D. Dynamic Leadership
1. A style is a personal method or manner of exerting influence.
2. Authoritarian leaders often see themselves as the source of power and authority.
3. The democratic leader often perceives the group as the source of authority and power.
4. Supervisors tend to do better when using the pattern of leadership that is most natural for them.
5. Social scientists suggest that the effective supervisor use the leadership style that best fits the problem or circumstances involved.
6. All four styles—telling, selling, consulting, joining—have their place. Using one does not preclude using the other at another time.

7. The theory X point of view assumes that the average person dislikes work, will avoid it whenever possible, and must be coerced to achieve organizational objectives.
8. The theory Y point of view assumes that the average person considers work to be a natural as play, and, when the individual is committed, he requires little supervision or direction to accomplish desired objectives.
9. The leader's basic assumptions concerning human behavior and human nature affect his actions, decisions, and other managerial practices.
10. Dissatisfaction among employees is often present, but difficult to isolate. The supervisor should seek to weaken dissatisfaction by keeping promises, being sincere and considerate, keeping employees informed, and so forth.
11. Constructive suggestions should be encouraged during the natural progress of the work.

E. Processes for Solving Problems
1. People find their daily tasks more meaningful and satisfying when they can improve them.
2. The causes of problems, or the key factors, are often hidden in the background. Ability to solve problems often involves the ability to isolate them from their backgrounds. There is some substance to the cliché that some persons "can't see the forest for the trees."
3. New procedures are often developed from old ones. Problems should be broken down into manageable parts. New ideas can be adapted from old one.
4. People think differently in problem-solving situations. Using a logical, patterned approach is often useful. One approach found to be useful includes these steps:
    a. Define the problem
    b. Establish objectives
    c. Get the facts
    d. Weigh and decide
    e. Take action
    f. Evaluate action

F. Training for Results
1. Participants respond best when they feel training is important to them.
2. The supervisor has responsibility for the training and development of those who report to him.
3. When training is delegated to others, great care must be exercised to insure the trainer has knowledge, aptitude, and interest for his work as a trainer.
4. Training (learning) of some type goes on continually. The most successful supervisor makes certain the learning contributes in a productive manner to operational goals.
5. New employees are particularly susceptible to training. Older employees facing new job situations require specific training, as well as having need for development and growth opportunities.
6. Training needs require continuous monitoring.
7. The training officer of an agency is a professional with a responsibility to assist supervisors in solving training problems.

8. Many of the self-development steps important to the supervisor's own growth are equally important to the development of peers and subordinates. Knowledge of these is important when the supervisor consults with others on development and growth opportunities.

G. Health, Safety, and Accident Prevention
1. Management-minded supervisors take appropriate measures to assist employees in maintaining health and in assuring safe practices in the work environment.
2. Effective safety training and practices help to avoid injury and accidents.
3. Safety should be a management goal. All infractions of safety which are observed should be corrected without exception.
4. Employees' safety attitude, training and instruction, provision of safe tools and equipment, supervision, and leadership are considered highly important factors which contribute to safety and which can be influenced directly by supervisors.
5. When accidents do occur, they should be investigated promptly for very important reasons, including the fact that information which is gained can be used to prevent accidents in the future.

H. Equal Employment Opportunity
1. The supervisor should endeavor to treat all employees fairly, without regard to religion, race, sex, or national origin.
2. Groups tend to reflect the attitude of the leader. Prejudice can be detected even in very subtle form. Supervisors must strive to create a feeling of mutual respect and confidence in every employee.
3. Complete utilization of all human resources is a national goal. Equitable consideration should be accorded women in the work force, minority-group members, the physically and mentally handicapped, and the older employee. The important question is: "Who can do the job?"
4. Training opportunities, recognition for performance, overtime assignments, promotional opportunities, and all other personnel actions are to be handled on an equitable basis.

I. Improving Communications
1. Communications is achieving understanding between the sender and the receiver of a message. It also means sharing information—the creation of understanding.
2. Communication is basic to all human activity. Words are means of conveying meanings; however, real meanings are in people.
3. There are very practical differences in the effectiveness of one-way, impersonal, and two-way communications. Words spoken face-to-face are better understood. Telephone conversations are effective, but lack the rapport of person-to-person exchanges. The whole person communicates.
4. Cooperation and communication in an organization go hand in hand. When there is a mutual respect between people, spelling out rules and procedures for communicating is unnecessary.
5. There are several barriers to effective communications. These include failure to listen with respect and understanding, lack of skill in feedback, and misinterpreting the meanings of words used by the speaker. It is also common

practice to listen to what we want to hear, and tune out things we do not want to hear.
6. Communication is management's chief problem. The supervisor should accept the challenge to communicate more effectively and to improve interagency and intra-agency communications.
7. The supervisor may often plan for and conduct meetings. The planning phase is critical and may determine the success or the failure of a meeting.
8. Speaking before groups usually requires extra effort. Stage fright may never disappear completely, but it can be controlled.

J. Self-Development
1. Every employee is responsible for his own self-development.
2. Toastmaster and toastmistress clubs offer opportunities to improve skills in oral communications.
3. Planning for one's own self-development is of vital importance. Supervisors know their own strengths and limitations better than anyone else.
4. Many opportunities are open to aid the supervisor in his developmental efforts, including job assignments; training opportunities, both governmental and non-governmental—to include universities and professional conferences and seminars.
5. Programmed instruction offers a means of studying at one's own rate.
6. Where difficulties may arise from a supervisor's being away from his work for training, he may participate in televised home study or correspondence courses to meet his self-development needs.

K. Teaching and Training
1. The Teaching Process
Teaching is encouraging and guiding the learning activities of students toward established goals. In most cases this process consists of five steps: preparation, presentation, summarization, evaluation, and application.

   a. Preparation
   Preparation is two-fold in nature; that of the supervisor and the employee. Preparation by the supervisor is absolutely essential to success. He must know what, when, where, how, and whom he will teach. Some of the factors that should be considered are:
   1) The objectives
   2) The materials needed
   3) The methods to be used
   4) Employee participation
   5) Employee interest
   6) Training aids
   7) Evaluation
   8) Summarization

   Employee preparation consists in preparing the employee to receive the material. Probably the most important single factor in the preparation of the employee is arousing and maintaining his interest. He must know the objectives of the training, why he is there, how the material can be used, and its importance to him.

b. Presentation
In presentation, have a carefully designed plan and follow it. The plan should be accurate and complete, yet flexible enough to meet situations as they arise. The method of presentation will be determined by the particular situation and objectives.

c. Summary
A summary should be made at the end of every training unit and program. In addition, there may be internal summaries depending on the nature of the material being taught. The important thing is that the trainee must always be able to understand how each part of the new material relates to the whole.

d. Application
The supervisor must arrange work so the employee will be given a chance to apply new knowledge or skills while the material is still clear in his mind and interest is high. The trainee does not really know whether he has learned the material until he has been given a chance to apply it. If the material is not applied, it loses most of its value.

e. Evaluation
The purpose of all training is to promote learning. To determine whether the training has been a success or failure, the supervisor must evaluate this learning.
In the broadest sense, evaluation includes all the devices, methods, skills, and techniques used by the supervisor to keep himself and the employees informed as to their progress toward the objectives they are pursuing. The extent to which the employee has mastered the knowledge, skills, and abilities, or changed his attitudes, as determined by the program objectives, is the extent to which instruction has succeeded or failed.
Evaluation should not be confined to the end of the lesson, day, or program but should be used continuously. We shall note later the way this relates to the rest of the teaching process.

2. Teaching Methods
A teaching method is a pattern of identifiable student and instructor activity used in presenting training material.
All supervisors are faced with the problem of deciding which method should be used at a given time.

a. Lecture
The lecture is direct oral presentation of material by the supervisor. The present trend is to place less emphasis on the trainer's activity and more on that of the trainee.

b. Discussion
Teaching by discussion or conference involves using questions and other techniques to arouse interest and focus attention upon certain areas, and by doing so creating a learning situation. This can be one of the most

valuable methods because it gives the employees an opportunity to express their ideas and pool their knowledge.

    c. Demonstration
The demonstration is used to teach how something works or how to do something. It can be used to show a principle or what the results of a series of actions will be. A well-staged demonstration is particularly effective because it shows proper methods of performance in a realistic manner.

    d. Performance
Performance is one of the most fundamental of all learning techniques or teaching methods. The trainee may be able to tell how a specific operation should be performed but he cannot be sure he knows how to perform the operation until he has done so.
As with all methods, there are certain advantages and disadvantages to each method.

    e. Which Method to Use
Moreover, there are other methods and techniques of teaching. It is difficult to use any method without other methods entering into it. In any learning situation, a combination of methods is usually more effective than any one method alone.

Finally, evaluation must be integrated into the other aspects of the teaching-learning process.

It must be used in the motivation of the trainees; it must be used to assist in developing understanding during the training; and it must be related to employee application of the results of training.

This is distinctly the role of the supervisor.